THE WORLD AS CULTURE

Other Books by D. Paul Schafer

Culture: Beacon of the Future (1998)

Revolution or Renaissance: Making the Transition from an Economic Age to a Cultural Age (2008)

The Age of Culture (2014)

The Secrets of Culture (2015)

Celebrating Canadian Creativity (2016)

Will This Be Canada's Century? (2017)

The Cultural Personality (2018)

The True North: How Canadian Creativity Changed the World (2019)

The Arts: Gateway to a Fulfilling Life and Cultural Age (2020)

THE WORLD AS CULTURE

Cultivation of the Soul to the Cosmic Whole

D. Paul Schafer

Rock's Mills Press
Oakville, Ontario
2022

Published by
Rock's Mills Press
www.rocksmillspress.com

For information about this title, including permissions requests and bulk orders, contact the publisher at:
customer.service@rocksmillspress.com

Contents

Preface vii
1. Why the World as Culture? 1
2. Cultivation of the Soul 21
3. The Arts 45
4. The Humanities 73
5. The Heritage of History 97
6. Personality Development 119
7. The Complex Whole or Total Way of Life 145
8. Societies, Social Systems, Communications, and Technology 169
9. Behaviour and Ways of Life of Other Species 193
10. Interactions with the Natural Environment 213
11. Mythology, Worldview, and Cosmology 235
12. Making the World as Culture a Reality 253
Notes 273
A Cultural Timeline, 1700–2000 281
Selected Readings 285
Index 295

Preface

This is a book about seeing the world from a cultural perspective—what I call for short *the world as culture.* I have written this book because I believe seeing the world in this way is necessary to come to grips with the dangerous and life-threatening problems that exist throughout the world today and going forward into the future, as well as to create more peace, harmony, happiness, equality, and sustainability in the world.

In order to achieve this, it is necessary to pass out of the world we are living in at present—a world dominated by economics, or, more briefly, *the world as economics.* By this phrase, I mean seeing the world exclusively or almost exclusively from an economic perspective and dealing with the world in these terms. This entails placing the highest priority on economics and the development of all the diverse economies in the world. This world began with the publication of Adam Smith's book *The Wealth of Nations* in 1776 and still exists today.

It wouldn't be difficult to justify the claim that this world as economics is the greatest human achievement in history. Billions of people throughout the world have had their standards of living and quality of life improved substantially over the last two and a half centuries. It is a phenomenal achievement.

However, it has become apparent in recent years that such a world is not sustainable in the future because it is incapable of coming to grips with the host of devastating and debilitating problems that exist in the world today, most notably climate change, the overall environmental crisis, huge disparities in income and wealth, conflicts between different races, genders, ethnic groups, religions, countries, and civilizations, the intermingling of people with very different worldviews, values, customs, and beliefs, the spread of COVID-19 and other infectious diseases, and the perpetual threat of a nuclear, biological, or chemical disaster. This is because the world as economics is designed to produce goods, services, and material and monetary wealth, and is not designed to deal with problems as vast, vital, complex, and multidimensional as these.

In order to deal with these problems, and others that have loomed above the global horizon in recent years, it is necessary to move out of the world of economics and into the world as culture. This is because culture in both its traditional and contemporary sense possesses the potential to confront and deal with these problems in one form or another.

Two major developments are imperative for this. The first is to come to grips with the nature and meaning of culture. The second is to capitalize on the profuse legacy of thoughts, ideas, ideals, and writings provided by cultural scholars over the centuries.

It is not difficult to determine why we must come to grips with the nature and meaning of culture. Over the course of history, culture has been seen and dealt with in many different ways, rather than in just one way (as is the case for most disciplines and activities). When two American cultural scholars, Alfred Kroeber and Clyde Kluckhohn, set out to clarify the nature and meaning of culture in the 1950s, they discovered that there were over 150 perceptions and definitions of culture in use throughout the world. This led them in 1952 to compile a comprehensive overview of the nature and meaning of culture, *Culture: A Critical Review of Concepts and Definitions*, which was published in book form in 1963. This same problem caused Raymond Williams, another cultural scholar, to contend that culture is one of the two or three most difficult words in the English language to pin down, understand, and define.

Fortunately, this problem of determining the nature and meaning of culture can be resolved to a significant extent by tracing the evolution of culture as an idea and a reality over the millennia. When this task is undertaken, it is possible to reduce the vast and unwieldy array of different perceptions and definitions of culture to a much smaller and more manageable number of *manifestations of culture*, since most of these perceptions and definitions are variations on the same theme or similar themes. While most of the discussions on this matter have taken place in Europe and North America, it is important to emphasize at the outset that these discussions have been strongly influenced by experiences, discoveries, research, and contributions with respect to the nature and meaning of culture in Asia, Oceania, Africa, South America, the Middle East, and elsewhere in the world, thereby making these manifestations of culture consistent with—and reflective of—practices in all parts of the world and not just the western world.

These manifestations of culture range all the way from culture as cultivation of the soul, the arts, the humanities, the heritage of history, and personality development, to culture as the complex whole or total way of life of people, societies, social systems, symbols, communications and technology, the behaviour and ways of life of other species, all the interactions that take place in the natural environment, and mythology, worldview, and cosmology. That is why this book is organized the way it is, with a separate chapter devoted to examining each of these main manifestations in some detail. These different aspects of culture, it should be emphasized, exist in the world not only in theoretical and idealistic terms but also in a practical and concrete sense.

When all the main manifestations of culture are pulled together and examined collectively, it is apparent that there has been a relentless trend throughout history towards expanding the nature, meaning, definition, and understanding of culture very substantially. That trend extends from the idea of "culture as philosophy or cultivation of the soul," which was espoused in ancient times by Marcus Cicero, the Roman orator and statesman, to "culture as an ordered and regenerative whole"—what I have called the "cosmic whole" for short, and something which is consistent with the meaning of cosmology and the views of some contemporary cosmologists discussed in the book. Hence the subtitle of this book.

When culture is seen and dealt with in these terms, there is virtually nothing in the world that is not concerned with culture in general, and cultures in particular, in one form or another. This fact is one of culture's greatest assets and most potent strengths, despite the fact that it is a very difficult concept to pin down. One reason for that lies in the reality that the more recent manifestations of culture are not limited to the human species, but include other species, the natural environment, and the universe as a whole. We desperately need a comprehensive idea and term like this if we are to succeed in coming to grips with the environmental crisis, the world's ever-increasing complexity and diversity, the true nature of reality, the human condition, the world system, and the vast array of human and non-human cultures that exist in the world.

If this first development in coming to grips with the nature, meaning, and importance of culture is essential, so is the second. It involves creating a prominent place for the thoughts, ideas, insights, and ideals of cultural scholars, who have a great deal to say about coming to grips with many of the contemporary world's most difficult problems and putting humanity in the strongest possible position to confront the future with optimism and confidence rather than pessimism and anxiety. While the works of cultural scholars are known, unfortunately they are known at present only by a limited number of people scattered across many different disciplines and areas. Nevertheless, it is amazing how many of the works of cultural scholars over the centuries are relevant to the world situation today and how it may or should evolve in the future, as we will see in the course of this book.

Capitalizing on the contributions of cultural scholars is crucial if we are to see the world from a cultural perspective, create strong theoretical and practical foundations for the world of the future, make culture and cultures the centrepiece of global development and human affairs, and create a better, safer, and more stable, sustainable, equitable, and peaceful world for all people, countries, and species. Hopefully, this will also make it possible for all people and all countries to enjoy reasonable standards of living and a decent quality of life without straining to the breaking point the globe's scarce resources, fragile ecosystems, and finite carrying capacity.

* * * * *

I would like to express my gratitude to many people who have helped me with my research and writing on these matters over the years.

First, I would like to thank my family—my wife Nancy, daughters Charlene and Susan, brother Murray, and sister-in-law Eleanor—for their constant companionship during my quest to broaden and deepen the collective knowledge and understanding of culture in general and cultures in particular, as well as to make the case that culture and cultures have a central rather than a marginal role to play in the world as well as in everyday life.

Secondly, I would like to thank many close friends and colleagues for their valuable contributions to my work. Included here are Jack Fobes, Guy Métraux, Gao Xian, Herman Greene, Biserka Cvjetičanin, Galyna Shevchenko, Prem Kirpal, Henri Janne, John Hobday, Alexander Schieffer, Diane Dodd, Erika Erdmann, Eleanora Barbieri Masini, Mochtar Lubis, Robert Vachon, Ervin Laszlo, S. Takdir Alisjahbana, Augustin Girard, Paul Braisted, Mark Riva, Federico Mayor, Grant Hall, Jeremy Geelan, Ronnie Lessem, Máté Kovács, Kurt Blaukopf, George Simons, Brian Holihan, Sascha Priewe, Andreas Johannes Wiesand, André Fortier, Walter Pitman, Sheila Jans, Frank Pasquill, Olimpia Niglio, Mira Sartika, Hans Köchler, Teressa Eca, Susan Magsamen, Ashfaq Ishaq, John Cimino, Meg Pier, Engelbert Rouss, Leslie Oliver, Thomas Legrand, Kevin Alexander Echeverry Bucuru, Nadarajah Manickam, Joyce Zemans, Fernand Harvey, Peter Mousaferiadis, Carmine Marinucci, Fawaz A. Bakhotmah, Jaber Alqallaf, Carlos A. Gonzalez-Carrasco, Fred Matern, Barry Witkin, Don McGregor, Real Bedard, Joy MacFadyen, Gariné Tcholakian, José Marín-Roig Ramón, Rana P. B. Singh, William Thachuk, Peter Sever, and many others.

Finally, and most importantly, I would like to thank my good friend and publisher, David Stover, for editing and publishing this book and others I have written on the subject of culture in general and Canadian culture and creativity in particular. Words will never convey how indebted I am to David for everything he has done to "get my message out" that culture has a mainstream rather than marginal role to play in the world, as well as all the important contributions he has made to this book, other books I have written, and my life in general.

D. Paul Schafer
Markham, Canada
2022

Chapter One

Why the World as Culture?

> The task is far from simple, yet understanding ourselves and the world we have created—and which in turn creates us—is perhaps the single most important task facing mankind [humankind] today.
>
> —Edward T. Hall[1]

We have arrived at a crucial point in history. We can go on living in the world as economics—the world we live in at present—or we can change direction and enter a new kind of world in the future. The decision is ours to make.

It is not difficult to determine why this decision is so necessary. Over the last few decades, many extremely difficult and dangerous problems have emerged that challenge human ingenuity, well-being, and survival in all parts of the world, and that threaten to escalate out of control. Most prominent among these problems are climate change and the overall environmental crisis; the spread of infectious diseases such as COVID-19 and its many variants; growing shortages of natural resources and basic foodstuffs; huge disparities in income and wealth; conflicts between different races, genders, religions, ethnic groups, countries, cultures, and civilizations; the intermingling of people with very different worldviews, value systems, and ways of life; and the constant threat of nuclear, biological, or chemical warfare. We don't need a psychic to tell us how severe these problems are—and will become—if they are not dealt with effectively.

What has brought this situation to a head is the devastating effect of the world as economics on the natural environment. Our world is driven and dominated by the development of economics, economies, and economic growth, and places the highest priority in the world on economic needs, wants, desires, aspirations, and expectations.

Without doubt, economics is the most powerful force in the world today. People, countries, and the world as a whole are so deeply immersed in the economic way of looking at things that it is taken for granted.

There is a reason for this. Economics is generally viewed as key to everything in the world and in life, especially when economics is understood as the production, distribution, and consumption of goods and services and creation of material and monetary wealth (as it is today in virtually all parts of the world). Economics is seen as the principal means of satisfying people's and countries' needs, requirements, and desires in all areas of life, as well as improving standards of living and quality of life everywhere in the world. It is also seen as the way to solve most—if not all—of the world's problems, regardless of whether they are economic *or non-economic* in nature.

It has taken a long time to develop the concept and reality of the world as economics and arrive at convictions and conclusions so fundamental and powerful. It all started back in 1776 with the publication of Adam Smith's book *The Wealth of Nations*. In this book, Smith created the theoretical and practical foundations for the world as economics by contending that specialization is the key to "wealth creation." If people specialize in certain production functions and pursue their own "self interest," according to Smith, things will work out for the best for all people, all countries, and, indeed, the world as a whole, because an "invisible hand" will ensure this happens. Over the next two hundred and forty years, this conviction developed slowly but relentlessly and eventually transformed itself into the world of economics we know and live in today. Well-known economists and their followers such as David Ricardo, Karl Marx, Alfred Marshall, John Maynard Keynes, Simon Kuznets, and many others contributed an immense amount to developing the world of economics and making it what it is today.[2]

Ricardo contended that economics is the most important activity in society and therefore should be given priority over all other activities in the political affairs of nations and in governmental policies. Marx argued that every society and country in the world can be divided into an economic base and a non-economic superstructure, with the economic base taking precedence over the non-economic superstructure because it is the "cause" and "basis" of this and everything else. In fact, Marx went much further. He reinforced this belief by formulating his economic interpretation of history, which is based on the conviction that humanity always has—*and always will*—live in a world dominated by economics because economics is by far the most powerful and important activity in societies, countries, and the world.[3]

Alfred Marshall's contribution was to examine how markets function and prices are determined in capitalist systems through the interaction of supply and demand in the marketplace, thereby satisfying the needs of both producers and consumers. For his part, John Maynard Keynes claimed that governments must get deeply immersed in the economic affairs of nations in order to deal effectively with business cycles and fluctuations in economic activity. In particular, governments must spend money in times of recessions and depressions in order to boost the aggregate demand for goods and services. Finally, Simon Kuznets and his colleagues quantified economics and the study of economies, by developing indicators such as gross national product, net national product, per capita income, and the rate of economic growth. This made it possible to measure and assess economic progress and performance, as well as create a system of "national accounts" to demonstrate and evaluate the achievements of countries in economic, commercial, and financial terms. This, in turn, allowed people to assess and compare countries according to the level of their economic attainment.

Many other tools and techniques have been developed over the last few centuries and especially over the last fifty years that are designed to generate economic activity, enhance economic performance and capabilities, and produce ever higher levels of income, output, wealth, growth, and profits. While these achievements were in the beginning limited largely to Europe and North America, slowly but surely they have been extended to include Australia, New Zealand, Asia, Africa, South America, the Caribbean, and the Middle East. The result has been significant improvements in these other areas of the world in economic terms, including the standard of living and quality of life of their citizens, through the process known as "globalization." Thus the world as economics became a universal and not just a western phenomenon.

What is most significant about all this is the fact that all people and countries in the world are now living in the world as economics. It is a world where economics is understood in terms of the production, distribution, and consumption of goods and services and creation of material and monetary wealth; the highest priority is accorded to economics, economies, and economic growth; and economic issues, problems, and concerns take precedence over all other issues, problems, and concerns because they are deemed to be the cause of everything and therefore most important.

As developments like this, and others, have taken place over the last few centuries, it has become commonplace to treat economics as "the whole" and everything else as "part of the whole" or as an element of economics, especially as more activities have been subordinated to economics and valued primarily if not exclusively for their economic impact, output, and benefits. Matters evolved to the point where humanity lost interest in seeing or understanding the world in any other way. The best illustration of this is the exclusion until quite recently of the natural environment from any serious consideration in the world as economics. Like fish in water, people, institutions, countries, and the world at large are now so deeply immersed in and dependent on the world as economics that it is taken for granted, seldom discussed, and virtually ignored.

At least until very recently! Over the last few decades, research undertaken by scientific, ecological, and environmental organizations, the Brundtland Commission on the Environment, the UN Intergovernmental Panel on Climate Change, and many others have caused some people to have serious reservations about the world as economics. Others have concluded that the status quo is no longer acceptable because the risks are too great. And still others feel that things must change and change substantially if environmental sustainability, human welfare, and the well-being of people, countries, and other species are to be assured in the future. This trend is confirmed by the fact that there have been many more—and more vigorous—protests in the world about contemporary policies and practices, as well as the need to confront the environmental crisis head on and deal with it effectively and without further delay. This is especially true for young people who are following the initiatives of such organizations as Greenpeace International as well as the activist activities of Greta Thunberg and many other organizations, institutions, and individuals.

These developments have been intensified by the COVID-19 pandemic as well as recent protests concerning systemic racism, the racial injustices done to Blacks, Indigenous peoples, Asians, and other oppressed minority and marginalized groups, as well as the unfair, inequitable, and abusive treatment of women and girls. As a result of these developments, and others, an objective and impartial assessment of the world as economics we are living in today is imperative, as was advocated and carried out in great detail in my earlier book *Revolution or Renaissance: Making the Transition from an Economic Age to a Cultural Age.*[4] It is impossible to undertake this assessment, however, without recognizing that economics dominates contemporary decision-making processes, the lives of people in all countries and parts of the world, and the affairs of nations in every area of the world. The need for this assessment is amplified even further when we consider the ancient Chinese proverb that states, "The beginning of wisdom lies in calling things by their right names." Surely the right name for this world or age we live in is "the world as economics" or "the age of economics."

It would be foolhardy to conduct this assessment without stating at the outset that the creation and development of the world as economics is the *greatest achievement in human history*. Despite the life-threatening problems that exist because of it today, no other achievement can match it or compare with it—not the agricultural revolution, the industrial revolution, the invention of the wheel, the printing press, the telephone, or the automobile; not the creation of the computer or the Internet; not our growing knowledge of the universe and the origins of life on earth; not sending people into space, landing astronauts on the moon, or any other miraculous human accomplishment.

Not only has the world as economics seen the production, distribution, and consumption of an astronomical volume of goods and services and creation of a vast amount of material and monetary wealth since it began in 1776, but it has also improved living standards and the quality of life for billions of people throughout the world over the last two and a half centuries. It has also facilitated countless other developments, such as remarkable achievements in the arts, the sciences, communications, health care, education, medicine, politics, recreation, sports, and many other areas of life. As a result of these advances and achievements, and countless others, it would be easy to conclude that we should continue living in the world as economics in the years to come—possibly even forever, as Karl Marx contended in his economic or materialistic interpretation of history

As tempting as this is or might be, there are a number of compelling and quintessential reasons why continuing to live in the world as economics would be a disastrous mistake. The costs, consequences, and dangers of this for people and countries in all parts of the world and the world as a whole are much too great and potentially life-threatening, especially as world population increases and more of the world's problems become multidimensional, complex, polarized, and complicated in nature.[5]

First of all, continuing to live in the world as economics will have a much more devastating effect on the natural environment, the world's scarce resources, the globe's fragile ecosystems, and the finite carrying capacity of the earth than it does at present if it carries on into the future. Not only will climate change worsen, but there will be more severe shortages and higher prices for natural resources and basic foodstuffs, deterioration in people's lives and threats to their existence, and diminution of the chances for survival of both human beings and other species. It will also increase the potential for many more conflicts, confrontations, and resource wars as people and countries fight for diminishing resources in a frantic attempt to maintain their standards of living and quality of life.

These problems will multiply if humanity does not change its present ways of doing things and create new ones for the future. This cannot be achieved as long as people, countries, and the world are entrenched in the world as economics and history is interpreted in economic terms. While this course of action might be possible if the population of the world were much smaller than it is today, it will not be possible as world population continues to increase, even if at a lower rate than in the past.

Why do these problems exist today? And why will they multiply rapidly in the future if nothing is done? During the entire time the world as economics was developing in the eighteenth, nineteenth, and twentieth centuries, the natural environment was taken for granted and ignored. As a result, the world as economics rests on faulty foundations. The architectural equivalent would be building a colossal office tower or huge condominium on sand or mud. At some point, it is bound to collapse because the foundations are unsound.

What makes this problem even more acute and potentially life-threatening is the fact that after ignoring the natural environment for more than two centuries, it is not possible at present or going into the future to insert the natural environment into the underlying ideology and theoretical and practical foundations of the world as economics **after the fact**. This explains why humanity is confronted with ever more serious, severe, and frequent environmental problems, including higher temperatures, rapidly melting glaciers, more intense and frequent forest fires, floods, hurricanes, tornadoes, typhoons, and the erosion or sinking of coastal areas. It also explains why human beings are making unsustainable demands on the natural environment. A way of life has been created, promoted, and promulgated throughout the world that is highly materialistic and quantitative in nature. This way of life is now so entrenched in people's minds, brains, lifestyles, behaviours, and ways of life that it cannot be changed as long as the world continues to be seen in economic terms.

This, in itself, is sufficient reason for passing out of the world as economics and entering another kind of world in the future. The world as economics ignores the most essential fact of all, namely that the natural environment provides the sustenance, resources, and wherewithal required for human survival and well-being, the survival and well-being of other species, and the context within which all human and non-human activities take place. This makes it imperative to strike out in a new direction in the future, especially as the carrying capacity of the earth is approached.

This first problem is compounded by a second problem that is also severe and potentially life-threatening. It is the huge disparities that exist in income and wealth throughout the world. These will get much worse if they are not addressed and dealt with effectively, thereby intensifying the tensions and protests that already exist.

The reason for this is also not difficult to detect. There is an inherent tendency in the world as economics and contemporary economic systems to produce greater and greater inequalities in income and wealth over time despite the best efforts to prevent this, especially between what are now deemed to be the two major classes in the world: the incredibly rich and everybody else. This is now crystal clear, especially after the protests against concentration of wealth in the hands of the "one percent."

As difficult as these two problems are, they are not the only problems inherent in the world as economics. As time marches on, it becomes ever more apparent that the world as economics is not capable of coming to grips with the complex conflicts that exist between different races, people, religions, countries, cultures, and civilizations, increased violence and terrorism, numerous immigrant and refugee difficulties, countless communications issues and technological concerns, and the inability to sustain some of humanity's most cherished values, goals, and ideals. This is because the world as economics is not designed to deal with problems as complex, crucial, fundamental, and multidimensional as these.

One final problem with the world as economics needs to be confronted here because it underlies all the other problems, and it is destined to get far worse in the future if it is not addressed head on. It is the practice of seeing and treating economics as "*the whole*" and everything else as "*part of the whole*" or "*part of economics.*" While it took a long time for this practice to evolve, this is the most serious and potentially life-threatening problem in the world today because the decision about what is deemed to be "the whole"—and what are deemed to be "the parts of the whole"—affects everybody and everything in every conceivable way.

When economics is seen and treated as the whole, everything is drawn into the realm of economics, reduced to it, and valued primarily if not exclusively for its economic impact and effects. While this practice has slowly but surely gathered momentum in the world over the last two and a half centuries, it has reached epic and alarming proportions today. This is inevitable as long as economics is seen and treated as the "cause" and "basis" of everything in life and the world, and history is interpreted and dealt with in economic and material terms.

The problem is that economics is not "the whole," despite its crucial role. While human beings are extremely dependent on economics, this does not mean—and will never mean—that everything in life has to do with economics and therefore economics should take precedence over everything else. There is a huge difference between saying that economics plays a crucial role in our lives, the development of countries, and the world at large—an undeniable fact that should always be seen and treated as such—and saying that economics is the whole and that everything else is part of it and should therefore be reduced or subordinated to it. There are many things in life and the world that have little or nothing to do with economics. These include love, compassion, friendship, beliefs, trust, truth, the creation of many remarkable inventions, ideas, and masterpieces, and a great deal else.

This problem of determining what is "the whole" and what are "the parts of the whole" is the biggest problem in the world today. Since the whole is greater than the parts and the sum of the parts, humanity must be exceedingly careful about what it considers the whole, what it considers the parts, and how this decision is dealt with at present and in the future, regardless of whether we are dealing with economics, politics, technology, communications, the arts, the sciences, or any other activity. The American cultural scholar Ruth Benedict foresaw this problem many years ago when she said, "The whole *determines* its parts, not only their relation, but their very nature."[6]

A great deal of light was shed on this problem in the latter part of the nineteenth century and early part of the twentieth, when western anthropologists began studying human societies and behaviour in depth and on the ground in many different parts of the world. What they discovered was that people had words to describe all the specific activities in which they were engaged as they went about the process of meeting their individual and collective needs and wants. What they did not have, and needed desperately, was a word that described how all these activities were woven together in different combinations and arrangements to create a whole or total way of life. *Culture, not economics, was the word anthropologists chose to designate this all-encompassing process and all-inclusive phenomenon.*

The breakthrough occurred in the late 1800s, when Edward

Burnett Tylor, one of the world's first anthropologists (if not *the* first), defined culture formally as "the complex whole" on the very first page of his book *The Origins of Culture*: "Culture or Civilization, taken in the wide ethnographical sense, is that *complex whole* which includes knowledge, belief, art, morals, law, custom, and any other capabilities and habits acquired by man [humans] as members of society."[7]

Since that time, use of the word "culture" in this all-inclusive, holistic sense has been confirmed by many institutions and scholars. For instance, at UNESCO's Second World Conference on Cultural Policies in Mexico City in 1982, delegates declared, "Culture ought to be considered today the *whole* collection of distinctive traits, spiritual and material, intellectual and affective, which characterize a society or social group."[8] Further confirmation came from Canadian cultural scholar Fernand Dumont when he said, "I have always considered a collective project as something mainly cultural. The economy is not an end in itself: culture is."[9] Wole Soyinka, the Nobel Laureate in literature and African cultural scholar, shared these convictions but carried them much further when he said, "We need therefore to constantly reinforce our awareness of the primacy of Source, and that source is the universal spring of Culture. It is nourished by its tributaries, which sink back into the earth, and thereby replenish that common source in an unending, creative cycle."[10] And, perhaps most importantly of all, this view of culture is confirmed by countless people throughout the world when they declare they are "the products of their culture." By this they usually mean they are products of everything that exists in their society or their culture "as a whole."

What is true for culture is also true for cultures. They are also wholes or total ways of life made up of many different and interrelated parts. Seen from this holistic perspective, it is apparent that the world is made up of culture and cultures at its very core and in its fundamental essence. This is because cultures, like culture, are concerned with the whole and therefore the entire way people see, understand, and interpret the world, organize themselves, conduct their affairs, act in the world, embellish and enrich life, and position themselves in the world.

Each of these components contributes a great deal to our overall understanding of culture in general and cultures in particular in one form or another. This is because people weave all the many different activities they engage in together to form a whole or total way of life.

How people see, understand, and interpret the world has to do with all the deeper philosophical, theological, cosmological, ethical, and ideological beliefs and convictions people possess. These beliefs and convictions constitute the foundation or cornerstones of culture and cultures because they provide the axioms, assumptions, and principles on which culture and all the diverse cultures of the world are based. As a result, they are intimately connected to the natural environment, the world situation, the human and cosmic condition, the relationship between mind and matter, and changing perceptions of time, space, and the universe.

How people organize themselves is concerned with all the decisions people make with respect to economic, social, and political issues, technological and scientific endeavours, military pursuits, defence installations, environmental policies and ecological practices, as well as the development of rural areas, towns, cities, regions, countries, and all other forms of human settlement. These "macro elements" of cultural life are undergoing profound change at the present time due to shifting trading practices, globalization, rapidly changing demographic patterns, and new economic, technological, digital, and political realities.

In addition to these macro elements of cultural life, there are also "micro elements." These are concerned with how people conduct their affairs and act in the world, the character of people's lives, and with these, decisions about consumer spending and behaviour, daily living practices, child rearing, family life, and personal preferences with respect to food, clothing, accommodation, and other amenities. These micro elements of cultural life are intimately related to the macro elements noted above.

The ways people embellish and enrich life are tied up with people's education and training, aesthetic preferences, scientific beliefs, religions and spiritual practices, moral and ethical ideals, and all those things that make life richer, deeper, and more meaningful than it would be otherwise.

Finally, how people position themselves in the world is related to people's geographical location, geopolitical situation, and territorial maneuvering in the world. These factors play a crucial role in determining the way people relate to their physical surroundings and other species, as well as to each other as members of groups, communities, countries, cultures, civilizations, and continents, as well as their international affairs. Clearly the potential for conflict and confrontation is always present at these *cultural contact points*, particularly as a result of rapidly changing demographic, economic, technological, social, political, and international conditions.

It follows from all these examples that very little in the world is not concerned with culture and cultures or connected with them in the all-encompassing sense in one form or another. This is confirmed by the many ways culture and cultures in the holistic sense manifest themselves in the world.[11] This was reinforced by the Croatian cultural scholar Nada Švob-Đokić when she said, "The systematic interpretation of culture brings us close to the thesis that global development is in reality the development of cultures and civilizations."[12]

Statements like these, and many others that could be provided, justify the claim that culture, not economics or any other discipline or activity, has the most legitimate claim to be seen and treated as "the whole" when it is used in the all-encompassing, holistic sense. This helps to explain why anthropologists, sociologists, ecologists, cultural historians, and many other scholars—as well as institutions like UNESCO—are embracing and using the holistic understanding of culture and cultures much more frequently as the most effective way of conveying and explaining this remarkable all-inclusive process and all-encompassing phenomenon. It also explains why people and countries in all parts of the world have developed and are developing cultures as wholes or total ways of life that are concerned with their involvement in many different types of activities—economic, social, political, artistic, scientific, technological, recreational, spiritual, environmental, and so forth. All these elements are combined to form wholes or total ways of life made up of countless interacting and interrelated parts.

This is not the only reason why culture in the all-inclusive, holistic sense has an indispensable role to play in the world. It is also because culture in general and cultures in particular—viewed in this way—

are consistent with the real nature of the world, the true character of reality, the nature of the human condition, and the direction humanity and the world should be headed in the future. This is not only because culture and cultures in the holistic sense include *all* activities and not just *some* activities, but also because culture and cultures possess many other qualities, characteristics, and capabilities that are required in the world of the present and the future.

One of the most important capabilities of culture in this respect is the potential to bring things together rather than split them apart, and therefore to *unite* rather than *divide*, since this is what the whole and wholes are really all about, regardless of whether it is culture, cultures, or any other whole or wholes. This potential is urgently needed in the modern world, where far too many things are divided into parts as a result of specialization and not enough are then brought together again through holism. While we have become remarkably skilled at breaking things up into parts and learning as much as possible from these parts—including what they are made of, how they function, and how they can be used to our individual and collective advantage—we are far less adept at re-assembling things and reconnecting or reuniting the parts in order to create wholes capable of producing more unity, togetherness, and cohesion in the world.

Yet another one of culture's qualities is the ability to see, understand, and deal with the "big picture," and with this, the many different relationships that exist—or do not exist—between the component parts of the big picture.

This is most essential in terms of the relationship between human beings and the natural environment. The findings of anthropologists serve a valuable function here because they confirm the fact that when societies don't look after the natural environment properly and respect it fully, they run the risk of overextending themselves and destroying not only the natural environment but also themselves. An excellent example is the collapse of the society located on Easter Island in the Pacific Ocean, but the same dire fate has befallen many other societies, communities, and settlements. This valuable lesson has been largely ignored since its discovery, as our inability to deal effectively with the environmental crisis readily confirms today.

Another important aspect of seeing the big picture lies in realizing that many of the tensions, conflicts, and wars that exist or have existed in the world result from failure to understand, respect, and come to grips with people's cultural differences. Many of the wars that have been fought in the twentieth and twenty-first centuries resulted from the inability to understand and deal effectively with differences in cultures, worldviews, values, value systems, customs, traditions, and ways of life. Such is the case with the recent killings in Myanmar, where more than 500,000 Rohingyan people have been driven out of the country and forced to become refugees. It is imperative to educate people in culture, cultural differences, and all the diverse cultures and civilizations of the world, as well as to create many more connections, exchanges, links, and relationships between diverse peoples, races, cultures, and civilizations of the world.

The same holds true for the capacity culture in the holistic sense possesses to shed light on what is required to create more balance and harmony in the world. The Dutch cultural scholar and historian Johan Huizinga provided us with a powerful and profound insight into this matter when, after examining numerous cultures in the world, he said that "The realities of economic life, of power, of technology, of everything conductive to man's [people's] material well-being, must be balanced by strongly developed spiritual, intellectual, moral, and aesthetic values."[13]

The power of this profound insight into one of the greatest challenges of all in the world should not be ignored. On the one hand, commitment to this insight will decrease the demands we are making on the natural environment and world's scarce resources because spiritual, intellectual, moral, and aesthetic values—and the activities grounded in them—are largely labour-intensive rather than capital- or material-intensive, and therefore don't make as many demands on nature's resources as most economic, technological, and manufacturing activities. On the other hand, it will create higher and loftier goals, objectives, and ideals for humanity, as well as decrease poverty and income inequality because a much higher priority will be placed on caring, sharing, compassion, and cooperation, all of which are key requirements in eliminating poverty and producing more equality in the world.

Focusing attention on the need to establish balance and harmony between the material and non-material (or quantitative and qualitative) dimensions of development and life also reveals how essential it is to develop other crucial relationships. This is especially true for the relationships among different genders, groups, races, and religions, those between technology and humanity, the arts and the sciences, the public sector and the private sector, people's rights and responsibilities, and, at the highest level, the relationships among all the diverse cultures and civilizations in the world. Imbalances and disharmonies exist in all these areas, and others, that need to be confronted and overcome. This also makes it necessary to achieve balanced and harmonious relationships not only *between* cultures but also *within* cultures.

It is necessary to position cultures effectively in the natural, historical, and global environment. Not only will this result in a great deal more environmental sustainability, but it will make it possible to come to grips with the cultural baggage we inherit from the past and carry with us in the present and into the future. This will help to improve relations and reduce tensions and conflicts among different peoples, groups, races, countries, and cultures, as well as to ensure that cultures are properly situated in time as well as in space.

This process of seeing and dealing with culture in the holistic sense is essential in understanding that economics is really part of culture rather than the reverse. Culture in the holistic sense provides the context or container within which economics, economies, and virtually all other human activities and disciplines in society and the world are situated and take place, just as the natural environment provides the context or container within which culture, cultures, and civilizations are situated and take place. Since context determines content, culture is the most important factor in terms of bringing about changes in people's worldviews, values, lifestyles, and ways of life that are imperative for coming to grips with the world's most difficult, debilitating, and life-threatening problems. The solutions are cultural rather than economic because it is culture that is concerned with making changes in people's ways of life and producing the transformations that are required in their attitudes, behaviour, and actions to achieve this. This is why many people in the world are talking more and more these days about the need to "*change the culture*" in order to come to grips with the environment crisis and many other problems.

It is benefits like these that make it essential to capitalize on culture's full potential at this crucial time in the history of humanity and the world. Clearly we have barely scratched the surface of the rich potential culture possesses to create a better, safer, and more stable, secure, sustainable, and harmonious world. Without a clear understanding of this idea and general acceptance of it, it will not be possible to take advantage of culture's most important strengths and benefits as well as deal with its most fundamental shortcomings and weaknesses. Nor will it be possible to bring an end to the problem Edward T. Hall, author of *The Silent Language, The Hidden Dimension,* and other books on culture and cultures, foresaw when he said, "In sum, though the concept of culture was first defined in print in 1871 by E. B. Tylor, after all these years, it still lacks the rigorous specificity which characterizes many less revolutionary and useful ideas." [14]

The most effective way to achieve what Hall calls "specificity" is to trace the evolution of culture as an idea and a reality over the course of human history. This makes it possible to see how expansive and all-inclusive culture as an idea and a reality really are, as well as to appreciate the many different values, virtues, attributes, and possibilities culture possesses. It also makes it possible to reduce the vast and unwieldy array of different perceptions and definitions of culture that have been created over the last two thousand years and more to a much smaller and more manageable number of *manifestations of culture*. This is because many of these perceptions and definitions are variations on the same theme or a similar theme.

In ancient, medieval, and early modern times, for instance, culture as an idea and a reality manifested itself in the world as cultivation of the soul, the arts, the humanities, and the heritage of history. This was needed to explain and focus attention on some of the most valuable and worthwhile assets, activities, and ideals in the world and in life that were evident at that time. In the nineteenth and twentieth centuries, culture began to manifest itself in far more expansive and all-encompassing ways, first as a major factor in personality development and development of the "whole person" as well as "the complex whole" or "total way of life" of people and their societies and social systems. More recently, culture has been manifesting itself in even more expansive terms as the behaviour and ways of life of other species, interactions among all life's diverse species and the natural environment, and in terms of mythology, worldview, and cosmology.[15]

Given the importance of these primary manifestations of culture—that is to say, all the most fundamental ways culture and cultures as ideas and realities manifest themselves today in the world in theoretical and practical terms—a separate chapter is devoted to each of these manifestations. This necessitates taking a long and captivating journey together. Our journey starts with seeing when each of these manifestations first appeared in history as well as what they were and are designed to accomplish, and concludes by determining why they remain relevant to the world of the present and have such an essential role to play in the world of the future. What will be most apparent when this journey is completed is that there is very little in the world or in life that does not have to do with culture and cultures to begin with or in the final analysis. This explains why there has been a progressive trend throughout history towards ever broader and more all-encompassing manifestations of culture. This has been necessary to maintain culture's relevance to the world and to life at each and every stage in the historical and life process, as well as to remain *au courant* with all the most important developments and changes in the world.

There is another fundamental aspect to culture that is also revealed by tracing its evolution as an idea and a reality over the course of history. It is the fact that, like all other ideas and activities in the world, culture manifests itself in negative as well as positive ways. On the one hand, it manifests itself in great artistic, humanistic, scientific, economic, social, political, technological, educational, and other advances and achievements. On the other hand, it manifests itself in the killing or maiming of millions of people, systemic racism, excessive nationalism, extremism, cultural genocide, and other atrocities. This makes it imperative to be ever mindful and watchful of the abuses and not just the uses of culture, as well as to ensure that culture is used in positive and constructive rather than negative and destructive ways as much as possible in the years, decades, and centuries ahead.

The key to this lies in taking the necessary precautions and establishing the requisite safeguards that are required, as well as to take maximum advantage of the thoughts, ideas, findings, insights, ideals, and wisdom of countless cultural scholars on these matters. For just as the theories and writings of economists such as Adam Smith, David Ricardo, Karl Marx, Alfred Marshall, John Maynard Keynes, Simon Kuznets, and many others were instrumental in laying the groundwork and establishing the theoretical and practical foundations for the world as economics and contributing a great deal to its content, character, and development, the same is true for cultural scholars. When the theories, findings, and writings of cultural scholars such as Cicero, Voltaire, Edward Burnett Tylor, Matthew Arnold, Jacob Burckhardt, Goethe, Franz Boas, Pitirim Sorokin, Johan Huizinga, Ruth Benedict, Margaret Mead, Bronislaw Malinowski, Edward T. Hall, Jacques Maritain, Joseph Campbell, Raymond Williams, S. Takdir Alisjahbana, Rex Nettleford, Stuart Hall, Néstor Garcia Canclíni, Joseph Ki-Zerbo, Ziauddin Sardar, Homi K. Bhabha, Clifford Geertz, Thomas Berry, and many others are brought together and examined collectively, they can be instrumental in providing the groundwork and creating the theoretical and practical foundations that are required for the establishment of the world as culture. In so doing, they possess the potential to contribute an enormous amount to the development of culture and cultures, and to the creation of a world visualized from a cultural perspective, as well as to its future direction, content, and character.

When their legacy is examined collectively and combined with the main manifestations of culture, a compelling and comprehensive portrait of the world as culture begins to emerge and take shape. While this portrait will require a great deal of filling out in the present and the future, it is predicated on the centrality of culture and cultures in all local, municipal, regional, national, and international developments, cultivating culture and cultures fully and situating them effectively in the natural, historical, and global environment, and opening up a commanding place for culture's highest, wisest, and most inspiring values, ideals, and activities in the overall scheme of things.

In order to achieve this, culture must no longer be seen and treated as a component of economics, part of the superstructure of societies, a means to other ends, or in any other limited or partial way. On the contrary, it must be seen and treated as the foundation for the world system, an end in itself, the heart and soul of life, living, global development, and human affairs, and the key to environmental sustainability, human welfare, and ecological and cosmological well-being in all parts of the world and for all species and not just the human species.

Chapter Two

Cultivation of the Soul

Culture is the philosophy or cultivation of the soul.
—Marcus Cicero[1]

One of the most interesting things about the world we live in today is that some of the most powerful ideas and fundamental forces in the world are thousands of years old. This is true for religion, philosophy, politics, and economics, but it is also true for culture.

As a reality, culture can be traced back to the very beginning. In human terms, this is when people huddled together in caves to protect themselves against nature's powerful elements, including wild animals. This era is depicted in many paintings of human beings and animals on the walls of caves in Indonesia, South Africa, France, China, and other parts the world.

As an idea, culture is also incredibly old. It first appeared in word form as *cultura* in Latin, which was derived from the Latin verb *colo*, meaning to plant, grow, nurture, and especially *to cultivate*. This is the sense in which Marcus Cicero, the great Roman orator and statesman, used this word for the first time in history more than two thousand years ago when he said "*Cultura animi philosophia est.*" Cicero's words are usually translated into English as "Culture is the philosophy or cultivation of the soul."

Discussions, speculations, and writings about the soul can be traced back much farther than this in many parts of the world. They were especially prominent in Hindu scriptures such as the *Vedas*, *Upanishads*, and *Bhagavad-Gita*, the Hebrew and Christian Bible, the beliefs of Indigenous peoples, Buddhism, and Greek philosophies such as those presented by Plato and Pythagoras. They were usually connected to thoughts and convictions about reincarnation, the concept of karma, the journey of the soul after death, and Indo-

European connections and relations connected to these matters. Nevertheless, Cicero was the first person to talk about the intimate connection between culture and the soul and how cultivation of the soul can be achieved through culture.

We owe Cicero a great debt of gratitude for this connection, for he linked culture to some of the most essential and worthwhile concepts and activities in life and in the world. The connection between culture, cultivation, nature, and the natural environment is especially important because all species depend on the natural environment for their survival and well-being. As a result, we have many words in our vocabulary today that are concerned with this connection, such as agriculture, horticulture, silviculture, viticulture, permaculture, and many others.

This connection is far too important to the world of the present and the future to be ignored. We need a world system in the future that is deeply rooted in nature, the natural environment, cultivation, and culture if we are to be successful in coming to grips with climate change and the overall environmental crisis. While focusing much more attention on this connection is necessary, it is not sufficient. We need a world system that is predicated on the intimate connection between nature, people, culture, and cultivation at its core and in its essence. Culture possesses the potential to do this, as Cicero rightly recognized more than two millennia ago.

This factor alone makes it imperative to commit fully and forcefully to culture and the inexorable connection it has to nature, the natural environment, people, and other species. Viewed from this perspective, Cicero performed a very valuable function when he linked culture to the soul, cultivation, human affairs, and philosophy. This link is of utmost importance for both the human and natural worlds as well as the intimate connection between them, despite the fact that it has been largely severed or taken for granted in the modern era.

As far as the natural world is concerned, the idea of culture as cultivation played a vital role in the development of agriculture thousands of years ago, much as it continues to do so today. This is also true for horticulture, or the cultivation of plants, flowers, and gardens; silviculture, or the growth and development of trees, shrubs, and forests; viticulture, or the development of grapes and the production of wine; and especially permaculture, or the creation and implementation of activities that work *with* nature rather than *against* it, which is so imperative going forward into the future. It is also true of many other terms we use, such as references to the culture and cultures of animals as living organisms. In fact, one of the greatest strengths of culture as we will see later is that it is not confined to human beings but applies to other species as well.

According to the Greek historian Thucydides, the importance of culture as cultivation can be traced back to the fifth century B.C. This is when people in the Mediterranean area began to emerge from barbarism and commence the long ascent towards civilization by learning how to cultivate grape vines and olive trees, which eventually led to the production of grapes, wine, olives, and olive oil for domestic consumption and commercial use. This occurred sometime between 3000 B.C. and 2000 B.C. in Asia Minor, Greece, the Cyclades Islands, and the Aegean. Recent research is revealing that winemaking started even earlier than this, probably around 6000 B.C. in sites located about 50 kilometres south of the Georgian capital of Tbilisi.

As time wore on, culture began to manifest itself more and more in the human realm and not just the natural realm, which is why Cicero was so prophetic when he linked culture to the cultivation of people, the soul, and philosophy and not just to nature and the natural environment. This was most apparent in Europe, although it may have been apparent in other parts of the world as well. By the late medieval ages, the idea of culture as cultivation was being associated in Europe not only with agriculture, but also with the development of people's manners, tastes, habits, morals, and enjoyment of the finer things in life.

No person was more committed to the idea of culture as cultivation in both the human and natural senses than Voltaire, the great French scholar and author. He was born François-Marie Arouet in 1694 in Paris. However, he adopted the pen name "Voltaire" to express countless thoughts and ideas about cultivation in the cultural sense that resonated strongly with people in France, Europe generally, and other parts of the world. Although he did not use the term "culture" as such, it is clear in retrospect that this is exactly what he meant in most of his writings.

Voltaire was concerned with culture in both individual and collective terms. In individual terms, he felt that it was necessary for every person to "plant," "build," and "cultivate," since this was the key to achieving a great deal, as well as living a full, upright, and meaningful life. In collective terms, Voltaire felt this was the best antidote of all against boredom, vice, violence, crime, and sorrow, something that this remarkable scholar deemed was imperative if societies were to be built up rather than torn down.

There is an interesting passage on this matter in Voltaire's book *Candide*. It can be paraphrased this way: *Above all, cultivate! Since this is a matter of conscience and character, it is essential to be constantly asking yourself such questions as: Do I plant? Do I build? Do I cultivate?* Voltaire answered these questions by assuming the role of the landlord of Ferney in *Candide*. He responded to these questions by saying that as a landlord he cared for his tenants by cultivating his mulberry bushes and feeding his silkworms, since this provided work for his employees and helped people who were engaged in spinning his silk.

This is not the only example drawn from nature that Voltaire used to make the case that culture as cultivation is essential for people in general and communities, societies, and countries in particular. He also expressed concern over the need to achieve "civilization"—and to build "civilizations"—which he epitomized by his oft-quoted phrase, "*We must cultivate our garden.*" By pooling the labour of all citizens, Voltaire believed it is possible to build societies, cultures, and civilizations—human gardens, if you will—that are capable of blending wisdom, morality, material welfare, order, and well-being together to form dynamic, organic, collective, and harmonious wholes. In order to do this, Voltaire felt that all factors must be present and in balance, since cultures, civilization, and civilizations require the presence, symbiosis, and synthesis of all the different factors, forces, and activities that comprise these complex entities.

One person who took Voltaire's insights in this regard to heart was the poet, philosopher, and cultural scholar Johann Gottfried Herder. He was born in Mohrungen, Prussia in 1744, twenty years after Voltaire's death.

While Herder was writing at a time when it was not commonplace to write about culture or cultures, he had a remarkable understanding of their all-encompassing character, as well as the way they can be cultivated most effectively. He likened culture and cultures to living organisms in order to emphasize their organic, dynamic, and all-inclusive character and capabilities.

For Herder, the most important factor in the development of cultures is not the individual, but the group. It is groups of people, not people as individuals, who create and cultivate cultures. Many factors contributed to this in Herder's view, such as history, heredity, tradition, education, interaction with other cultures, and especially climate, geography, landscape, and nature. In one of the most telling passages in Herder's *Outlines of a Philosophy of the History of Man*, he states:

> Man [woman] is no independent substance, but is connected with all the elements of nature; he [she] lives by inspiration of the air; and derives food and drink from the most unlikely productions of the Earth; he [she] employs fire, absorbs light, and contaminates the air he [she] breathes; awake or asleep, at rest or in motion, he [she] contributes to the change of the universe; shall not he [she] also be changed by it?[2]

Herder was committed to Voltaire's idea that creating and cultivating cultures and civilizations is very much like creating and cultivating gardens. However, his captivation with culture, cultures, cultivation, and gardens does not end here. He also said, "Culture is the flower of a people's existence," equating culture with one of the most important and highest objectives people can aspire to and achieve, namely cultivating activities and creating things that are beautiful and worthwhile, and using this horticultural example to make his case.

It was but a short step from this for Herder to conclude that human cultures are very much like gardens with all sorts of plants, trees, shrubs, flowers, and trees growing and being cultivated in them. Every culture, like every garden, has its own special fragrance, appeal, appearance, design, and distinctive features. The challenge is to make it possible for every culture to develop its own specific properties, identity, and characteristics—its own "circle of happiness" as Herder called it—to the greatest possible extent.

By the time Herder was writing about culture and cultures and how they can be developed most effectively, many people in Germany, France, England, and other parts of Europe thought that a "European culture or civilization" was beginning to emerge, take shape, and might just become the crowning achievement of Europe and possibly even the entire world. Herder was strongly opposed to this idea, as was Voltaire before him. Both scholars felt that no one culture or civilization was more important than the others. In their opinion, every culture, like every garden and every civilization, has its own special properties and specific characteristics, regardless of where it is situated in the world or what group of people created and cultivated it.

The connection Herder made between culture, nature, gardens, plants, flowers, and people—much like Voltaire before him—is very important. There is an enormous amount to be learned about culture and cultures in general—as well as the intimate connection between culture, cultures, nature, people, horticulture, and human culture in particular—from nature and especially gardens because the similarities between them are striking.

Consider nature as an example. Being in tune with nature and bonding fully with nature is essential because it makes us much more aware of nature's many different elements, cycles, characteristics, rhythms, patterns, and themes. Not only does nature dance to its own drummer and have a life, personality, character, and presence all its own, but it is full of all sorts of elements and ingredients that have been immortalized throughout history for their medicinal qualities and soothing, relaxing, and healing properties.

What is true for nature is also true for the cultivation and functioning of nature's many different elements. While we have spent a great deal of time over the last few centuries ignoring nature and emphasizing the differences human beings have with it as well as with other species—largely for the purpose of capitalizing on nature—much more time and attention will have to be accorded to embracing nature and understanding and appreciating the many similarities and differences that exist between human beings, nature, and other species. One of the best ways to do this is through gardening, and especially creating, studying, and cultivating gardens.

I discovered this many years ago when I became fascinated with a specific plant in our garden—a monkshood. I watched this plant very closely for several months one summer to see if it would bloom. It had been a long, hot, dry summer with very little rain. Moreover, this fascinating plant—which possesses the ability to thrill as well as to kill because it is very beautiful on the one hand and poisonous on the other—was situated in a part of our garden surrounded by huge trees and large shrubs that were sucking all the moisture out of the ground before this plant could get a crack at it. I knew that monkshoods tend to bloom a little later in the season but was wondering if our monkshood would bloom at all that year due to the poor growing conditions.

Then it happened. It bloomed and bloomed magnificently. It was certainly the most exquisite plant and flower in our garden that year, perhaps any year. With its long slender stems, delicate leaves, and exquisite purple-blue flowers—which really do look like monks' hoods when they are in full bloom—it stands proudly in any garden and towers over most other plants. This immediately got me thinking about the similarities between plants, flowers, gardens, and people—horticulture and human culture—because plants, like people, are living organisms that bloom at different stages in the life cycle and their lives.

As far as plants and flowers are concerned, there are "early-bloomers," "mid-bloomers," and "late-bloomers." Early-bloomers burst forth in all their glory at the first signs of spring, announcing that "spring has sprung" and "the grass has ris" as the old saying goes. Then there are mid-bloomers. They tend to hit their stride at different times over the summer. Finally, there are late-bloomers, which flower in the fall. There are even "non-bloomers," plants that do not bloom at all because the growing conditions were not right. This explains why I was watching the monkshood in our garden very carefully that year to see if it would bloom.

People are like this, too. There are early-bloomers, mid-bloomers, late-bloomers, and—alas—even non-bloomers. A few people bloom very early in life. When they do, they are often called "child prodigies" because they manifest unusual talents and exceptional abilities at a very early age. Then there are the mid-bloomers. Most people are like this because they hit their stride later in life, usually in their thirties, forties, and fifties. These people are followed by the late-bloomers. They bloom much later in life—often in their sixties, seventies, eighties, and now perhaps even in their nineties—but may go on to produce things that are very beautiful and valuable. Finally, there are non-bloomers. These are people who do not bloom at all because they received too little attention, recognition, and encouragement during their lives and consequently the growing conditions were not right.

These are not the only similarities between plants and people. Plants come in many different shapes, sizes, colours, and types, much as people do. Some plants are annuals or biennials, blooming once or possibly twice and then—regrettably—dying out and never returning. Others are perennials, and come back every year to bless us with their beauty and dependability. Moreover, some plants are tall; others are short. Some grow horizontally and spread out along the ground; others grow vertically and stretch upwards towards the heavens. Some are top heavy and need propping up; others have strong spines and stems and do not require any outside assistance.

People are like this, too. They come in all shapes, sizes, and types. Some flower once—or possibly twice—but never again. Others flower continuously. Some are seven feet tall; others are four feet short. Some have highly developed minds but need propping up in other areas. Others are fully developed in all areas and require little external assistance. Some are Africans, Asians, and Oceanics, others are Americans, Europeans, Middle Easterners, or South Americans. And this is the point. No two people—like no two plants—are exactly alike. Each has his or her own specific qualities and characteristics—qualities and characteristics that make every person distinctive and unique.

And the similarities do not end here. Some plants and flowers love the sun and thrive on it; others prefer the shade and are happy to be situated in it. To this must be added the "show-offs" and the "wallflowers." Plants and flowers that derive from bulbs, such as gladiolas, irises, and lilies, are often show-offs. They produce magnificent flowers when they are looked after properly. Others are wallflowers, constantly shrinking from view and attention. People are like this, too. Some like the heat, and perform best when they are in the limelight. Others prefer the shade and perform best when these conditions prevail. Moreover, show-offs often muscle other people out of the way in order to grab all the attention and recognition for themselves. However, wallflowers—or "shrinking violets" as they are sometimes called—hold back and stay out of the limelight, thereby providing a great deal of relief from the show-offs.

Every gardener knows all about the special qualities and characteristics of plants and flowers and gives this matter a great deal of attention in the design, layout, and cultivation of gardens. If gardens are to delight the eye, tickle the imagination, and soothe the senses and the soul—and if they are to thrive throughout the entire growing season and not just specific parts of it—it is imperative to know an enormous amount about the strengths, shortcomings, and idiosyncrasies of plants and flowers. What would a garden be without its show-offs and wallflowers, its annuals, biennials, and perennials, plants that flourish in the sun and plants that flourish in the shade, and plants that bloom at different times in the season?

Shakespeare knew all about this. In fact, plants, flowers, and herbs figure prominently in many of his plays. In *A Midsummer Night's Dream*, for example, Oberon begins his famous speech with the words:

> I know a bank where the wild thyme blows,
> Where oxlips and the nodding violet grows,
> Quite over-canopied with luscious woodbine,
> With sweet musk-roses and with eglantine.

With such an intimate knowledge of horticulture, Shakespeare may well have been an excellent gardener—which in fact he was, because he cultivated a garden of his own for many years—and not just a remarkable playwright.

What is true for plants, flowers, and people is also true for gardens. This explains why the connection Voltaire and Herder made between cultures and gardens is so striking, informative, and captivating.

This is not only because cultures are wholes made up of many parts much like gardens, but also because there are many different types of gardens and cultures in existence throughout the world.

In the case of gardens, some are composed of all the same flowers—roses and tulips, for example—and are uniform and homogenous. These gardens are incredibly beautiful when they are in full bloom—think of the rose gardens in England and the tulip gardens in the Netherlands, for instance—but are far less attractive when they are not in full bloom. Other gardens are composed of many different flowers, which makes them diverse and heterogeneous. These gardens have many different types of plants and flowers in them that bloom at different stages throughout the season and not all at once. The human equivalent to this would be homogeneous and heterogeneous cultures—monocultures and multicultures, if you like—which is why Voltaire and Herder were so committed to the cultivation of many heterogeneous cultures in Europe and not a single and homogeneous "European culture."

The similarities between cultures and gardens do not end. Cultures, like gardens, are designed and cultivated in many different ways and for many different purposes. Some cultures, especially western and northern cultures, are designed and cultivated with a great deal of care and attention to detail. An incredible amount of time, energy, and effort goes into ensuring that every part of these cultures is cultivated properly, from the arts and sciences to politics, economics, education, sports, recreation, technology, social affairs, and so forth. Many European cultures are like this, especially urban cultures where everything is attended to with special care to ensure it serves the purpose for which it is intended. In other cases, cultures may be left much more to their own devices, as is the case with some cultures in Africa, South America, and the Caribbean, where things are much freer to evolve in their own way and style.

Regardless of what type of culture or garden it is, the litmus test is always the same. Does the culture or garden work? Are people's needs and wants dealt with successfully? Have dynamic and organic wholes been created that achieve balance and harmony between and among the many different parts? Without doubt, there is a great deal to be learned from the creation and cultivation of gardens that is relevant to the creation and cultivation of cultures if we are wise enough to realize this fact.

Over the course of history, many famous gardens have been created and cultivated in the world, revealing how gardeners have attempted to deal with the problems, challenges, and opportunities that confront them. In Europe and North America, for instance, there are the Kew Gardens in England, the Tivoli Gardens in Denmark, the Tuileries and Versailles Gardens in France, the Villa d'Este Gardens in Italy, the Generalife Gardens in Spain, the Butchart and Royal Botanical Gardens in Canada, and the Japanese Gardens in San Francisco. This is also true for many other gardens, such as the famous gardens in Suzhou, China that date back to 600 B.C., the Hanging Gardens of Babylon, which were watered by the Euphrates, built on roof-tops, had columned terraces, and were deemed to be one of the seven ancient wonders of the world; the Chinampas or "floating gardens" of the Aztecs in Mexico; Claude Monet's famous lily and flower gardens in Giverny, France; the internationally-famous tulip garden at Keukenhof in the Netherlands; and many others. All these gardens, and others, required a great deal of cultivation, as well as some central organizing principle or principles that made it possible to combine all their various parts together to form balanced, harmonious, and orderly wholes.

Some gardens are cultivated in great detail because they are based on the belief that every petal, leaf, plant, flower, tree, shrub, and stone should be situated in just the right place in order to achieve the maximum effect. Many Japanese gardens are laid out and cultivated in this way, such as the world-famous Kenroku-en and Kōraku-en gardens. These gardens are not overly large, but every element is situated in just the right place and every effort is made to achieve the greatest possible effect.

This contrasts sharply with gardens that are embellished very little, since they are based on the belief that it is better to achieve a more natural, spontaneous, and random effect. Many English gardens are organized and laid out this way. While an enormous amount of time, energy, effort, and ingenuity goes into their design, development, and cultivation, they possess a natural, spontaneous, and random quality that is difficult to describe but easy to appreciate. This gives the viewer the sense that nature is being experienced firsthand rather than through some form of human intervention, although nothing could be further from the truth. This helps to explain the popularity of many English country gardens as well as many other gardens in England, such as the ones at Wisley in Surrey, Rosemoor in Devon, Hyde Hall in Essex, and Harlow Carr in North Yorkshire. It also explains why Percy Grainger, the Australian-born composer and arranger, wrote a delightful piano piece called "Country Gardens," based on popular English melodies and folk tunes.

Interestingly, comparisons are often made between western and eastern gardens to show how gardeners in these different parts of the world attend to their duties and use their talents to best advantage. Japanese gardens, for instance, are usually organized, designed, and cultivated as "single units" or "unitary wholes." The focus is on creating a single unit or unitary whole that shines the spotlight directly on nature and its diverse elements. Since the viewpoint of the observer is crucial, Japanese gardens are usually seen from a single perspective, or, at most, a few perspectives if the viewer happens to be walking along a path. Water is extremely important in Japanese gardens, but only in its natural form and never in an artificial state. It can be manifested as a stream, pond, or waterfall since these are all found in nature. However, it is seldom if ever used in a fountain because fountains are not found in nature. Moreover, common plants and shrubs are used often in Japanese gardens to achieve a desired effect. This is done to prevent some parts of the garden from dominating other parts or the whole.

This contrasts sharply with most western gardens. Whereas nature and its many different elements are celebrated in Japanese gardens, human dominance over nature is celebrated in many western gardens. This aim is manifested in a variety of ways. Western gardens are usually planned and laid out as a series of units or wholes, rather than as a single unit or whole. This makes it possible to break western gardens into sections—wholes within the whole, so to speak—in much the same way that smaller community and municipal cultures are incorporated into larger regional and national cultures. This makes it possible for every section in a western garden to possess some special theme or specific characteristic, as well as to separate the different sections by hedges or shrubs. These gardens can then be seen from a variety of perspectives—rather than a single perspective—because the observer is able to walk from one section to another.

Given all this talk about plants, flowers, gardens, people, and cultures, it is not surprising that botanical images and horticultural examples are used in virtually every culture and country in the world today to shed light on the complex connection between horticulture and human culture in general and culture, cultures, gardens, plants, flowers, and people in particular. The similarities between the two are really very striking and quite remarkable, though perhaps not all that surprising because both are organic and dynamic rather than non-organic and static entities.

An interesting illustration of the use of botanical images and horticultural examples to describe or explain certain situations in the human realm are the references the Arts Council of Great Britain—now Arts Council England—used to make to roses (and possibly still does today). When the Council spoke of "few, but roses" in several of its annual reports many years ago, the intention was to focus on the Council's belief at that time that the priority should be placed on cultivating fewer arts organizations capable of achieving outstanding results, rather than on many arts organizations capable of achieving only mediocre results. By concentrating on the cultivation of a few organizations—but superb ones—the Council felt such organizations would provide excellent examples for all other organizations to follow and would eventually elevate all arts organizations.

The more these matters are thought about and reflected upon, the more it becomes obvious that there is an incredible amount to be learned from the cultivation of gardens, plants, and flowers. As every gardener knows, it is essential to plant plants properly in the ground and "root them effectively" if they are to grow and develop properly. It is also necessary to have excellent soil if this is to be achieved. If the soil is rich in nutrients such as nitrogen, phosphorous, and potassium—and if it holds moisture well and the plants are rooted properly and get a lot of sunshine—they are likely to spring forth in all their majesty and bloom magnificently. However, if the soil is deficient in nutrients, if it does not hold moisture well and if plants are not properly rooted in the soil and don't get enough sunlight, they are likely to grow poorly and even shrivel up and die. It is a well-known fact in gardening that "if you look after the roots, everything else will take care of itself."

The same holds true for people. If they are able to profit from excellent nutrients and are rooted properly during the first years of life, it is very likely that they will grow up to be mature and responsible adults. If children have loving parents, devoted families, numerous opportunities for growth and development, wonderful playmates, stable neighbourhoods, healthy environments, and are able to use their individual and collective talents to the full during the formative years of their lives, they are likely to grow up to be fulfilled adults and responsible citizens. However, if they are not able to profit from these amenities and requirements, they are likely to experience numerous problems and hardships in life. As the old saying goes "as the twig is bent, so grows the tree."

Are there additional lessons to be learned from the cultivation of gardens, plants, and flowers that are relevant to the development and cultivation of culture, cultures, groups, and people? Indeed there are. One of the most important of these lessons is how essential it is to give people and groups enough space to grow, develop, and mature.

One of the biggest mistakes that can be made in gardening is to place plants too closely together. When this happens, normal growth is cut off because there is insufficient room to spread out and plants must compete for sunlight, water, and other nutrients. This spatial problem is often encountered when new subdivisions are built and new homes are constructed. There is a tendency to plant saplings, trees, and shrubs too close together. This is either because people are too anxious to fill up the empty spaces on their properties, or because they have a difficult time visualizing how large saplings, trees, and shrubs will be when they are full grown. In either case, by the time saplings, trees, and shrubs mature, they will probably be blocking each other out and struggling to survive because they can't get enough sunlight, water, and other nutrients.

The same holds true for people and groups. They need enough room and space to grow, spread out, and develop as well. They should never be packed too tightly together, since this restricts their mobility, freedom, and growth. They need to be able to spread their wings, so to speak, as well as to develop their creative abilities, energies, and talents to the maximum extent. This is why one of the biggest mistakes that can be made in education is to put too many students in a classroom, since there is insufficient room for growth and teachers are unable to attend to the needs, interests, and problems of every student and group. Clearly all people and groups need enough space to grow and develop if their abilities are to be cultivated effectively and they are to soar to great heights.

This same need for space is evident in town planning and urban design. When people and groups are packed too tightly together, the result can be frustration, crime, and violence because human densities are too high. Indeed, one of the greatest challenges in town planning and urban design is to provide enough space for people and groups to grow and develop properly while simultaneously preserving the sense of community, identity, solidarity, and belonging that comes from bringing people and groups together, enabling them to share the same space together, and living in harmony and happiness.

Given these examples, and others that might be provided, is it any wonder that Voltaire, Herder, and many others have been captivated by the intimate connection between gardens, plants, flowers, and cultivation on the one hand and people, groups, culture, and cultures on the other?

For one thing, gardens, plants, flowers, and cultures are all cultivated by people or groups. They are reflective of the way people and groups imprint their thoughts, ideas, plans, visions, and actions on very specific pieces of the world's natural environment and globe's geography. Whereas plants, flowers, and gardens are cultivated through the application of tools and techniques to the wonders of nature, culture and cultures are cultivated through the application of tools and techniques to the wonders of human creativity and ingenuity.

In the cultivation of gardens, plants, and flowers, it is always wise to have an overall plan in mind even if this plan must be revised many times during the actual execution. In the cultivation of cultures, it is also advisable to have an overall plan in mind, even if it must also be changed many times during the implementation process. Just as care must be taken in the cultivation of gardens, plants, and flowers to ensure that tools and techniques are applied with a masterful hand and skilful eye, so care must be exercised in the cultivation of cultures to ensure that tools and techniques are applied with sensitivity, sensibility, and compassion—the kind of sensitivity, sensibility, and compassion that raises the development and cultivation of cultures from a science to an art.

Moreover, gardens, plants, flowers, and cultures all exist to satisfy a variety of human needs and yield a great deal of satisfaction and delight. In this case, it is the need for rest, relaxation, recuperation, and communion with nature, which is why gardens, plants, and flowers have been prized throughout history in all parts of the world and are often closely associated with thoughts and images of heaven, paradise, and the sublime. "We plant the tree so we can enjoy the shade" is how the ancient Chinese proverb puts it, as well as how Handel expressed it in the exquisite aria *Ombre mai fù* in his opera *Serse*, which is, in effect, "an ode to a tree." In the case of cultures, it is the need for social, economic, educational, artistic, spiritual, and environmental well-being. Nevertheless, the objective is the same: to satisfy a variety of needs and create a great deal of harmony, fulfillment, and delight.

This explains why most countries use elements drawn from nature for cultural purposes, especially as national symbols and emblems that convey important messages and images. These symbols and emblems are closely associated with countries' cultures and are symbolic of those cultures in many ways.

This is especially true for plants, flowers, trees, and animals. The lotus, for instance, is the national emblem or symbol of India, just as the fleur-de-lis is of France, the black orchid is of Belize, the jasmine is of Tunisia, the copihue is of Chile, and the cherry blossom is of Japan. In fact, cherry blossoms and cherry trees go back many centuries in Japanese culture, where blossoms represent the beauty and fragility of life and serve as a reminder that life can be incredibly beautiful and long but also remarkably brutal and short. In addition, cherry tress and blossoms are symbolic of springtime in Japan and many other parts of the world, and therefore a sign of regeneration, renewal, and rebirth.

While Canada, where I live, does not have an official national flower, every province and territory does have a flower as its emblem. In Ontario, the province where I reside, the symbol is the white trillium. It is a beautiful three-petal flower in the shape of a triangle that usually grows in wilderness areas. It can be, and often is, ubiquitous in these areas, and most frequently is white but occasionally deep wine or dark red in colour. It is illegal to pick this flower due to its importance as a provincial symbol.

Canada has many other important elements or symbols drawn from nature that perform a similar function for the country, its citizenry, and its culture. They include the maple leaf, beaver, polar bear, moose, loon, and Canada goose.

The maple tree is ubiquitous in most parts of the country and the maple leaf is accorded a prominent position at the very centre of the Canadian flag where it is surrounded by two red bars and situated on a white background. It is representative of Canada and Canadian culture in many ways because maple leaves turn many different shades of red, gold, orange, yellow, and brown in the fall, in a sense epitomizing the multicultural character of the Canadian population.

For its part, the beaver is symbolic of some of the most important traits and characteristics of Canadians and Canadian culture, such as persistence, dedication, and hard work. The beaver manifests these qualities when it is building its dams and lodges. The polar bear, moose, loon, and Canada goose manifest and represent something else. The polar bear and moose signify power and the ability to live in difficult climatic and geographical circumstances. The loon and Canada goose signify something different—the loneliness and isolation that many Canadians feel and experience due to the colossal size of the country and its small population. This is personified by the loon's plaintive and haunting call on countless Canadian lakes, as well as Canada geese flying in a V-shape over much of the country, especially during the fall.

Regardless of whether they are animals, leaves, trees, or flowers, elements drawn from nature perform an extremely valuable and often indispensable function for all cultures, countries, and citizens in the world. They are so symbolic, ubiquitous, metaphoric, and revered that they contribute a great deal to people's identity, character, and cohesion. This is why many Canadians sew images of maple leaves and the national flag on their jackets, jerseys, and backpacks when they are travelling abroad. Doing so helps to identify them and epitomize their country and culture in other parts of the world. It is also why many Canadian designers and clothing manufacturers use "cultural symbols" drawn from nature in the design and creation of their clothing, especially hats, toques, jackets, mittens, and parkas.

What is true for Canada, Canadians, and Canadian culture is true for other countries, citizens, and cultures as well. Just as the beaver is symbolic of Canadians culture, so the giant panda is of Chinese culture, the kiwi of New Zealand culture, the bald eagle of American culture, the snow leopard of Afghan culture, the giraffe of Tanzanian culture, the peregrine falcon of the United Arab Emirates' culture, and the bear of Russian culture. Of these, it is probably the bear that is the most powerful and revered national symbol in a cultural sense. Not only does it appear frequently in Russian folk tales, sayings, proverbs, and literary works—often as a protagonist—but also it has been the mainstay of Russian circuses for decades. Misha the bear was the mascot at the twenty-second Olympic Games in Moscow in 1980, and appeared once again during the closing ceremonies at the Winter Olympics in Sochi in 2014, this time alongside a leopard and a rabbit to snuff out the Olympic flame to signify the end of the Games.

We could go on, but the point has been made. There is an intimate connection between nature, people, culture, cultures, gardens, plants, animals, other species, and symbols in all parts of the world. The connection dates back centuries and manifests itself in many different ways. All this explains why Cicero's insights into this matter more than twenty centuries ago were so significant at that time and even more so today.

We cultivate many things in life—skills, abilities, talents, minds, friendships, relationships, personalities, identities, cultures, countries, ways of life, plants, flowers, gardens, agricultural crops, and so forth. All require a great deal of care and attention to detail if they are to be cultivated successfully. Moreover, we constantly search for new and better ways of cultivating things, as well as struggle to do things more efficiently and effectively. It is impossible to do so without mastering the art of cultivation and realizing it to the best of our individual and collective abilities.

As important as cultivation is, the connection between people, nature, culture, cultures, and the natural environment that Cicero foresaw more than two thousand years ago is far more essential. Since nature and the natural environment provide the wherewithal and resources that are essential for our survival, existence, and well-being—*as well as the context within which all human and non-human activities are situated and take place*—humanity must place nature and the natural environment at the very centre of its world. Despite the fact that we have developed countless devices and technologies that have reduced our dependence on nature and the natural environment—as well as caused untold environmental damage and destruction, it must be quickly added—it is mandatory to create strong bonds and intimate connections between nature, people, groups, other species, culture, and cultures in the years and decades ahead.

These bonds and connections have been badly frayed in the modern era and must now be recreated, reinforced, and revitalized. This is because culture and cultures, like nature and the natural environment, are evolutionary, organic, fluid, and flexible rather than static, non-organic, inflexible, and fixed. They are constantly evolving and mutating as living organisms as a result of the changes going on in their various parts and the way these parts are woven together to form wholes. Numerous transformations will be needed in all the diverse cultures in the world in the years ahead.

More than any other activity or discipline, culture possesses the needed potential and capabilities to achieve this. Not only will this make it possible to reduce humanity's huge ecological footprint by making the changes in worldviews, values, lifestyles, individual and collective behaviour, and ways of life, but it will make it possible to create a better world and develop this world in reality and in fact.

The key to this lies in treating nature, the natural environment, and other species with all the dignity, respect, and reverence they deserve, as well as reducing the colossal demands we are making on them. Consequently, nature and the natural environment must be revered and respected in the way Brian Swimme and Thomas Berry suggest in their book *The Universe Story*, as well as in other books that are concerned with what Berry called the "Great Work" of humanity. This is also why Pope Francis wrote a papal encyclical—*Laudato Si': On Care of Our Common Home*—that deals with the need for human beings to accept responsibility for the current state of the natural environment and the planet as well as their prospects for the future.

It is this same reverence and respect for nature and the natural environment that Jean Sibelius had uppermost in mind when he wrote many of his most important musical works and especially his fifth symphony. The last movement of this symphony is especially revealing, since it is based on a number of evocative calls Sibelius heard from a flock of swans flying over his farm in Finland one fall afternoon. This renowned composer of Finlandia and many other remarkable musical works exclaimed, "This is one of the great experiences of my life! God, how beautiful," after witnessing this memorable event. (We should also mention his second symphony, which Sibelius said is a real "confession of the soul.")

We have come full circle, since Sibelius's comment reminds us of Marcus Cicero's insightful statement more than two thousand years ago that "culture is the philosophy or cultivation of the soul." For nature and the natural environment are not only the keys to our survival, existence, and well-being, but also the key to understanding how essential it is to cultivate the soul in a personal, group, national, and international sense.

In a personal sense, cultivation of the soul is without doubt one of the most important developments in our lives, if not the most important development. One of the best ways to cultivate the soul is to bond with nature at every opportunity. This is best achieved by studying nature's patterns, rhythms, cycles, themes, elements, and possibilities intensively, as noted earlier. Not only is nature filled with elements that have been immortalized throughout history for their soothing, healing, and spiritual qualities, but it has a life and character all its own. This information is helpful when applied to our lives and souls, since life is more fluid, relaxed, spiritual, and ethereal when it is in tune with nature and we incorporate nature fully and intentionally into our lives. It is simply a matter of getting in sync with nature and paying close attention to its moods, methods, melodies, and mysteries. This is probably why John Muir—the Scottish-American naturalist and one of the major founders of the national parks movement in the United States—said, "It's into the forest I go, to lose my mind and find my soul."

What is true for the soul in a personal sense is also true for the soul in a group and national sense. Just as there are "individual souls," so there are "collective souls," which result from uniting different groups of people, such as tribes, ethnic groups, citizens, countries, and cultures to form unitary entities. This is what Mahatma Gandhi had in mind when he said, "A nation's culture resides in the hearts and in the soul of its people." And what is true for a country's national culture is also true for its community, municipal, regional, ethnic, rural, and other cultures. That is why Oswald Spengler devoted an entire chapter in his book *The Decline of the West* to "The Soul of the City."

And this is not all. Spengler was keenly interested in the "souls of cultures." In the aforementioned book published in 1918, as well as revisions to this book published in a second volume called *Perspectives of World History* in 1923, Spengler went to great lengths to talk about the souls of cultures. He rejected the Eurocentric view that history is a series of distinct periods or phases—such as the division of history into ancient, medieval, and modern eras that was popular in his time and even today—and embraced the notion that history is really about developing a number of different cultures as evolving and dynamic organisms.

For Spengler, there were three major cultures that have evolved throughout history in this sense: the Apollonian, the Magian, and the Faustian. These are better known today as the Classical, Arabian, and Western cultures. Each of these cultures had a beginning, a period of growth and flourishing, and a decline. This latter period occurs when a culture reaches its full potential and final stage and therefore becomes a "civilization" according to Spengler, meaning that it has actually "arrived" rather than is still "becoming."

Each of these cultures has a "distinct soul" that is its "driving or life force," thereby constituting its most important characteristic or feature. In Spengler's view, the Apollonian culture was centred around ancient Greece and Rome, and had a soul characterized by appreciation for the beauty of the human body and a preference for the local and present moment. The Magian culture, which included the Jewish peoples from about 400 B.C., early Christians, and later different Arab tribes and groups up to and including adherents to Islam, had a soul that revolved around the concept of the world as cavern and is epitomized by the domed mosque and a preoccupation with "essence." The Faustian culture, which began in western Europe in the tenth century and now encompasses much of the world, has a soul inspired by an unusually dynamic and expansive psyche and the concept of "infinitely wide and limitless space." This for Spengler is most accurately expressed in modern mathematics and especially its notion of infinity.

For Spengler, the spaciousness of Gothic cathedrals, the voyages of the Vikings, the Crusades, the great geographical discoveries, the age of colonization, the idea of "go west, young man, go west," and "rational restlessness" are all manifestations of the soul of Faustian culture. Spengler sums things up this way: "The Faustian soul—whose being consists in the overcoming of presence, whose feeling is loneliness and whose yearning is infinity—puts its need of solitude, distance, and abstraction into all its actualities, into its public life, its spiritual and its artistic form-worlds alike."[3] This is why religious, spiritual, heritage, artistic, and architectural signs, symbols, metaphors, and so forth—such as cathedrals, mosques, public monuments, famous paintings, and cherished musical works—are often seen, used, and referred to as the "keys" to the different cultures of the world and especially their souls.

This was most obvious in the case of cathedrals and cherished monuments when a tragic and unexpected fire brought down and gutted a large part of the 800-year-old timbered roof of the Notre Dame Cathedral in Paris in 2019. The deep and heartfelt remorse this event caused was shared by people all over France, as well as in many other parts of the world. This explains why there was an instant desire to restore this venerable architectural edifice and national symbol to its former glory.

However, back to *The Decline of the West* for a moment longer. This book's conclusions were rejected for many years because people in the western world didn't like Spengler's pessimistic conviction that

Faustian or Western culture was in decline. Nevertheless, the book eventually received a more favourable reading and assessment as events unfolded.

Consider developments in the United States in recent years. In the present century, two major books have been written about the soul of this country and its culture. The first is Jacob Needleman's book *The American Soul: Rediscovering the Wisdom of the Founders*, published in 2003, and the second is Jon Meacham's book *The Soul of America: The Battle of Our Better Angels*, published in 2018. The arguments made in both books have proven to be prophetic, especially during the 2020 presidential election, which many saw as a fight for "the soul of America." This fight, which many observers contend is going in other parts of the world as well, makes the notion of "the soul" of a culture and country a major and contemporary concern, not something merely of historical interest.

Spengler was not the only cultural scholar to write about the soul of a people, city, country, or culture. Carl Jung's idea of the "collective soul" is also connected to this idea as well as concerned with it. Jung believed that there is a "universal soul" that unites all people as members of the human species. Mark Riva had a similar idea in mind when he launched his online *IMAGINEzine* project in 2021 to call attention to the "collective imagination" and "collective consciousness."

For Jung, the collective or universal soul is based on such shared instincts and archetypes as Mother Earth, the Tree of Life, Water, and so forth. While the collective or universal soul is part of Jung's "collective unconscious," perhaps the time has come for humanity to focus attention on the development of a collective or universal soul as an "all-encompassing, universal, and transcendental soul." Such a soul would be concerned with the spiritual and sublime side of human nature and life and not only the material and physical side, as well as "the essence of life" and not just "the details and specifics of life." As such, it would be concerned with both the "ideals" and "realities" of life.

It is culture, more than any other activity, discipline, or factor in the world and in life, that possesses the potential to realize this. It is through culture, for instance, that it is possible to create a very different type of relationship with the natural environment and "the land" in the future, reduce humanity's demands on the world's scarce resources, and celebrate the profundity, magnificence, and sanctity of the natural realm at every opportunity and in every possible way. It is also through culture that it may just be possible to create a world where all people and all countries are able to enjoy reasonable and realistic standards of living and a decent and enjoyable quality of life without straining the globe's finite resources and limited carrying capacity to the breaking point, as well as to reach for and achieve higher, wiser, and more important goals and objectives.

Is there anything more important to the world, the world system, and humanity at present and going forward into the future? This is what makes Cicero's belief that "culture is the philosophy or cultivation of the soul" so compelling, captivating, and essential. Not only is it a necessity worthy of a great deal of thought, reflection, and attention, but also it is symbolic of the best humanity, culture, and cultures have to offer and are capable of achieving. What makes this even more remarkable is the fact that the intimate connection between culture, cultures, humanity, cultivation, nature, the natural world, and the soul was espoused more than two thousand years ago and still stands as one of culture's highest, wisest, and most cherished ideals today. We have Marcus Cicero to thank for this.

Chapter Three

The Arts

> The arts are not for the privileged few but for the many ... their place is not at the periphery of society but at its center ... they are not just a form of recreation but are of central importance to our well-being and happiness.
>
> —Rockefeller Panel Report, *The Performing Arts: Problems and Prospects*[1]

If culture as cultivation of the soul can be traced back to ancient times, so too can culture as the arts. While there is a great deal of debate, controversy, and uncertainty about when and where music, literature, painting, drama, and so forth first appeared, there is no doubt about the fact that the arts have been in existence for countless millennia in virtually all parts of the world.

A good example of this is the practice of painting images of animals and people on the walls and ceilings of caves. Such paintings have been traced back to 70,000 B.C. in Indonesia and 40,000 to 50,000 B.C. in France, South Africa, China, and possibly elsewhere in the world, indicating a strong bond between culture and the arts that is thousands of years old. This is also true of the emergence of the decorative and ceremonial arts—the painting of faces, making and wearing of masks, creation of colourful costumes, celebration of rituals, burials, and the like. These practices likely originated at a much later date than cave paintings. Nevertheless, these arts became popular and commonplace almost everywhere, among the Indigenous peoples of North and South America as well as Oceania, not to mention countless tribes in Africa, early and numerous dynasties in Asia, and diverse groups of peoples in Europe, the Middle East, and other parts of the world.

This bond between the arts and culture was strengthened by the powerful role the Muses played in Greek mythology and antiquity, most notably as sources of divine inspiration in the arts and in many other areas and avenues of life. In some cases, the Greeks believed there were three Muses, those of poetry, the arts, and the sciences. In other cases, they thought there were nine Muses, namely those of epic poetry, lyric poetry, music, tragedy, hymns, history, dance, comedy, and astronomy. In both cases, the Muses were deemed to be daughters of Zeus who lived on Mount Helicon near Mount Olympus. They have been written about countless times in history, especially by such well-known authors as Homer, Virgil, Dante Alighieri, Chaucer, Shakespeare, and Milton. The Muses were, and still are, often invoked by people in many different walks of life and parts of the world as a source of inspirational thoughts, ideas, and insights, especially during the formative stages of the creative process.

Despite the bond established between the arts and culture in ancient times and the important role the Muses eventually played, the *artistic manifestation of culture* did not begin to assert itself in earnest until much later. In Europe, for instance, this occurred most notably in the medieval period and early modern times, especially the Renaissance. During this period, there was a powerful connection between the arts and religion, as there has been in many other parts of the world as well. This brought with it a great deal of religious painting, music, and architecture. Countless contributions were made to this by such Italian painters, architects, sculptors, and composers as Giotto, Fra Angelico, Luca della Robbia, Leonardo da Vinci, Michelangelo, Brunelleschi, Donatello, Claudio Monteverdi, Giovanni Gabrieli, and many others. During this period, the arts in Europe burst forth in all their magnificence and rose to great heights, first in Italy, then elsewhere in Europe, and eventually throughout many other parts of the world. The world has never been the same since. For this reason, it is fair to say the artistic manifestation of culture is one of the most essential manifestations of culture of all. It also illustrates how the arts, culture, and cultures fit together as nicely as a hand in a glove.

Whereas the arts were viewed somewhat narrowly in earlier times, they are seen in substantially broader terms today, and are generally deemed to include music, opera, dance, drama, painting, sculpture, literature, and poetry, as has been the case for more than two thousand years. Many people also include language, architecture, town planning, urban design, landscaping, photography, gastronomy, cinematography, photography, and horticulture in this list of the arts, and with good reason. There are also many people who include the material and decorative arts and the crafts in their definition of the arts and the artistic manifestation of culture and rightly so, since they require a great deal of aesthetic ability and artistic expertise and are among the world's oldest and most ubiquitous artistic activities.[2] More recently, it has become commonplace to include the "cultural industries" of publishing, radio, television, film, video, sound recording, digital technologies, and so forth as part of the artistic manifestation of culture, although there is much less agreement on this because most of these activities can be reproduced by mechanical means or technological devices and are therefore not "one of a kind" in the way most artistic activities are. It should also be noted here that some people consider any activity as an art form if it is executed with flair, imagination, creativity, and excellence.

Regardless of how the arts are defined, it is necessary to be very clear about what is included and what is not. This can vary significantly from one country to another and one part of the world to another. In China and Japan, for example, tree dwarfing, flower arranging, and calligraphy are deemed to be arts, just as tattooing is in Tanzania. Then there is Bali, which is rich in the arts and elevates many activities to art forms because everything is done to "the very best of people's abilities."

Just about everything that exists in the world involves the arts in one form or another when the arts are seen in this much more expansive and all-encompassing way. This means the arts play a crucial role in the world and in life—a role that is much more important and valuable than is commonly assumed, as will be demonstrated in this book. Not only do the arts open up vast vistas and fertile avenues for exploration and discovery, but everything is there in one form or another: nature, the natural environment, the human species, other species, personality development, communities, towns, cities, countries, cultures, civilizations, history, geography, the past, the present, the future, and a great deal else. This is why some people believe that "art imitates life" and "life imitates art." An enormous amount can be learned from the arts about life, living, reality, the human condition, and the world situation. It also explains why Jean Cocteau believed that "art is not a pastime, but a priesthood." In doing so, he stretched a point to make a point, as many good artists do.

Time spent examining the arts is richly rewarded. One begins to see why the arts are so important and deserve such a prominent place in our lives as well as at the centre of culture, cultures, and the world. When the American psychologist Rollo May asked, "What if art and culture are not the frosting at all, but rather the fountainhead of human existence?" he put his finger on the crux of this matter. For the arts, like culture, are *not* frills, luxuries, or the icing on the cake, but rather the elixir that is needed to live happy, meaningful, and contented lives at each and every stage and age, from the earliest signs of life to its final days of life. They also provide the key needed to learn a great deal about life, living, the world, and the life process in all their diverse forms.

While there has been a tendency in the modern world to value the arts primarily as forms of entertainment that are pleasant to look at, watch, listen to, and appreciate—something they obviously are and which should not be discounted or downplayed—this should not be allowed to obscure the fact that the arts have deep aesthetic, symbolic, philosophical, and spiritual significance when they are viewed as they should be, namely from a cultural rather than an economic, recreational, or entertainment perspective. As such, they possess the potential to expand, enhance, and enrich people's lives and the world condition in a multitude of diverse ways.

We experience the arts even before we are born. Regardless of where we are born in the world, we are exposed to some of the most important aspects of the arts when we are still in the womb. This is true for language and the language arts—among the most important arts and art forms of all but, unfortunately, usually taken for granted and ignored because they are so commonplace—but also for music, literature, and other artistic activities. Many mothers throughout the world sing to their babies and read stories to them when they are still in the womb, knowing intuitively or consciously how important the arts are for getting a good start in life. This is why many parents want music lessons, art lessons, singing lessons, or dance lessons for their children, even if they have been deprived of such opportunities themselves.

After we are born, our encounter with the arts escalates rapidly. This is especially true for the material arts or crafts, since babies and infants manifest a keen desire to have sensorial experiences by touching, holding, smelling, and feeling everything they come into contact with, including pillows, blankets, dolls, hands, fingers, and toes. Not long after this, they play with blocks and other materials. They also sing, dance, perform, and clown around, either by themselves or in public. They also experiment with paint, applying it to paper and other materials with their hands, feet, and brushes, as well as throwing it against walls to see what this will look like, much to the consternation of their parents.

One person who had a keen interest in the arts and especially the education of children in the arts was Sir Herbert Read, the British author and educator. He produced a powerful rationale for the arts and arts education in childhood and youth—and indeed throughout life—in books such as *Education through Art, Culture and Education in a World Order*, and others. He also participated in the establishment of the International Society for Education through Art as an executive arm of UNESCO in 1954.

One organization that has capitalized on Read's remarkable vision in this area and carried it further is the International Child Art Foundation, which was created by Ashfaq Ishaq in the United States several decades ago. This remarkable organization employs the power of art in all its diverse forms and especially in the visual arts to nurture children's creativity and imagination and imbue children with empathy, sensitivity, and compassion. As a promoter and developer of children's artistic abilities and experiences, it produces the Arts Olympiad and World Children's Art Festival, publishes *ChildArt Magazine*, and provides many Peace through Art programs and initiatives.

For many centuries, the arts were seen and treated as "ends in themselves" rather than "means to other ends." As a result, the focus was on the many benefits that could be derived from the arts themselves. From the visual, material, and architectural arts, for example, there is much we can learn about mass, texture, density, form, shape, proportion, colour, and perspective; from dance, drama, and literature, one learns a great deal about balance, movement, muscle control, physical coordination, tragedy, comedy, satire, and pathos; and from music, sound, rhythm, melodies, harmony, counterpoint, composition, and orchestration. Much can also be learned about discipline through participation in artistic activities, including playing musical instruments, painting pictures, acting in plays, writing poems, telling stories, and the like. The underlying assumption in most cases is that people will not grow up to be artists or have artistic careers later in life, but they can still enjoy the arts and derive a great deal of satisfaction from them.

In recent years, there has been a tendency to treat the arts more as means to other ends rather than ends in themselves. This is apparent in many parts of the world. It results from the many benefits that can be reaped from the arts, such as cultivating people's creativity, imagination, and commitment to excellence; developing a battery of skills, abilities, and techniques that can be applied to other activities; mastering other disciplines; producing numerous economic benefits; bringing people together; learning about nature and the natural environment; and contributing to the realization of a more harmonious and sustainable world. Learning about the arts in this sense and not only as ends in themselves is essential if people are to be prepared properly for life.

While some art forms are individual in character—the visual and material arts, for example—others are more collective, such as drama, dance, opera, and music. It is impossible to put on a play, produce a symphony, or stage an opera, ballet, or dance without engaging many people in the process and achieving a great deal of cooperation and teamwork. This ranges all the way from working together on the construction of sets and props and the rehearsal of scenes and movements to polishing up specific parts and putting on final performances. Through the preparation and presentation of works of art, people learn to work collectively in the realization of common causes, goals, and objectives, thereby developing the collaborative skills and cooperative abilities that are in great demand throughout the world today. This also produces more human interaction and social engagement, countering the isolation and estrangement that often arise from the use of contemporary technology, not to mention the social isolation produced by such events as the COVID-19 pandemic.

Recognition of these two distinct strengths of the arts—as ends in themselves and as the means to other ends—has resulted from the work of UNESCO and many other organizations, the involvement of countless artists and arts organizations in a variety of social causes and humanistic concerns, the advocacy of distinguished experts in the arts such as Sir Kenneth Robinson, and recent research into and assessments of the role the arts play in society, people's lives, and the world at large. Without the ability to create, innovate, work together, think critically, respond imaginatively, deal with a host of internal and external problems, and apply what is learned from the arts to other areas of life, people will face severe disadvantages in the future.

Contemplation of these facts should encourage us to open up a commanding place for the arts in our lives, communities, towns, cities, cultures, countries, and the world. This will help in numerous ways, including the development of our personalities, identities, careers, and lives, the raising of children, the enjoyment of family life, the cultivation of friendships and relationships, connection with other people, the sharing of experiences, and a great deal else. Not only should we reach out to the arts whenever and wherever possible, but we should allow the arts to penetrate into the interior of our being and our consciousness. There is no better way to explore the many different ways the arts can broaden, deepen, intensify, and enrich our lives, enhance our understanding of ourselves and others, contribute to our development, confidence, identity, and well-being, and strengthen our connections with other people, nature, and the world around us. It doesn't matter whether this happens on a part-time, full-time, casual, or comprehensive basis. It can still produce transformative changes and transcendental experiences.

Take, for instance, the remarkable amount of joy and happiness that the arts bring into our lives as a result of listening to beautiful music, watching superb plays, enjoying exciting operas and dance performances, gazing at evocative paintings, cherishing precious craft objects, reading fascinating books, savouring memorable stories, poems, films, architectural masterpieces, and exquisite cuisines, and viewing majestic monuments, especially if we fully open our hearts, minds, souls, spirits, and senses to these experiences. Surely this is what Walter Pater had in mind when he declared, "Art comes to you proposing frankly to give nothing but the highest quality to your moments as they pass."

There are billions of people all over the world who are enjoying artistic experiences like these and many others as audience members, active participants, or both. While forms of engagement in the arts differ for different people and groups—with diverse implications, consequences, and outcomes—they bring an enormous amount of pleasure into people's lives and help them to deal with the stresses and strains of modern life. Regardless of the art form, every person in the world, no matter where they live, young or old, male or female, rich or poor, derives an immense amount of satisfaction from the arts every minute of every day, whether in an elite, popular, or folk sense, or in any other way. It is impossible to live in any part of the world today without encountering and enjoying the arts in a variety of settings on a daily, weekly, monthly, and yearly basis.

One of the most fascinating things about the arts is that they can be enjoyed in reproduced or recorded form, not just "live." The arts are not only accessible through live concerts, plays, exhibitions, performances, festivals, and so forth, but also through the cultural industries of radio, television, film, video, sound recording, and publishing, as well as by means of a rich array of technological devices, channels, platforms, and vehicles. In recent years, this accessibility has been enlarged and enhanced substantially through incredible advances in communications and major breakthroughs in the social and mass media as well as digital technologies, especially during the COVID-19 pandemic.

There is hardly a person in any part of the world or any walk of life today who is not able to access the arts through computers, iPads, iPhones, smartphones, tablets, the Internet, YouTube, Facebook, Twitter, virtual reality, and other digital, technological, and communications platforms and devices, whether owned by themselves or by family members, friends, schools, community centres, libraries, or local associations. The ability to access works of art of the highest calibre in every art form by virtually every artist and arts organization in the world—past and present, ancient and modern, eastern, western, northern, and southern—as well as the ability to "walk" through any art gallery, museum, street, or city in the world today through virtual reality and other means is an achievement of monumental proportions. As people in all parts of the world are discovering much to their delight, this achievement will undoubtedly be amplified many times over in the future as more digital, technological, and communications vehicles and capabilities are conceived, created, and employed.

Enjoying the arts doesn't have to cost a great deal of money. While it can be expensive to attend concerts and plays or take singing, painting, craft, dance, or music lessons, there are still numerous opportunities to enjoy the arts in every community, city, country, and culture in the world without having to pay an exorbitant price, provided we are willing to work at this and seek them out. The joy and satisfaction that comes from the arts over a lifetime is immeasurable and immense, as is evident on the faces of young children, teenagers, adults, and seniors whenever and wherever we see them enjoying or participating in the creation or presentation of a work of art. As Glenn Gould, the well-known Canadian pianist, said, "The purpose of art is not the release of a momentary ejection of adrenaline but is, rather, the gradual lifelong construction of a state of wonder and serenity."

While the arts have a great deal to do with the world and everything in the world when they are looked at in totality, one of the most fascinating things about them is that every art form possesses some special quality or ability that makes it distinctive and unique. This is true not only for the performing, exhibiting, and literary arts, but also for the cinematographic, architectural, culinary, and all other arts, as I discuss in my book *The Arts: Gateway to a Fulfilling Life and Cultural Age* (Rock's Mills Press, 2020).

Consider music as one of the best examples of this fact. In this case, it is sound, rhythm, and melodies that make music distinctive. Composers and musicians use these qualities and capabilities to create musical experiences and compositions that express their (and our) hopes, dreams, aspirations, and ideas, often in deep, profound, sublime, and ethereal ways. This is what gives music its incredible power and universal appeal, and that is why some people contend that music is the highest art form of all. This is also likely why

Henry Wadsworth Longfellow, the American poet, described music as humanity's "universal language," and the Danish author Hans Christian Andersen declared that "where words fail, music speaks." Millennia earlier, Plato said in *The Republic* that music should play a central role in the development of our lives and the "ideal state" because it gives "soul to the universe, wings to the mind, flight to the imagination, and gaiety to life and to everything." Or, as Walter Pater observed, "all art constantly aspires toward the condition of music."

Music possesses an awesome power to move people in profound and multifarious ways, to the very depths of their being. We have all been so touched by specific pieces of music at various times in our lives that we feel we have transcended the world and entered a sacred place.

In the western musical tradition, melody-makers such as Schubert, Mendelssohn, the Beatles, and countless others possessed a special ability in this regard. Chopin seems to have had a particular talent for the creation of melodies. Some of his most beautiful melodies occur at the very beginning of pieces, or, in a few cases, throughout entire pieces such as his *Étude Op. 25, No. 1* in A-flat major (also known as the *Aeolian Harp*). Others, however, are buried in the middle of pieces and only revealed much later, such as the exquisite melodies in his *Fantaisie-Impromptu Op. 66*, *Scherzo No. 2 in B-flat minor, Op. 31*, and *Ballade No. 1 in G minor, Op. 23*. We have to wait for some time to hear the exquisite melodies in these pieces, something that is also true in the second movements of his first and second piano concertos. And these are only a few examples of melodies drawn from the western musical tradition. There exists a vast cornucopia of beautiful melodies in the works of composers and musicians in every culture, country, tradition, and part of the world, as well as in classical, popular, folk, historical, and contemporary genres.

What sound, rhythm, and melodies are to music, representation, perspective, proportion, and the use of colour are to the visual arts. Painters use these properties all the time and in many different ways to produce paintings that express feelings, emotions, ideas, thoughts, impressions, and visions that border on the sublime. An excellent example of this practice in the western visual arts tradition are the paintings of Joseph Mallord William Turner, the renowned Romantic landscape painter. He created a wealth of paintings of scenes and events in his native England and on the European continent that are incredibly beautiful and most revealing in their use of colour, perspective, proportion, and representation. I am thinking here, for example, of his *Morning after the Wreck*; *The Moselle Bridge, at Coblenz*; *The Fighting Temeraire, tugged to her last berth to be broken up*; *The Grand Canal, Venice 1835*; and *The Lake, Petworth: Sunset, a Stag Drinking*. There is a mystical and ethereal quality about these paintings that borders on the sublime.

Just as colour, perspective, proportion, and representation are central to the visual arts, so is simplicity a key element of poetry. While every artist and art form aims to express things simply—often doing so because this is one of the keys to creating great works of art—poetry seems far more concerned with simplicity than other art forms, as well as manifesting this quality most profusely. In fact, it is probably fair to say that poetry relies more heavily on simplicity than on any other quality. This is because the challenge in poetry—regardless of whether poems are oriental or occidental, long or short, traditional or contemporary—is to express things as simply and succinctly as possible, achieving the maximum effect with the minimum number of words.

Examples of this abound. John Keats' line "A thing of beauty is a joy forever" resonated strongly with people because it expressed a powerful idea in eight short and simple words. Interestingly, Robert Schumann's musical piece, "The Poet Speaks," also achieves this and does so deliberately because Schumann was attempting to demonstrate this specific ability of poets and poetry in this intriguing piece of music. It is undoubtedly one of the simplest pieces of music ever written, along with J. S. Bach's *Prelude No. 1*, which is also very simple but incredibly beautiful and powerful.

Poetry's claim to profundity and power through simplicity is also illustrated by William Blake in his poem *Auguries of Innocence*. This poem says so much in so few words that it possesses an awesome power and profundity that is difficult to describe but easy to appreciate:

To see a World in a Grain of Sand
And a Heaven in a Wild Flower

Hold Infinity in the palm of your hand
And Eternity in an hour

It took a poet of Blake's stature to put these thoughts and ideas into words and express them in such a succinct way that they resonate so strongly with people. This is equally true of the next two lines of this poem, which also possess a remarkable power and profundity and are famous for their ability to convey an enormous amount in a few simple words:

A Robin Red breast in a Cage
Puts all Heaven in a Rage

These two lines resonate strongly with countless people concerned about freedom and the many constraints imposed on it. They also speak to those opposed to putting animals in cages or zoos, a practice increasing numbers of people around the world want to see ended.

Interestingly, on the other side of the world and a century earlier than Blake, the great Japanese poet Matsuo Basho was creating short and powerful haiku verses in the Edo period in Japan. These poems were eventually revered and became world famous. Consider his most celebrated poetic masterpiece:

An old pond
A frog leaps in
Sound of water

Basho, Keats, and Blake are only three examples of myriad poets throughout the world who have expressed powerful ideas with great simplicity. There are many others, including Elizabeth Barrett Browning ("How do I love thee? / Let me count the ways") and William Shakespeare ("All the world's a stage / And all the men and women merely players") in the western poetic tradition. Talk about saying powerful things with the utmost simplicity and minimum number of words! Countless other poets in the world have done so as well, such as Robert Browning, Pierre de Ronsard, Omar Khayyam, Emily Dickinson, Pablo Neruda, Federico Garcia Lorca, Rabindranath Tagore, Li

Po, Wang Wei, Du Fu, Robert Frost, Jorge Luis Borges, Maya Angelou, and numerous others.

What simplicity is to poetry, movement and physicality are to dance. Here, too, many examples abound in different idioms and parts of the world. In ballet, for instance, Tchaikovsky's *Swan Lake* and *Sleeping Beauty* are masterpieces filled with many graceful solos and steps as well as elegant *pas de deux* that border on the sublime and possibly even the divine. But these are only two examples among many. Countless dances performed in all parts of the world are incredibly beautiful and coveted for their grace, elegance, and charm, regardless of whether they are classical, popular, folk, contemporary, or multicultural in character. This includes, among many others, the *Adumu* performed by the Maasai in Africa, the Bharatanatyam in Southern India, the Samba in Brazil, the Dragon Dance in China, and the dances performed by the Whirling Dervishes in Turkey, the Maori in New Zealand, Flamenco dancers in Spain, and major dance troupes in the Caribbean, just to cite a few. Surely this is why Martha Graham, the legendary American dancer and choreographer, described dance as "the hidden language of the soul."

Then there is architecture. What movement and physicality are to dance, mass, density, form, design, matter, and texture are to architecture. Architects use these elements all the time and in many different ways to produce exquisite buildings and other structures. Some refer to architecture and architectural masterpieces as "frozen music." Indeed, some buildings are so enticing and ornate that they really do look like music that has been frozen in time and space.

While the Taj Mahal in India is perhaps the best example of this since it is deemed by many people to be one of the most beautiful architectural masterpieces in the world—if not *the* most beautiful—there are countless others. Included here would undoubtedly be the Hagia Sophia and Blue Mosque in Turkey, the Jameh Mosque and Shah Mosque in Iran, Kinkaku-ji (the Temple of the Golden Pavilion) in Japan, the Shwedagon Pagoda in Myanmar, Angkor Wat in Cambodia, the Temple of Heaven in China, Mezquita-Catedral de Córdoba in Spain, the Hindu temple Prambanan in Indonesia, the Sydney Opera House in Australia, and the famous cathedral in Milan, Italy. All these architectural marvels, and myriad others, use mass, form, matter, design, density, and texture to enhance their impact and appeal.

This is true for large buildings and small. While many Gothic and Romanesque buildings achieve beauty by enclosing vast spaces and doing so in such a way that they stretch upwards towards the heavens—think of the great Gothic cathedrals of France and England, for example—many Byzantine buildings achieve beauty by enclosing small spaces and decorating them as exquisitely as possible. The many beautiful Byzantine basilicas in Russia, Eastern Europe, and Ravenna, Italy, do this and do it extremely well. By decorating the walls, ceilings, and floors with glittering frescos, tiles, inlays, icons, and images, these buildings are predicated on the belief that "small is beautiful" and "less is more." As a result, they provide excellent examples of how beauty can be achieved in small places and spaces.

Turning to theatre, literature, opera, and film, these arts are characterized by the use of story, doing so in fascinating, informative, and illustrious ways. Stories communicate things that are simple and profound, mundane and momentous, timely and timeless. Consider the works of Shakespeare. His stories are full of keen insights into different personality types, diverse social, political, and societal situations, human triumphs and tragedies, and individual foibles and insecurities. For these reasons, his plays are as revered today as when they were first written—perhaps more so. What is true for Shakespeare is also true for many other authors, including Charlotte Brontë, Jane Austen, George Bernard Shaw, Molière, Charles Dickens, Jalāl ad-Dīn Muhammad Rūmī, Alice Munro, and countless others. What a powerful, endearing, and enduring effect stories can have, regardless of whether they are epic tales or everyday adventures, who is telling them, or how they are presented.

Operas also tell stories. We need think only of the operas of Puccini, Verdi, Wagner, Handel, Monteverdi, Leon Cavallo, and many others. And while great stories can be told in operas, they can also be told in music without words. This is hard to believe but easy to illustrate, since there are thousands of examples. In the European tradition, Telemann was a master of this form. Think of such compositions as his *Don Quixote at Camacho's Wedding* and *La Bourse* (*Stock Exchange*) suites. You can almost see Don Quixote tilting at windmills and people running around on the Stock Exchange floor buying and selling bonds while listening to these compositions.

There are countless stories in every culture, country, and civilization in the world that ring true because they are so captivating and compelling, regardless of the art form used to tell them. These stories run the gamut of possibilities, from the remote past to the immediate present. They extend, in fact, from Homer's *Iliad* and *Odyssey* to Chinua Achebe's *Things Fall Apart* and Paulo Coelho's *The Alchemist*. In the western literary tradition, there are countless literary masterpieces, including Dante Alighieri's *Divine Comedy*, Miguel de Cervantes' *Don Quixote*, Alexander Dumas' *Count of Monte Cristo*, Emily Brontë's *Wuthering Heights*, Mary Shelley's *Frankenstein*, Herman Melville's *Moby-Dick*, J. R. R. Tolkien's *The Lord of the Rings*, Harper Lee's *To Kill a Mockingbird*, Leo Tolstoy's *War and Peace*, Mark Twain's *The Adventures of Huckleberry Finn*, Toni Morrison's *Song of Solomon*, and J. K. Rowling's Harry Potter series. These works, and many others, expose the light and dark sides of human nature and the human condition. And what is true for the western literary tradition is also true for all other literary traditions. Every country in the world has its own cornucopia of outstanding stories and cherished literary masterpieces, regardless of whether it is situated in the south, north, east, or west.

Likewise with film, an art form that possesses the potential to tell stories in visual and auditory terms, as well as to preserve them for posterity. This is epitomized by such epic films as *Gone With the Wind, How Green Was My Valley, Rashomon, Seven Samurai, Frida*, and many others, which are all great stories that have been enjoyed by millions of people around the world since they were first released. (Admittedly, some films such as *Gone With the Wind* and others have been criticized for being racially biased as well as having a number of other deficiencies and shortcomings.)

Then there are the culinary arts. As everyone knows, their special qualities are taste, texture, smell, and aroma. The culinary arts rose to prominence after the internationally renowned French master chef Auguste Escoffier popularized them as well as the major gastronomic achievements of France in the nineteenth century. Not only did he capitalize on many techniques and recipes created by Marie-

Antoine Carême—also a famous master chef—but he systematized French cooking in his book *Le Guide Culinaire*, which is still used by chefs throughout the world today. He also made French sauces popular, especially the "famous five"—béchamel, velouté, espagnole, hollandaise, and tomato.

Not long after this other countries picked up on Escoffier's and Carême's initiatives and inspirations to draw attention to their own culinary masterpieces and gastronomic traditions. This helped to stimulate international interest in the great cuisines and traditions of the world, including Chinese, Indian, Japanese, Thai, Italian, and Turkish cuisines. Also playing a part more recently were the many television programs made by Julia Child, Anthony Bourdain, and others who travelled to many different parts of the world to focus attention on local restaurants and their cuisines as well as their intimate connection to the other arts, local people, neighbourhoods, and community and national cultures. The world hasn't been the same since these and other programs were created, with far more interest in food, foodstuffs, and the many diverse cuisines of the world as well as the crucial role the culinary arts play in many different aspects of life, from family celebrations, community events, ethnic festivals, and fairs to banquets, diplomatic affairs, cultures, and international culinary exchanges of many types.

All this is documented in detail by the International Institute of Gastronomy, Culture, Arts, and Tourism (IGCAT) in Barcelona through its quarterly reports, examples of creative and indigenous cuisines, and numerous other activities. Co-founded and spearheaded by Diane Dodd, this organization has done a great deal since its inception a decade ago to celebrate cultural and food diversity, largely by providing awards to outstanding chefs and regional cuisines that connect different sectors in an effort to promote a more sustainable future and show how gastronomy is intimately connected to people's overall health and well-being, other artistic and cultural experiences, responsible tourism, environmental conservation, and sustainable development. In so doing, they are making a strong case for the fact that food, foodstuffs, and the culinary arts, like other art forms, are major keys or gateways to culture and cultures with a great deal to teach us.

Thelma Barer-Stein knows all about the culinary arts and culinary possibilities, especially those of different ethnic groups. In her book, *You Eat What You Are: A Study of Ethnic Food Traditions*, she states, "Without food we cannot survive. But food is much more than a tool of survival. Food is a source of pleasure, comfort, security. Food is also a symbol of hospitality, social status, and has ritual significance. What we select to eat, how we prepare it, serve it, and even how we eat it, are all factors deeply touched by our individual (and collective) cultural inheritance."[3] Interestingly, many people no longer ask if you would like to have fish, chicken, or steak for dinner, but rather if you would like to eat "Indian," "Moroccan," "French," "Italian," "South American," or "Caribbean."

It is clear from experiences like these and many others that every art form possesses specific qualities, abilities, and features—in addition to sharing many general characteristics—that are unique and can be used to great advantage to produce powerful artistic and aesthetic experiences that influence people in a variety of ways. And this is not all. Different art forms—and different elements and ingredients in art forms—are capable of evoking strong emotions, responses, feelings, images, and sensations. There is a big difference, for instance, between the feelings and emotions aroused by a play by Molière compared to one by August Strindberg, a painting by Jackson Pollock compared to one by Ai Weiwei, or a musical composition by Palestrina compared to one by Prokofiev. And what is true for plays, paintings, and musical works is also true for musical instruments and colours. Whereas the feelings, emotions, and sensations evoked by an oboe or a saxophone tend to be melancholy, soothing, and haunting, the feelings, emotions, and sensations aroused by a trumpet or drum are much more strident and assertive. This is also true for colours. Think of the different emotions, feelings, and sensations evoked by the colours red, green, white, blue, and black, as well as the different effects these colours can and often do have on people, something well known by advertisers and marketing experts.

If the arts and artists bring an incredible amount of joy and happiness into our lives, they also help us to express ourselves in more sensitive, humane, and compassionate ways. This makes it possible for us to feel better about ourselves, as well as to connect with other people on a deeper, richer, and more fundamental level. While the arts, artists, and arts organizations can be provocative and destructive at times—*and must be if they are to fulfill one of the most essential roles and responsibilities in their mandate, in society and in the world*—the feelings and emotions evoked and aroused are far more positive than negative. Artists and their works rarely injure people, destroy things, or incite violent and destructive forms of behaviour. They also help people to develop their capacity for creativity and excellence. As a result, they are ideal vehicles for helping people to respond imaginatively, intelligently, and energetically to the demands and dictates of the modern world.

The arts also have a valuable role to play in training people for jobs, professions, and careers. At one time, people were trained for a single job and profession. As a result, education was focused on learning specific skills and specialized abilities. With the high rate of occupational turnover and technological change today—it is now estimated that people may have ten to fifteen jobs over the course of their lives, in very different areas and professions—this view is changing and changing rapidly. It is now apparent that narrowly trained and highly specialized people may not be able to deal with new employment situations, realities, and possibilities, or with jobs that are constantly changing, evolving, mutating, being downsized, or even disappearing entirely.

Clearly much more attention will need to be paid to helping people to become more creative in finding jobs and employment opportunities. It is creativity rather than conformity that will enable people to do this, as well as to create jobs for themselves and fashion the new types of employment situations, practices, and entrepreneurial skills and abilities that are required. Nothing does this better than involvement in the arts—the kind of involvement that brings out the best in people and makes it possible for them to express themselves in innovative and imaginative ways.

What is true for creativity is also true for excellence. Regardless of what occupations or professions people end up in over the course of their lives, achieving excellence is essential in all. The arts tend to value excellence more highly than many other activities because it is imperative for mastering aesthetic challenges and producing outstanding artistic results. Nobody likes to watch inferior or mediocre performances! In order to prevent this, it is necessary to aspire to and achieve excellence in all artistic endeavours, which often turns out to be the key to realizing excellence in other areas of life as well. This is why we have terms in our vocabulary such as "the art of science," "the art of politics," and "the art of business." Each of these areas is an art form when performed with excellence. Henry David Thoreau went a step further in this regard when he said, "The highest condition of art is artlessness."

The same holds true for diversity. The arts are incredibly diverse because they are constantly evolving rather than remaining constant, thereby exposing us to new, better, and different ways of doing things. While many techniques in the arts have to be repeated over and over again in order to master them, one of the most salient things about the arts is that they are always changing and diversifying, not only in time but also in space. What is commonplace today will likely not be commonplace tomorrow, as the history of all art forms reveals. The arts are always on the move, so to speak, thereby helping people to deal more effectively with diversity, complexity, and a world that is in perpetual motion and constant flux.

The arts are also capable of strengthening our perceptual and sensorial abilities. This should begin by cultivating the art of seeing, since it is largely through sight in general and the eye in particular that we learn to see and comprehend the world, much as Goethe, Ken Wilber, Fritjof Capra, and many others have advocated. This ability is cultivated most effectively through the visual arts, including taking art lessons as well as going to art galleries, museums, and so forth. Doing so enables us to develop our capacity for seeing, perceiving, and perspective, comprehending foreground and background relationships, discovering links and connections, and focusing on the whole and not just the parts of the whole to a much greater extent.

This is merely the first in a long sequence of steps that is required to strengthen our other sensory capabilities. For the arts improve our ability to hear, taste, smell, and touch and not just to see. These other capabilities can be cultivated through music, sculpture, the material, culinary, and literary arts, and many others. While it may not be recognized as much as it should be, people who take art or craft lessons, modern or ballroom dancing, or cooking courses are more likely to have better sensorial abilities than people who do not engage in these activities. For involvement in activities such as these makes it possible to write more convincingly, speak more clearly, express ideas more simply, hear more acutely, touch more gently, taste more discerningly, and see more precisely.

The arts also have an essential role to play in bringing people, groups, communities, societies, and countries together. They do this through the ability of artists and arts organizations to create music, poems, pictures, paintings, stories, plays, and so forth that can be and often are *shared,* regardless of whether this is in live, visual, virtual, or digital terms. This does more than anything else to create strong bonds, connections, and a sense of belonging between people, regardless of whether they live in small towns, big cities, or rural areas.

This ability to create social bonds and cultural connections is urgently needed in the world of the present and the future. A good example of the arts' ability to bond and connect people is the work of Gareth Malone, the British choral conductor, who created many choirs in England and other parts of the world, especially in schools, communities, corporations, among military personnel, and for the Invictus Games. Malone's work in this area attracted a great deal of international attention, in part because of the depiction of many of his achievements in a television series, *The Choir*, produced by the British Broadcasting Corporation.

Especially important in this respect were the choirs Malone created in South Oxhey, a suburb of Watford in Hertfordshire, England. South Oxhey was economically depressed. Malone brought the whole community together by ferreting out many people who had never sung in a choir before and encouraging them to join the South Oxhey community choir. This culminated with highly successful performances in the Watford Coliseum, St. Albans Cathedral, and other venues. Members of the choir waxed eloquently about how frightened they were to join initially, how persistent Malone was in getting them involved, how well trained they were for their performances, and how exciting and enriching these experiences were in their lives. Not only did the choir do a great deal to rejuvenate South Oxhey in social and musical terms, but also it helped to bring the community back from the brink of economic disaster.

South Oxhey is not alone in this regard. Towns, cities, and countries all over the world are benefiting from the remarkable capacity the arts, artists, and arts organizations possess to activate and stimulate major urban developments. It is no coincidence that the cities that are the most developed in economic terms are often the cities most developed in artistic terms. What would Paris be without the Eiffel Tower and the Louvre, Vienna without the Ring and the Vienna Philharmonic, Florence and Venice without their remarkable art galleries and museums, Beijing without the Forbidden City and its incredible aesthetic treasures, and New York without Carnegie Hall, Broadway, and many other musical venues and theatrical organizations? These and countless other cities throughout the world are rich in artistic treasures and anxious to display their aesthetic accomplishments to residents and visitors alike, as well as to capitalize on the social, economic, and financial rewards that are derived from this.

Indeed, the arts are "making things happen" in towns and cities all over the world. This is being achieved through the creation of artistic hubs, districts, corridors, neighbourhoods, platforms, clusters, and centres that yield many by-products and spin-offs. Included among these are commercial developments, the stimulation of a great deal of investment, burgeoning marketing, tourist, and culinary activity, and the transformation of many aspects of community and urban cultural life. Examples include Beijing's Olympic Green, Singapore's Esplanade, Hong Kong's West Kowloon Cultural District, Chicago's Millennium Park, Dallas's Arts District, and Toronto's Distillery District and Liberty Village. All these places, and countless others, do a great deal to activate other possibilities, engage citizens in the developmental process, attract tourists, and entice corporations and commercial entrepreneurs and enterprises to locate in these and other municipal surroundings, creating a "sense of place" that people want to live and work in as well as be associated with and enjoy.

Yet another valuable contribution that the arts make is challenging existing ways of doing things and creating new ones. For the arts not only bring a great deal of joy and happiness into our lives, and create numerous economic benefits and social opportunities. They should, and often are, abrasive, dangerous, demanding, and unsettling, and must be if they are to shake us out of our lethargy and indifference when this is necessary to compel us to create new and better ways of doing things and look at things in fresh and original ways.

A good example is the first performance of Igor Stravinsky's *The Rite of Spring* in Paris in 1913. It caused an uproar in the City of Light when it was first performed by Vaslav Nijinsky due to its pulsating rhythms, carnal melodies, boldness, and audacity. But much of Stravinsky's music is like this, even if not as throbbing, penetrating, and abrasive as *The Rite of Spring*. This is also true for many compositions by other Russian composers, most notably Prokofiev and Shostakovich. Following on the heels of the more soothing music of such Russian masters as Tchaikovsky, Rimski-Korsakov, and Borodin in earlier periods, the music of Prokofiev, Shostakovich, and Stravinsky was meant to express strong feelings, pent-up emotions, and bring about change, especially change that was compatible (and in many clever ways not compatible!) with the dictates, objectives, and ideals of the Soviet state. Not all the music of Prokofiev, Shostakovich, and Stravinsky did this, nor was it intended to. Nevertheless these composers transformed musical tastes, traditions, and practices in Russia and elsewhere. As such, they helped to usher in the world we are living in today.

This is also true for the ability artists possess to advocate for social and political change. The best-known examples of this in an international sense are probably the activist and advocacy activities of American folk singers such as Woody Guthrie, Pete Seeger, the Weavers, Joan Baez, Bob Dylan, Peter, Paul, and Mary, Johnny Cash, Bruce Springsteen, and others. Each of these artists, and many others, was involved in a number of social causes and political movements designed to bring about social change, principally in the United States, from the days of the Great Depression to the civil rights era. In the process of doing this, the aforementioned artists produced many activist songs that became famous internationally, such as "Where Have All the Flowers Gone?", "This Land is Your Land," "Blowin' in the Wind," "We Shall Overcome," "If I Had a Hammer," and "Born in the USA."

The advocacy of artists for social change is not, of course, limited to the United States. As Carlos A. González-Carrasco, the Chilean cultural scholar, pointed out to me recently, artists play the same role in Latin America, where, he said, "In the cultural field and particularly against the background of brutal and murderous dictatorships a massive and vibrant popular Latin America art movement emerged in the 1970s, 1980s, [and] 1990s, involving poetry, murals, music, theatre, cinema, and paintings depicting the social, political, economic and repressive reality from a non-western perspective." The movement revived many older Latin American traditions and but also promoted "new homegrown Latin American cultural expressions by Latin American artists."

What makes the activist and advocacy activities of artists and the arts so essential is the fact that they help to create new insights, attitudes, perceptions, values, lifestyles, and forms of behaviour. Nowhere is this more apparent or necessary than in broadening and deepening knowledge and understanding of the natural world and appreciation, awareness, and reverence for it. Only by doing so can we create an entirely new relationship between the natural world and the human world.

While the arts are not the only activities capable of doing this, it is amazing how much can be learned about nature, the natural environment, other species, and nature's countless elements from the arts. There is a huge cornucopia of artistic works in all cultures and countries in the world that is concerned with nature in all its diversity, complexity, and grandeur, as well as how it expresses and manifests itself. In the western artistic tradition alone, there are millions of artistic works that are concerned with nature and its elements, most notably the sun, moon, stars, sky, planets, landscapes, seascapes, stages in the day, seasons of the year, rivers, lakes, forests, mountains, plants, animals, and a great deal else.

Another important ability buried deep in the arts, and one that might possibly be the most important of all, is the capacity for holism. It derives from the fact that *every work of art is a whole made up of many parts.* While this is most apparent in the visual arts, it is true of all other art forms as well. Regardless of whether it is a play, painting, musical composition, poem, story, dance, or architectural edifice, every work of art is a whole composed of myriad different parts that are all woven together in different combinations and arrangements. The resulting wholes are greater than the parts and the sum of the parts. This is because new properties and entities are brought into existence when these wholes are created that are not present in the parts taken separately. This makes the arts an ideal vehicle for seeing and experiencing things in holistic and not just fragmented terms.

This has major implications for the world of the present and the future as well as for the development of people and their personalities and lives because it addresses one of the greatest problems facing humanity. While we have become remarkably skilled at breaking things up into parts in order to study those parts in detail, we have lost our capacity for putting the parts back together again to create wholes, as indicated earlier. Since the arts involve the mind, body, heart, soul, spirit, senses, emotions, and intellect, they make it possible to bring most if not all human faculties and activities together to form balanced and harmonious wholes made up of many interconnected parts. This explains why artists, arts organizations, and the arts were in the vanguard of the movement to create "the whole person" more than a century and a half ago. This capacity in the arts to put the parts back together to form wholes is not only helpful for people, but also for towns, cities, regions, countries, cultures, and the world at large.

The arts are able to achieve results like this because artists and arts organizations produce works that move us deeply, transport us to exquisite places and ethereal spaces, and reach right into our hearts, minds, souls, spirits, and intellects. While every person in the world finds beauty, motivation, inspiration, and the sublime in different places as well as in different art forms, music seems to do this better than other art forms. Perhaps that explains why so many people like the famous saying, "We are the music makers and the dreamers of dreams." These words are voiced by Willy Wonka (played by Gene Wilder) in the 1971 film *Willy Wonka and the Chocolate Factory*, and while often attributed to Roald Dahl (whose novel served as the basis for the movie), in fact are from the first stanza of the poem "Ode" by Arthur O'Shaughnessy, published in 1874.

In my own case, there are numerous pieces of music that I find incredibly beautiful in this sense, such as the *Minuet* from Handel's opera *Berenice*, the aforementioned Étude Op. 25, No. 1 by Chopin, Mascagni's *Intermezzo* from his opera *Cavalleria Rusticana*, Rachmaninoff's *Piano Concerto No. 2*, Schubert's *Impromptu*, Opus 90, No. 3, Franz Liszt's transcription of Robert Schumann's exquisite song *Widmung*, Richard Strauss's *Morgen!*, Ennio Morricone's *Gabriel's Oboe* from the 1986 film *The Mission*, and the second movement of Beethoven's *Fifth Piano Concerto*.

This is also true for many popular pieces of music, such as "If I Loved You" and "You'll Never Walk Alone" from *Carousel*, "Climb Ev'ry Mountain" from *The Sound of Music*, "Stranger in Paradise," "Smile," "Moon River," "Tammy," "It's a Wonderful World," "Imagine," "You Raise Me Up," and many others. Works like these never fail to move and inspire me through their remarkable beauty and their ability to transport me to lofty heights whenever I hear them or feel despondent or depressed, to exhort me to "stay the course" when things look bleak, to visualize a world full of happiness, hope, and harmony rather than pessimism, anxiety, and despair, and to encourage me to embrace the need for a world where people "live as one."

While this capacity is most evident for me in the realm of music, it is by no means limited to music. It is also very evident in other art forms, especially the visual and architectural arts. Looking at exquisite paintings by Impressionist artists and brush painters as well as architectural masterpieces in Europe, the Middle East, China, Japan, Thailand, and elsewhere in the world can put me in a transcendental state. There is something about our need to reach above and beyond ourselves in the search for the sublime and possibly even the divine that gives works of art and artistic experiences like this, and many others, a profundity that is lacking in many other activities and experiences in life. Nothing does this better than the arts. We need to look to the arts, artists, and arts organizations if we want to be "raised up" and lifted to great heights in the future.

It is clear that all art forms have an essential role to play at all stages and ages in life. As recent research is revealing, this is not only true for childhood, youth, and adulthood, but also for old age and the final years and days of life. These latter requirements can be realized through activities that people can engage in on their own or that are provided for them by a variety of arts therapy groups, community organizations, senior citizen homes, health care centres, and so forth. This explains why institutions like these, and others, are increasing their commitment to activities and programs in the arts for people during their final years. This is a perfect time to listen to music, sing songs or join a choir, paint pictures, make craft objects, read books, enjoy dancing, movies, comedy, and humour, and derive all the other benefits the arts are able to provide.

While this is true for people who are getting older but still enjoying good health, it is especially true for people suffering from debilitating diseases and illnesses such as heart disease, stroke, cancer, depression, dementia, anxiety, Alzheimer's, Parkinson's, multiple sclerosis, ALS, and so forth. It is also true for people who are experiencing other physical and mental ailments, such as those struggling with disabilities, autism, post-traumatic stress disorder, and various other conditions.

Over the last few decades, there has been a phenomenal increase in the number of organizations, books, articles, research studies, and other developments devoted to coming to grips with these and other illnesses and diseases. What is being discovered in countless hospitals, health care clinics, medical and palliative centres, organizations like the Society for the Arts in Dementia Care, Partnerships in Dementia Care Alliance, the National Ballet School of Canada, and many others—as well as through the publication of such books as *The Creative Arts in Dementia Care: Practical Person-Centred Approaches and Ideas* by Jill Hayes and *Dementia Arts: Celebrating Creativity in Elder Care* by Gary Glazer—is that the arts can be very helpful in assisting people suffering from these and a host of other difficulties and illnesses. They can help people breathe and hear better, improve their memory, enhance their creativity, improve their balance so as to avoid falling, and help them interact more effectively. While the arts are not the only activities that can do this—and, it should be said, are not able to cure these and other maladies and health problems—they can make life easier for people who are suffering with these and other ailments, as well as for caregivers and family members helping them deal with some of life's greatest challenges.

What is true for older people and those suffering with difficult diseases is rapidly becoming true for people of all ages. Recently created, the NeuroArts Blueprint offers a set of bold, culture-changing steps to cultivate the emerging field of *neuroarts*—the study of how the arts such as dance, music, theatre, visual arts, and others produce aesthetic experiences that measurably change the brain, body, and behaviour and how this knowledge can be used to improve people's general health and wellbeing. This initiative is led by Susan Magsamen, executive director of the International Arts + Mind Lab (IAM Lab) Center for Applied Neuroaesthetics at the Pedersen Brain Science Institute at Johns Hopkins University School of Medicine and Ruth J. Katz, executive director of the Health, Medicine and Society (HMS) Program of the Aspen Institute. By inviting communities to create the neuroarts ecosystem of today, the Blueprint offers concrete principles, findings, recommendations, and action steps to realize the transformative potential of neuroarts. It presents both a five-year plan and a longer-term vision of a mature neuroarts field dedicated to advancing people's health at every level, strengthening communities, and promoting cultural change.

When all the multifarious benefits to be derived from the arts at all ages and stages in life and the life process are added up and considered collectively, it is obvious that the arts must be seen in a totally new light. The arts, artists, and arts organizations have a central rather than marginal role to play in the world and in life, especially given the present state of the world and prospects for the future. This must be based on the realization that there are art forms and artistic activities to satisfy every mood, need, situation, and occasion. They invigorate, stimulate, and motivate us, ignite and challenge us, soothe and relax us, inspire and delight us, enable us to soar to great heights, give us hope and a sense of awe, wonder, and ecstasy, make it possible for us to express our feelings, emotions, love, affection, and compassion, and allow us to experience the sublime and even the divine. They also connect us to other people, make it possible for us to share stories and experiences, depict specific times, places, and events, intensify our awareness, appreciation, and care for the natural world, and generate a great deal of economic activity.

Nowhere is this more in evidence than in the intimate connection that exists between culture and the arts. Not only are the arts and culture bound together in a whole series of deep, dynamic, profound, and inexorable ways, but they share common bonds and intimate connections that date back thousand of years. This is why "the arts" and "culture" are often viewed as one and the same.

It is also why most people immediately think of the arts when they hear the word culture. And it explains something else—something of great importance to the future. It explains why the arts are the most essential "gateways" to culture and cultures, although not the only ones. Not only do the arts open the doors to culture and cultures in all their diverse forms and manifestations, but they expose and convey many of the most salient and symbolic features of culture, cultures, and cultural life. Indeed, there is very little in the world that is not revealed through the arts.

This is why the arts should be seen and treated as the centrepiece of culture and cultures in much the same way that culture and cultures should be seen and treated as the centrepiece of the world as a whole. When it comes to understanding what is going on in the world, interacting with nature and the natural environment, bringing people, ethnic groups, races, religions, countries, cultures, and civilizations together, inspiring people and transporting them to higher and loftier heights, and showcasing where the world should be headed in the future, the arts are in a class by themselves.

The arts in general and artists and arts organizations in particular need and deserve a great deal more support and funding from governments, corporations, foundations, private benefactors, and the public at large at present and going forward into the future. Without this, the full value, potential, and capabilities of the arts will not be realized and the world as culture will not come to be. It is as simple as that.

Chapter Four

The Humanities

> Three things in human life are important. The first is to be kind. The second is to be kind. The third is to be kind.
>
> —Henry James[1]

Just as the arts can be traced back to ancient times, so can the humanities. Much like the arts, the humanities did not really rise to prominence in Europe until the late Middle Ages and especially during the Renaissance, although there was a great deal of interest in them in the classical period not only in Europe but also in many other parts of the world.

The rise of the humanities to prominence in Europe took place largely in Italy, where there was a concerted attempt to conceive, treat, and deal with the humanities as a separate area of activity distinct from many others. This occurred when Italian scholars became interested in examining how humanity was documenting its experiences in general and how specific people and groups were documenting their personal and collective experiences in particular. Thus the word "humanities" derives from the Renaissance Latin term *studia humanitatis*, meaning "the study of the humanities." This study was initially linked to the study of the classics of Greece and Rome—most notably philosophy, literature, and the arts—and therefore to culture understood in terms of refinement, cultivation, and appreciation of the finer things in life. All these things were considered part of the education and training of people who wanted to be "civilized" and "cultured." This was consistent with the way the term "culture" was used in the early modern period of European history and for some time thereafter in most parts of Europe.

What should be included in the humanities and what should be excluded has been hotly debated for centuries. A short list would probably include philosophy and religion, which were subjects of intense interest and activity in all parts of the world during the classical period in Europe and in many cases much earlier, as well as literature, history, linguistics, and the study of classical languages such as Greek and Latin. A longer list would likely include all the aforementioned areas, as well as the arts, ethics, morality, jurisprudence, archeology, and perhaps even politics, depending on what scholar or institution was compiling the list. Speaking generally, it is common practice in most universities and institutions of higher learning in the world today to divide academic courses and programs into three main groups: the arts and humanities; the physical, natural, and social sciences; and professional activities such as law, medicine, dentistry, and so forth. This categorization confirms the impact that European perceptions have had on the classification and compartmentalization of academic disciples and activities in most if not all parts of today's world.

Determining how specific groups of people document the human experience in general and their own experiences in particular has been popular for centuries everywhere in the world. This has led to the creation and accumulation of a great deal of valuable information with respect to how different groups of people the world over have lived their lives, evolved in both the individual and collective sense, and achieved many things by living together rather than living apart. This is deemed to be important not only in terms of recording these experiences for everyday use as well as posterity, but also learning how ways of life can be improved in all the diverse human collectives, communities, and countries throughout the world.

These factors make the term "humanities" a descriptive term first and foremost, since it describes different ways and processes of recording experiences and focuses on documenting these ways and processes in detail and in depth. However, this matter can also be understood in a more prescriptive, conceptual, and analytical sense, especially when assessments are made of human processes and experiences that are used to educate people, assist them with the development of their personalities and their lives, improve their theoretical and practical capabilities, enhance their capacity for critical thinking, self-evaluation, reflection, learning, and creativity, and enabling them to change their modes of behaviour and actions in life when it is necessary to do so.

According to the National Endowment for the Humanities in the United States, the humanities deal with what is fundamentally and essentially "human." As such, they focus primarily on abilities and attributes that differentiate the experiences and behaviour of human beings from those of other species. These include not only self-consciousness or self-awareness, but also the ability to reason and reflect, create and use complex languages, espouse values, hold aspirations, experience what it means to "be human," examine these matters, assess them, interpret and refine them, and add to them over time if this is necessary.

Creation and development of the humanities in this sense eventually gave rise to the intimately connected but much more specific idea and term "humanism." This idea and term is derived from the Latin word *humanus*, meaning "centred on humans or human beings." While this is largely a descriptive term as well, it came to be associated with specific ways of seeing, thinking, acting, behaving, living, being, believing, and becoming, and, as a result, subject to a wide variety of meanings, interpretations, and perspectives.

In Europe, for instance, the humanist movement started in the fourteenth century and reached its zenith during the Reformation and Renaissance when humanists reacted strongly against medieval scholasticism by emphasizing human, intellectual, and cultural achievements and capabilities rather than various forms of divine intervention, the brevity and miseries of life, and the different ways of escaping from this. As often happens in intellectual movements like this, the term "humanism" was actually used for the first time several centuries after the Renaissance, when the eighteenth- and nineteenth-century theologian Friedrich Niethammer created the term to describe this movement.

Over the centuries, many people in the western world and elsewhere have been associated with certain aspects and branches of the humanities that have proven helpful in paving the way for the creation and development of humanism as a formal and fundamental activity. In ancient times, for instance, Epicurus, Xenophanes, Aeschylus, Thucydides, Anaxagoras, Protagoras, Confucius, and especially Marcus Cicero were all concerned with such matters. In medieval and early modern times, so were Thomas Aquinas, Geoffrey Chaucer, Dante Alighieri, Enea Silvio Bartolomeo Piccolomini (Pope Pius II), Petrarch—deemed by some people the real "founder" of humanism because he studied the classics and classical literature intensely—as well as Erasmus, who edited the works of the Church Fathers and the Greek New Testament. More recently, such people as John Dewey, Mark Twain, H. G. Wells, Albert Einstein, Betty Friedan, Edward Said, Gloria Steinem, Isaac Asimov, Alice Walker, Margaret Atwood, and many others have been viewed as humanists and often associated with humanism.

It is probably for reasons such as this that many definitions of humanism have been advocated by organizations over the last few decades, some of which can be found on the American Humanist Association's website. This organization itself defines humanism as "a progressive philosophy of life that, without theism or other supernatural beliefs, affirms our ability and responsibility to lead ethical lives of personal fulfillment that aspire to the greater good." For its part, the International Humanist and Ethical Union defines humanism as "a democratic and ethical life stance which affirms that human beings have the right and responsibility to give meaning and shape to their own lives. It stands for the building of a more humane society through an ethics based on human and other natural values in a spirit of reason and free inquiry through human capabilities. It is not theistic, and it does not accept supernatural views of reality."

The Humanist magazine defines humanism as "a rational philosophy informed by science, inspired by art, and motivated by compassion":

> Affirming the dignity of each human being, it supports the maximization of individual liberty and opportunity consonant with social and planetary responsibility. It advocates the extension of participatory democracy and the expansion of the open society, standing for human rights and social justice. Free of supernaturalism, it recognizes human beings as a part of nature and holds that values—be they religious, ethical, social, or political—have their source in human experience

> and culture. Humanism thus derives the goals of life from human need and interest rather than from theological or ideological abstractions, and asserts that humanity must take responsibility for its own destiny.

Finally, the Humanist Society of Western New York defines humanism much more fully, but also in a rather similar way:

> A joyous alternative to religions that believe in a supernatural god and life in a hereafter. Humanists believe that this is the only life of which we have certain knowledge and that we owe it to ourselves and others to make it the best life possible for ourselves and all with whom we share this fragile planet. A belief that when people are free to think for themselves, using reason and knowledge as their tools, they are best able to solve this world's problems. An appreciation of the art, literature, music and crafts that are our heritage from the past and of the creativity that, if nourished, can continuously enrich our lives. Humanism is, in sum, a philosophy of those in love with life. Humanists take responsibility for their own lives and relish the adventure of being part of new discoveries, seeking new knowledge, exploring new options. Instead of finding solace in prefabricated answers to the great questions of life, humanists enjoy the open-endedness of a quest and the freedom of discovery that this entails.

While there are some interesting variations in the content of these definitions, by and large they are similar in most respects. Among the most important similarities are the way religion, religions, and supernatural powers are seen and treated; the importance of ethics, morality, and acting in an honest, upright, humane, compassionate, and responsible manner; the fundamental roles, rights, and responsibilities of humanity in general and individuals in particular; aspiring to and achieving higher ideals and forms of behaviour for humanity; making the best of our own lives and improving the lives of other people; taking responsibility for the state of the natural environment in all its diverse forms and manifestations; and cherishing freedom and democracy. These similarities provide a feeling for the meaning, character, and aspirations of the humanities in general and humanism and humanists in particular, as well as their close connection to culture in both broad and narrow terms.

In the beginning, religion, religions, and various types of supernatural powers were a very important part of the humanities because most people adhered to a specific religion, attended services in churches, synagogues, mosques, and other religious facilities on a regular basis, and incorporated religion and religions as a very important part of their lives. Many of the qualities that religions espoused had to do with how people should live their lives, the amount of time, attention, contributions, and donations they should make to religions and religious institutions, and how to live a good, upright, and moral life by following the beliefs and practices of a specific religion.

This was especially true with respect to what was (and still is) called "the Golden Rule," which calls on us to treat other people in the same way we expect and would like to be treated ourselves. Here are several examples of the Golden Rule as set out by some of the most prominent religions in the world:

- This is the sum of duty: Do naught unto others which would cause you pain if done to you. (Brahmanism: *Mahabharata* 5:1517)
- Hurt not others in ways that you yourself would find hurtful. (Buddhism:*Udanavarga* 5: 18)
- Is there one maxim which ought to be acted upon throughout one's life? Surely it is the maxim of loving-kindness: Do not unto others what you would not have them do unto you. (Confucianism: *Analects* 15: 23)
- What is hateful to you, do not to your fellow man. That is the entire law: all the rest is commentary. (Judaism: *Talmud, Shabbat* 31a)
- All things whatsoever ye would that men should do to you, do ye even so to them: for this is the law of the Prophets. (Christianity: *Matthew* 7:12)
- No one of you is a believer until they desire for their brother that which they desire for themselves. (Islam: *Sunan*).

One of the most interesting things about religions is that they all seem to hold the Golden Rule in common. However, the same cannot be said for humanism. In many ways, humanism became a reaction against religion, religions, religious institutions, and supernatural powers—a reaction that has broadened, deepened, and intensified right up to the present day.

This reaction had its origins in the Enlightenment when the motivating factor was to break intellectual thought free of the shackles of religion, prioritizing knowledge of this world and in particular scientific knowledge over assurances of God's infinite powers and mercy. This movement continued to gain ground throughout the nineteenth and twentieth centuries with Darwinism, Freudianism, quantum mechanics, and the works of authors such as Dostoevsky, Emile Zola, and especially Auguste Comte. As a result, the term humanism began to denote an anti-religious position in which human beings were not only "the measure of all things" but also "the only true measure of all things." This intensified when Walter Lippmann introduced the concept of "scientific humanism" in his book *A Preface to Morals*. This book emphasized the need for "a philosophy based on science and morals without religion." This is why secular humanism today "emphasizes human worth and the rights of human beings, and its *atheism* is as dogmatic and uncompromising as the religious *fundamentalism* which led to its rise in the first place."[2]

This is primarily because many humanists are anxious to place the highest priority and focus virtually all their attention on human beings, their lives, and their responsibilities, behaviour, strengths, weaknesses, and decisions, and not on religion, religions, religious institutions, and supernatural powers. As the preceding definitions of humanism reveal and readily confirm, humanism is an attempt to explain life, living, behaviour, responsibilities, and actions in human and humanistic rather than religious and supernatural terms—in short, in terms that place the emphasis largely on rationality, reason, science, and being human rather than on God, gods, supernatural powers, and the tenets of the various religions of the world.

These developments are intimately connected to the growth and development of science. The more science and scientific activities have evolved and developed over the last few centuries and particularly over the last fifty years, the less emphasis has been placed on religion, religions, and supernatural powers by humanists, most notably in terms of the origins, nature, and meaning of life and living. This has caused a discernible shift in different parts of the world away from religion, religions, and religious explanations and towards science, the sciences, and scientific explanations of many important things in life and the world.

This development was strengthened in many ways and many parts of the world when C. P. Snow's book *The Two Cultures and the Scientific Revolution* was published in 1959.[3] In this book, Snow made the case that intellectual life in Britain and generally throughout the western world—and more specifically in educational systems and institutions—could be divided into two distinct cultures: the *humanistic culture* (which included the arts), and the *scientific culture*. This was a problem, according to Snow, because it prevented us from coming to grips with some of the most urgent and pressing problems in the world. This was because a great deal of attention and too high a priority were placed on the humanistic (and artistic) culture and too little attention and too low a priority was placed on the scientific culture in Britain and other western countries and their educational systems.

Snow made such a powerful case for paying more attention to science and the scientific culture that a shift away from the humanities, the arts, and humanistic (artistic) education toward science and scientific education then began and gathered speed. It wasn't long after this that the sciences began to be seen and treated as "hard" and the humanities and the arts as "soft" in most educational institutions in the western world. This was accompanied by an increase in funding for the sciences and scientific education and a decrease in funding for the humanities and the arts and humanistic and artistic education.

Had this practice been confined to education and to Britain and the western world, Snow's case might not have had the powerful effect it eventually had. But Snow's ideas soon became popular in the western world *as a whole* and not just educational institutions. This was because science was linked to economics, politics, industry, and technology—and therefore the beliefs of many business people, politicians, civil servants, corporations, and governments—and viewed as the key to solving the world's most pressing and prevalent problems.

As this occurred, it was no longer a case of treating the sciences as hard subjects and the humanities and the arts as soft subjects. Rather, and much more fundamentally, it was a case of treating the sciences as "hard activities" and the humanities and the arts as "soft activities," not only in the west but in virtually all other parts of the world as well. This view became firmly entrenched not only in the minds of many business people, politicians, and civil servants, but also in the minds of countless other people. As a result, the "Snow thesis"—as it was called at that time and is still called today—became a worldwide phenomenon. Hard activities were concerned with "the basics" in life, and therefore what life and living were really all about; soft activities were concerned with "the frills," and consequently relegated to people's leisure time. Visualized and dealt with in this way, humanistic and artistic activities might be appropriate pursuits for one's spare time, but had little to do with the necessities, essentials, and realities of life. Their principal purpose was to "round people out" and make them more civilized and sophisticated, as well as to prevent them from becoming bored and help them enjoy their leisure time more.

When Snow saw what was happening after *The Two Cultures and the Scientific Revolution* was published, he wrote a second book on this matter entitled *The Two Cultures: And a Second Look: An Expanded Version of the Two Cultures and the Scientific Revolution*, which appeared in 1963.[4] In this book, Snow tried to explain the need for science, education in the sciences, and the growth of the sciences in more detail in order to rectify the imbalance and rift that had developed between the humanities and the arts on the one hand and the sciences on the other hand. But it was too late. The pendulum was swinging and swinging rapidly away from the humanities and the arts and towards the sciences in most countries and parts of the world and neither Snow nor any other person in the world was able to prevent this, as is often the case when situations become polarized like this. The problem, as has been demonstrated throughout history, is that pendulum swings like this can be and often are so powerful and pervasive that a great deal of damage is done before the pendulum swings back.

In the years that followed, courses and programs that were deemed part of the humanistic-artistic culture and education were cut in more and more educational jurisdictions and systems throughout the world. A much lower priority was placed on them in both the curricular and extracurricular sense compared to the sciences. This intensified in the final decades of the twentieth century and first decades of the twenty-first.

As this occurred, educators in the humanities and the arts found themselves in a very difficult situation, forced to decide what courses and programs in the arts and humanities needed to be cut and what courses and programs could be maintained. With the arts and humanities treated largely as recreational, entertainment, and leisure-time activities—valued primarily for their ability to make people more refined and produce economic, commercial, and financial benefits—educators in the humanities and the arts struggled to make the best of a debilitating and depressing situation.

This was not an easy task. However, they fought back and began to justify the humanities and the arts not only in terms of their ability to expose students to such subjects as philosophy, religion, languages, music, drama, dance, the visual and literary arts, classical subjects, jurisprudence, archaeology, and so forth, but also for their ability to help students come to grips with a much broader range of human, social, and cultural issues and problems, as well as to develop their ability to think critically, communicate clearly, analyze and evaluate effectively, integrate complex ideas and concepts, engage in cross-cultural understanding and exchange, communicate and cooperate, develop a strong sense of civic pride and responsibility, cultivate good manners, judgement, and aesthetic sensibilities, and develop a greater sense of humanity, humility, and compassion. This helped to prevent the humanities and the arts from slipping farther down the academic ladder, as well as justifying their relevance in terms of educating people to be more human, humanistic, and humane.

This was essential because another powerful factor was emerging in many educational institutions and countries throughout the world during this time. This was the emergence of scientific theories concerning the creation of the universe. The origins of this development can be traced back to 1922 when the Russian mathematician Alexander

Frieidmann proposed that the universe is constantly evolving and expanding. About the same time the Belgian astronomer and Catholic priest Georges Lemaître was advocating what later came to be called the "big bang theory." According to this theory, the universe came into existence when what Lemaître called the "cosmic egg" exploded billions of years ago, setting off an incredible series of developments that included the formation of the stars and galaxies, the creation of our solar system (including the sun and the planets), and, eventually, the emergence of life on earth.

In the hundred years since Friedmann and Lemaître first introduced these ideas, the big bang theory has been expanded, refined, and elaborated upon to an enormous extent. Astronomers have also sought evidence to confirm the theory, of which the most important has turned out to be the existence of "cosmic background radiation," first detected in the mid-1960s. This faint radiation permeates the entire universe, and (so far at least) the most compelling and convincing explanation for it is that it is the fading afterglow of the big bang itself, greatly attenuated during the nearly 14 billion years since the moment of creation.

Over the last few decades, the big bang theory has slowly but surely been embraced by more and more scientists, educators, and people in other walks of life as the most feasible and legitimate explanation for the creation and evolution of the universe, to the extent that it has tended to overshadow other explanations—both competing scientific theories and, especially, religious explanations involving a single God, many gods, or some other divine authority or supernatural force. As a result, religious explanations of this miraculous process are today given less attention, downplayed, and even ignored in some educational curricula and institutions. This is consistent with the desire of many educators to design courses and curriculums that are grounded in hard facts and scientifically verifiable theories rather than abstract ideas, unproven facts, unverifiable theories, or supernatural beliefs, regardless of whether they are religious or non-religious in nature.

This swing of the pendulum from one extreme to the other seems shortsighted in view of the fact that religious explanations for the creation and evolution of the universe and the world have been included and studied in most educational systems and institutions throughout the world for centuries, but, far more importantly, have a legitimate claim to being studied as *one* possible way of explaining the origin and purpose of the universe. While the proper place for such study would not necessarily be in science courses and curricula, surely it would be useful to offer a course that might be called "Views on the Origin and Nature of the Universe," that would not only discuss modern scientific theories (including but not limited to the big bang theory) but also the many different ways the world's religions have addressed such matters. Such a course would embody the core principle behind the idea of "the world as culture," for it would endeavour to examine human views of the nature of the universe in their totality—as a whole—rather than in separate "silos" devoted to each discipline. Such a course would show that science and religion are not necessarily opposed but often intertwined and complementary. (It is worth reiterating that Georges Lemaître was a Catholic priest. Indeed, members of many Catholic religious orders have played a significant part in the development of modern science.)

The development of such courses seems especially important as religion still plays a prominent if not dominant role in the lives of billions of people throughout the world and there is still a great deal of debate, discussion, and uncertainty about who—or what—was and is responsible for the creation of the universe, the evolution of life on planet earth, and the creation of other planets, solar systems, and galaxies. A course like this would be an appropriate forum to discuss another important but unanswerable question: Is it possible than a God, many gods, or some other supernatural power or divine force caused or created the "big bang" in the first place? Surely this possibility should at least be included in educational curricula, especially when there is still so much that is unexplained about the world and about life, as well as the origins of good and evil, right and wrong, the creation of beauty, awe, compassion, and so forth.

This situation discussed above has been exacerbated over the last few decades by the fact that there has been a significant decline in involvement in some religions and religious institutions in at least some parts of the world. This has been accompanied by a decrease in attendance at religious services and events, as well as commitment to certain religious institutions and beliefs. There are many reasons for this, such as the inability of religions and religious institutions to deal successfully with people's current circumstances and needs, scandals over such issues as gender biases, birth control, abortion, and women's rights, and corruption in some religious institutions. This has been intensified by an unwillingness or reluctance to accept any belief or theory that cannot be verified in scientific and empirical terms, the increased separation of religion and politics in general and church and state in particular, commitments to political correctness, the teaching of some religious beliefs in schools and not others, and preoccupation with secularism, materialism, contemporary communications, and remarkable advances in digital and other technologies.

Speaking generally, while some people believe developments like these are a positive development and should have occurred much sooner, others characterize these changes as negative ones, with serious implications and consequences for all people and countries in the world and humanity as a whole.

This raises a timely and relevant question. What is lost when religion is downplayed or eliminated in educational systems, political policies, governmental practices, and people's lives?

The most obvious consequence of this is surely the loss of many remarkable achievements in the world and in life that were and are inspired by religion, religions, and religious institutions and beliefs, and with this, the ability of people to reach above and beyond themselves in both the individual and collective sense in the search of the sublime and possibly even the divine.

Without doubt, an incredible amount is lost when belief in religion, god, gods, and supernatural powers is downplayed, minimized, or eliminated entirely from human affairs. This inspiration has been, and in many cases still is, necessary to produce magnificent paintings and inspirational music, drama, architecture, literature, and so forth. Think of all the phenomenal works that have been created as a result of humanity's commitment to religion, religions, and religious institutions, as well as to religious causes, beliefs, concerns, and ideals. The list is endless and enormous: millions of temples, pagodas, cathedrals, mosques, synagogues, stupas, and other sacred buildings; the creation of a virtually limitless cornucopia of religious relics and exquisite artifacts; the writing of millions of religious and spiritual texts; the creation of exquisite works of art; the production of countless sacred songs and dances, myriad hymns, anthems, and choral works; and a great deal else.

Where are the contemporary counterparts to religious masterpieces and works by such composers as Hildegard of Bingen, Monteverdi, Palestrina, Corelli, Bach, Handel, and Fauré, painters such as da Vinci, Raphael, Rubens, and El Greco, architects like Cramonte and Wren, sculptors like Michelangelo, and cathedrals, temples, stupas, mosques, and synagogues including the Basilica of Saint Paul Outside the Walls in Rome, the Ahmed Mosque and the Blue Mosque in Istanbul, Princes Road Synagogue in Liverpool, the Mormon Tabernacle in Salt Lake City, the Lotus Temple in Delhi, and millions of others? All these works, and countless others, have a "religious quality" and "spiritual presence" about them that results from the feeling that they transcend the commonplace and the mundane, reach upwards towards the heavens, and provide sublime experiences the moment they are seen, entered, or experienced. This is especially true for architectural edifices of a religious character. As Richard Kieckhefer observed many years ago, entering a religious building is a metaphor for entering into a very spiritual relationship.

While many beautiful artistic works and architectural masterpieces are still being produced in the religious domain and motivated by strong religious beliefs, convictions, and ideals, there is no doubt that there has been a significant decline in works of this type in recent years compared to earlier periods of history. This is largely because composers, painters, playwrights, sculptors, artisans, architects, and so forth are turning to more secular subjects and sources for their motivation and inspiration. Nevertheless, when a colossal office tower, huge condominium, or newly minted government building is entered today, is it not a very different kind of experience and relationship that is felt compared to entering a religious edifice?

Added to this is the decline that is taking place in the sacred side of life compared to the secular side, as well as commitment to higher and loftier goals and ideals for humanity compared to commitment to materialism, technology, and economic growth. This has caused a decline in ethics in the modern world, as well as difficulties in creating an effective theory of ethics based on secularism and humanism rather than sacredism and religion. This goes to the heart of how difficult it is to realize humanism without some religious or spiritual context, content, and underpinning, as well as create an effective ethical theory when belief in god, gods, or some supernatural power or divine source is minimized or eliminated.

There has also been an increase in individualism, commitment to the "me generation," and the tendency to focus more on "the self" than "the other" in many parts of the world over the last few decades. Many factors are contributing to this, such as the increase in wealth that makes it possible for people to depend less on religion, religions, communities, and other people, and the development of technological devices such as smartphones and a variety of other communications vehicles that are tending to turn people inward rather than outward, causing them to focus more on themselves and their own needs and interests than on the needs and interests of other people. This also seems to be affecting the pursuit of ideals that are external and shared collectively, as well as the ability to transcend the self, secular interests, individualism, and preoccupation with oneself rather than others.

This explains why the World Commission on Culture and Development, which was created by the United Nations and UNESCO in 1993, devoted the first chapter of its final report (released in 1995) to the need for "a new global ethics."[5] This would certainly not have been the case had the report been published twenty years earlier, since the first chapter would undoubtedly have been concerned with the arts and humanities that were then deemed, along with what are now called the cultural industries, as the most important aspects of culture to be addressed. However, this was not the case in 1995, and surely would not be the case today or in the future if things keep moving in the same direction they are at present.

Surely the biggest problem in this area is the difficulty involved in creating an effective system of global ethics that is predicated on science rather than religion, due primarily to the fact that behaving in an ethical manner does not seem to be compatible with, or susceptible to, scientific verification or empirical confirmation. Although science has many uses and produces countless benefits, rewards, and opportunities, the inability to produce a scientifically based and empirically justified system of global ethics poses an enormous problem and seemingly insurmountable obstacle for humanity at present and going forward into the future. This is not dissimilar to the problem encountered in "aesthetics" where beauty is in "the eyes of the beholder," and therefore what beauty is for one person is or may not be beauty for another person.

This same problem seems to be true of ethics at this time, where different people and different groups have different "takes"—and often conflicting ideas and opinions—about what is and what is not ethical behaviour. It wouldn't be far off the mark in this regard to suggest that things *seem* to be veering towards the belief that if you can get away with something then it is ethical. Since many contemporary laws have their origins and are still predicated on religious convictions in many parts of the world, humanity seems to be incapable of creating what might be called "a new system of global ethics" that is based totally on science and not on religion and religious beliefs in some way.

Creating this system is obviously one of the most difficult but quintessential challenges confronting humanity and the world today and going forward into the future, especially a system that is based on humanism and secularism, has teeth in it, is legal, and is universally accepted and practiced by most people and countries in the world. This is especially true for the humanistic dimension of this system, which is facing the greatest and most severe test of all because it means creating a system of ethics that puts the onus, emphasis, and responsibility on people and humanity rather than on God, gods, supernatural powers, or divine forces.

Without this, there is the constant danger of getting so caught up in secularism, materialism, and technological developments that the need to aspire to and achieve higher goals, objectives, and ideals for humanity is lost and preoccupation with the self prevents the development of higher standards of ethical behavior. The problem here is that ethics and ethical problems will never go away. They will always be there in one form or another, and will fester in the side of humanity like a deep soar or cut until they are addressed and dealt with effectively.

This new system should be based on looking *outside the self* to see and connect with other people and assist them whenever possible and necessary; looking *upwards* to achieve higher goals, objectives, and ideals for humanity; and looking *inside oneself* to get in touch with those deeper feelings, emotions, sensitivities, and sensibilities that are connected to our hearts, souls, and spirits.

There are many possible approaches to the development of an ethical system like this. However, the most promising one in a humanistic sense would seem to be basing this system on the Golden Rule referred to earlier, since it would be predicated on putting the onus, responsibility, and emphasis with respect to ethics on people rather than things, god, gods, or supernatural powers. Despite the fact that the origins of the golden rule are religious and cultural rather than humanistic in character, this "faith-based" rule has withstood the test of time throughout the world.

In individual terms, there is much to be gained from basing this new system of ethics on the Golden Rule and treating other people in much the same way that people would like and expect to be treated themselves. Not only would this compel us to be more concerned with the needs and requirements of others and not just ourselves, but it also would produce a great deal more caring, sharing, compassion, and cooperation in the world. Initially and writ small, this may only affect people in their own particular areas, vicinities, neighbourhoods, and communities, especially people who may be suffering from various types of illnesses, diseases, and health problems, or don't have sufficient means or financial resources to cover their expenses and most pressing requirements. However, if most people did this and did it consistently, it would eventually—and writ large—have a powerful effect on people well beyond their own immediate areas, vicinities, neighbourhoods, and communities, as well as help to address and redress some of the most basic disparities, discrepancies, and inequalities in income, wealth, and social requirements between people, societies, and countries.

This would also produce more sensitivity, civility, and decency in the world, as well as respect for other people and other countries for who they are, what they have rather than what they don't have, and what they have achieved. The ultimate and overall outcome of this would be like dropping a small stone in a large pond, with ripples emanating outward in broader and broader circles until ultimately the entire world is affected. It would also assist people and countries that are struggling to survive in life beyond the bare minimum.

What is true in the individual sense is also true in the collective sense. Looking around the world today, it is clear that there is a major imbalance between people's rights on the one hand and their responsibilities on the other. There is a reason for this. When the United Nations Declaration of Human Rights was signed in 1948, it was only three years after the end of the Second World War. Many people had lost all their rights or had them confiscated or taken away, due to aggressive actions on the part of oppressive leaders and governments. As a result, the most obvious need and concern at that time was to address and assert people's rights in virtually all areas of life and all parts of the world in both legal and political terms, as well as to enshrine these rights in a comprehensive and powerful international declaration.

A great deal has been achieved since the signing of the Universal Declaration of Human Rights in 1948, though admittedly a lot remains to be accomplished. By identifying people's rights in economic, social, political, educational, and other terms, as well as their right to freedom of speech, expression, and mobility and to a higher standard of living and better quality of life, a major step was taken in an ethical and humanistic sense in this respect.

Once people's rights were enshrined in the Universal Declaration of Human Rights, it was understandable that the bulk of attention at that time and for a long time thereafter would be focused in most if not all countries and parts of the world on creating similar declarations at the local, regional, and national level, as well as ensuring that these rights were binding and enforceable in municipal, regional, and national courts of law and not only in international courts. This is largely were matters stand today. Many countries have created national, regional, and/or municipal declarations of human rights capable of protecting their citizens that are monitored on a regular basis both inside and outside these countries.

In principle and in theory, this is helping to ensure that the rights of people and citizens are not violated, and, if they are, that violations can be dealt with through judicial rulings in their favour in courts of law. And what is true for countries is also true for the world, where similar monitoring and concern for the enforcement of human rights have been going on for some time through the International Court of Justice, the International Criminal Court, and others. In practice and in fact, however, a very different situation in many countries often prevails, due to the actions of oppressive regimes, corrupt governments, and powerful leaders, as well as the inability to ensure the enactment of legal decisions made in courts of law. Clearly it is one thing to claim that the "rule of law" and "people's rights" are sacrosanct and being respected and enforced; it is quite another to manifest this in reality and concrete terms.

While significant strides have been made with respect to the recognition and articulation of people's *rights* since the Universal Declaration of Human Rights was signed in 1948, unfortunately the same cannot be said for people's *responsibilities*. In fact, so much time and attention has been focused on the articulation and realization of people's rights since 1948 that little or no time or attention has been devoted to similar developments with respect to people's responsibilities, except perhaps in a few select cases or esoteric places in the world. As a result, there is a void in this area in the ethical and legal sense that needs to be addressed and overcome without delay. Without doubt, the time has come to focus much more attention on people's responsibilities, since both requirements—people's *rights* and people's *responsibilities*—must be dealt with successfully if an effective theory of ethics, as well as higher standards of human conduct and character, are to be achieved. This is needed to create the balance and harmony necessary in all human actions and facets of life, especially given that rights and responsibilities fit together as tightly as do the arts and culture, something discussed earlier.

What are people's most important responsibilities? Among others, surely they consist of showing concern, compassion, and respect for other people and especially people who are sick, elderly, disadvantaged, distressed, poor, oppressed, or marginalized; treating all genders, races, ethnic groups, and peoples fairly, equally, and without prejudice; learning about other people's cultures, civilizations, and ways of life and showing interest in this at all times and in all places; pursuing peace, harmony, liberty, security, democracy, and freedom of expression and movement; manifesting cooperation and compromise rather than conflict, confrontation, war, and aggression; protecting the natural environment and other species at every opportunity; conserving resources and never taking more from the natural environment than is necessary for a reasonable standard of living and decent quality of life; giving back to the neighbourhood, community, and country where people were born, to which they moved, or in which they are living and working today; making the transition from wealth to well-being; and creating values, beliefs, and lifestyles that are consistent with the state of the world at present and prospects for the future. These responsibilities, especially if they are articulated clearly, taken seriously, and addressed fully, would ensure that people develop the sensitivities, capabilities, behaviours, and ways of life that are required to be responsible citizens in human, humane, humanistic, and ethical terms.

Cultivating these responsibilities in deeds and actions and not just in words and ideas would go a long way towards putting countries in all parts of the world in the strongest possible position to come together and collaborate on creating a *Universal Declaration of Human Rights and Responsibilities* that would be applicable to all people and all countries. It is impossible to do this without dealing with and embracing the other and not only the self, since it means giving back to other people, communities, cultures, and countries and not just taking from them.

These developments would also go a long way towards creating the ethical ideals, standards, and objectives that are necessary throughout the world today, as well as creating the new system of global ethics that the World Commission on Culture and Development felt was so imperative and urgently needed. This is affirmed when one examines the principal ideas and ideals that the World Commission felt should constitute the core of this new ethical system, namely human rights and responsibilities, democracy and the elements of civil society, protection of minorities, commitment to peaceful conflict resolution and fair negotiation, and equity between and within governments.

According to the Commission, this system of global ethics and the individual and collective modes of ethical behaviour to be included in it are consistent with the centrality of culture and involve and address culture in many different ways. As the Commission put it:

> It is not difficult to see that the search for a global ethics involves culture and cultural aspects in numerous ways.To begin with, such an endeavor is itself an emphatically cultural activity, including questions such as Who are we?, How do we relate to each other and to humankind as a whole? and What is our purpose? *These questions are at the centre of what culture is all about.* Moreover, any attempt to formulate a global ethics must for its inspiration draw on cultural resources, on people's intelligence, on their emotional experiences, their historical memories and their spiritual orientations. *Culture, unlike scarce resources, will in this process be invigorated and enhanced rather than depleted.*[6]

We have come full circle. We set out at the beginning of this chapter to show how the humanities and humanism in general and the humanistic manifestation of culture in particular came into being initially and evolved over a long period of time, particularly after the Renaissance, the Enlightenment, and, more recently, the development of the sciences, as well as to indicate how these matters are intimately connected to culture. For like culture, the humanities, humanism, and the humanistic manifestation of culture are concerned with life and living seen from a human and humane perspective, as well as living life on a higher plane of ethical existence—one that human beings can create and take responsibility for on their own, drawing on humanism, science, and religion in a broad and diverse variety of ways.

This cannot be achieved successfully at present or moving forward into the future without creating a *system* of ethical behaviour and a global ethics that is manifested in practical and concrete and not just in theoretical, idealistic, or verbal terms. This requires giving as well as taking, compatibility with both religion and science, and capitalizing on the strengths and addressing the shortcomings in both these areas and others. This is a fundamental aspect of culture, since it is difficult to see how matters as crucial as the environmental crisis, vast inequalities in income and wealth, and countless injustices to races and groups such as Blacks, Indigenous peoples, and other oppressed and marginalized minorities can be confronted and overcome without this.

Are there grounds for optimism in this regard? Indeed there are. While the COVID-19 pandemic and the Black Lives Matter movement have had a powerful effect on the world and all its people and countries in many different ways, they have also brought out many ethical and moral values, ideals, practices, actions, and behaviours in people, thereby revealing what it is to be truly "human," "humane," and a "humanist" in the best sense of these terms. At the most basic level, this manifested itself through the vast majority of people respecting other people's personal space, avoiding physical contact as much as possible, saying "hello," "good morning," or "good afternoon" to people who were totally ignored prior to this, and respecting, valuing, and appreciating the countless deeds and actions of numerous "front-line workers" who risked their lives to help people, especially in the earlier stages of the pandemic.

And this is not all. These people are and have been accompanied by many others who put the interests and needs of other people ahead of their own. This includes artists who gave freely of their time and talents to provide art, music, drama, and dance to millions of people despite the fact that they had lost their sources of income and were forced to stay at home. Nevertheless, they found ways to communicate their feelings and emotions to others through digital devices, virtual reality, and other technological means. While these observations may not be true of all people, they are true for enough people to conclude that these unselfish acts of kindness, humanity, humanism, and altruism did not go unnoticed and could form the basis for the development of an effective new system of global ethics in the years ahead.

The big question now is whether these acts of kindness, generosity, altruism, and compassion will be sustained after the pandemic and racial protests subside, or if they will disappear after things return to normal and business as usual resumes. For what the pandemic and these protests have revealed is that there are not only important lessons to be learned from these tragic and devastating events that are

Chapter Five

The Heritage of History

> Culture in general as a descriptive concept means the accumulated treasury of human creation: books, paintings, buildings, and the like; the knowledge of ways of adjusting to our surroundings, both human and physical; language, customs, and systems of etiquette, ethics, religion, and morals that have built up throughout the ages.
>
> —Alfred Kroeber and Clyde Kluckhohn[1]

Like culture as the arts and culture as the humanities, culture as the heritage of history can be traced back thousands of years. However, it was not really until the eighteenth and nineteenth centuries that interest in this particular manifestation of culture began to assert itself in earnest.

This interest was most apparent in Europe and among European cultural scholars. Especially noteworthy were Johann Christoph Adelung, whose *Essay on the History of Culture of the Human Species* was published in 1782, as well as Gustav Klemm, whose first volume of a ten-volume *Cultural History of Mankind* was published in 1843. This book, which was devoted to the study of the gradual development of humankind as a species, was followed by a two-volume work, *Science of Culture*, that was published in 1854 and 1855 and focused largely on the nature and meaning of culture. In these works, Klemm paid a great tribute to Voltaire, who, he said, was the first person to set aside lists of kings, dynasties, and wars in order to focus on culture, even if he did not use the term as such.

It is important to emphasize here that there are really two aspects of the heritage of history. The first is general and all-inclusive. It includes everything that people, countries, and the world have created and inherit from the past, both positive and negative, superior and sinister, constructive and destructive, old and new, large and small, valuable and valueless, and timely and timeless. No distinction is made in this version between the nature and character of particular items inherited from the past; it is the *totality* of what is inherited from the past that is important. The second version is much more specific, selective, and exclusive. It tends to be confined to accomplishments and artifacts that people have created and value most highly, cherish most deeply, and consequently are most anxious to preserve, protect, enjoy, share, and pass on from one generation to the next.

It bears repeating: The first, all-inclusive version of our heritage from history includes elements that are deplorable and not just those that are highly cherished. This makes it imperative to be ever mindful of the distinction and difference between good and evil, right and wrong, the need to correct mistakes made in the past, and the necessity of ensuring that these mistakes are not repeated in the future.

Just as the artistic and humanistic manifestations of culture possess many qualities, characteristics, and capabilities that are relevant to the overall understanding of culture as an idea and a reality and have a crucial role to play in the world, so too does the historical manifestation of culture. This is especially true of the second version of the heritage of history, since it emphasizes the fact that humanity has inherited a rich legacy of material and non-material achievements from the past that represent its hopes and dreams, knowledge and wisdom, ideas and ideals, objects and artifacts, aspirations and accomplishments, together with the tangible and intangible creations of previous generations of people in all countries and parts of the world and the world at large. As such, the past exercises an incredible influence over the present and the future.

This is especially true for the positive and cherished dimension of the heritage of history. It anchors humanity in the world and creates an intimate bond between the past, present, and future. It also contributes to humanity's solidarity, identity, and sense of belonging, being, and becoming, giving people a sense of cohesion, coherence, and rootedness in time as well as in space. This is needed more than ever in a world characterized by rapid and relentless technological change as well as increased globalization, computerization, and polarization.

Every person in the world has an individual heritage that begins when they are born. This includes their biological heritage—their genetic inheritance—as well as their cultural heritage, including their ethnic origins and ancestral heritage.

From these beginnings, every person creates and acquires countless things throughout their lives that form an integral and indispensable part of their personal cultural heritage. This heritage is the summation of all the things people do, think, experience, create, and acquire during their lives. It evolves progressively from day to day, week to week, month to month, and year to year, and includes all the friendships, associations, relationships, memorabilia, tangible and intangible accomplishments, and artifacts they create, inherit, or acquire from the moment they are born until the final days of their lives.

In the holistic sense, these individual cultural heritages have a great deal to do with who people are, where and what they work at over their lives, what they achieve in life—their good deeds and bad deeds—and how they lived their lives in all their various forms and manifestations. An important part of these heritages is the imprint people make on a very specific part of the world's geography and natural environment during their lives. While much has been made of this specific part of people's individual cultural heritages in recent years—largely because it relates so much to their ecological footprint on the natural environment—their imprint is substantially broader, deeper, and more fundamental than this. It is their total *cultural* imprint that matters most, since it includes everything they do, create, write, record, achieve, inherit, and accumulate in life.

After people die, many aspects of their individual cultural heritages remain behind and are perpetuated by their family members, friends, the places they worked and visited, the educational institutions they attended, even the country or countries they lived in. This includes all the public and private records that are available about them and their lives, all the photographs that were taken of them and kept by family members, relatives, friends, and others over the years, the memoirs they have written during their lives, the memorabilia they have collected, stored, and left behind, and all the other things they created and produced in life.

The size of this heritage varies substantially from individual to individual according on how much present and future generations decide to preserve and how much they decide to discard. For most people, it probably includes many photos that were taken of them, the memories of them that remain in the minds, hearts, and souls of family members, relatives, friends, and others, the stories that are told about them after they are gone or have been written about them, clothing they might have worn at one time that family members can't bring themselves to throw out, and much more.

These individual cultural heritages—or *bio-archives* as some people like to call them today—are built up by everyone. Their size is growing with increasing rapidity as a result of living in a digital world and being surrounded on all sides by technological devices capable of documenting one's life in great detail.

(Of course, no one can live a life devoid of at least some unpleasant experiences and adverse occurrences, whether they be hurting or exploiting another person, insulting people with different ideas, ideals, values, beliefs, or ethnic and racial origins, beating up someone in a schoolyard fight, having a car accident and injuring someone, and so forth.)

What is true for people and their individual cultural heritages is also true for families, organizations, ethnic, and racial groups. They all have cultural heritages composed of countless items, both in the positive and negative sense. While not all families, organizations, and ethnic and racial groups document their heritages or keep formal or informal records of them, it is amazing how many do, making it an important and integral part of life and living. Many people do this to carry on traditions lasting decades and possibly centuries, or to ensure that these heritages are not stamped out or forgotten.

The collective heritage of the Jewish people provides an excellent example of this, since they have sustained and documented their collective cultural heritage for millennia. This includes being driven out of Egypt thousands of years ago, being ostracized in many countries and communities and forced to live in ghettos with intolerable living conditions, the killings, horrors, and atrocities experienced by millions of Jews during the Holocaust, and many other threats to their existence as a people. Despite this, they have endured and maintained detailed records of their collective cultural heritage, which reached a climax in many ways when the state of Israel was founded in 1948. This made it possible for many Jewish people to return to their ancestral homeland, preserve and maintain their collective cultural heritage in a more systematic, sustained, and comprehensive way, and cherish and celebrate this heritage today.

The same holds true for countless other ethnic and racial groups. Every ethnic group in the world has its own collective cultural heritage which includes myriad accomplishments as well as a great deal of information about how it came into existence, evolved over time, what it has done right and what it has done wrong, what it is achieving and cherishing today, and what it has contributed to other people and the world at large. And what is true for all ethnic and racial groups is also true for all other human collectives.

The same holds true for towns, cities, rural areas, regions, and countries. Each of these entities possesses a collective heritage that is rich in information, and which is preserved, protected, and stored in government buildings, museums, libraries, and archival and custodial institutions all over the world, as well as by individual citizens and the public at large. While the heritages of towns and cities are exceedingly important—especially as an increasingly percentage of the world's population is now living in urban areas—the heritages of rural areas are also extremely important.

Interestingly, many towns, cities, rural areas, and regions are creating programs, projects, and even special institutions that are designed specifically to reflect images of themselves and display their collective cultural heritages. This is especially true for what are called *eco-museums*. These are institutions where many things from and about a town, city, rural area, or region are represented, thereby encouraging residents and visitors alike to explore and experience these cultural heritages in the settings where they are actually located and not just in a formal institution or venue.

This can and should be carried much farther than it is today in terms of depicting and displaying the cultural heritages that towns, cities, rural areas, and regions all over the world have built up, manifest, and imprint on the world. Paris provides an excellent example. It is subdivided into twenty *arrondissements* or *cultural districts*. Its distinctive neighbourhoods and features range all the way from the Louvre and Palais Royale in the centre of this remarkable City of Light to Montmartre, the Parc de la Villette, Belleville, the Père Lachaise cemetery, and so forth. Each arrondissement, district, or area has its own special cultural character and characteristics as well as its own distinctive heritage, all of which contribute a great deal to the city's overall cultural heritage.

Many countries are manifesting similar developments, which enable them to display their distinctive cultural heritages, character, and features in museums, galleries, archives, and other institutions. This is especially true for many European countries, which have long been recognized as international leaders in heritage conservation. Entire countries in Europe are often subdivided into distinct cultural districts, zones, regions, or areas similar to those in France, with cultural maps of the different regions of the country.

It is the sum total of all these individual, group, institutional, urban, rural, regional, and national cultural heritages that constitutes the cultural heritage of humankind. It includes everything that has been created and kept by human beings in terms of both aspects of the heritage of history discussed earlier, but especially in regard to the second version, which is more restricted, valued, and cherished. Not only is this heritage colossal in size, but it is growing at a phenomenal rate and includes an incredible array of items and artifacts from every period in history, part of the world, and aspect of cultural life.

This heritage is the birthright of all citizens and all countries and belongs to the whole of humanity, not just specific peoples or nations, thereby providing a sense of collective identity, well-being, and belonging for all the world's inhabitants and humanity at large. It is a living heritage in the sense that it is constantly evolving, mutating, and growing.

A substantial part of this heritage has been maintained, preserved, protected, and sustained by women throughout the course of human history, since they have been actively engaged in, and highly committed to, ensuring that the community, local, municipal, regional, and national heritages of people, ethnic groups, tribes, races, and countries—as well as the entire cultural heritage of humankind—is passed on from one generation to the next and one century to the next. Without this vital contribution from women, it is obvious that the total cultural heritage of humankind would be substantially less than it is today.

While the value and importance of the cultural heritage of humankind has been recognized for a very long time, it is only rather recently that steps were taken in official and systematic terms to recognize this heritage. A major development in this regard took place in the 1960s when the United States linked the idea of *cultural conservation* to the idea of *natural conservation*. This resulted largely from the seminal role the United States played in recognizing the world's natural heritage, primarily through the creation of national parks such as Yosemite and Yellowstone, as well as the role that many other countries, the United Nations, UNESCO, and so forth played in conserving the most cherished and highly valued dimensions of these heritages.

An historic step forward occurred in 1965 when the United States convened a conference at the White House where it was decided that a World Heritage Trust should be created to preserve "the world's most superb natural and scenic areas and historic sites for the present and the future of the entire world citizenry." What was most significant about this event was the fact that it laid the foundation for the passage of the *Convention Concerning Protection of the World's Cultural and Natural Heritage* that was signed in Paris on November 16, 1972 by 187 member states of UNESCO in addition to the Holy See, Niue (a self-governing state in free association with New Zealand), and Palestine. At long last, the idea of a universal cultural and natural heritage of humankind became a reality and was inscribed into international law. It was based on the conviction that specific elements of the total natural and cultural heritage of the world and humankind should be held in trust for future generations and protected from exploitation.

Some of the most important groundwork for this historic achievement was set out in the preamble to a 1954 convention signed in the Hague that called for the protection of cultural property in the case of armed conflict. This was then tied to the protection of oceans, sea beds, and outer space in 1967, and accorded a much broader and more fundamental connotation with the signing of the aforementioned *Convention Concerning Protection of the World's*

Cultural and Natural Heritage. The convention identified a *World Heritage Site* as a place listed by UNESCO as being of special cultural or natural importance to humanity. In 2016, there were 1,073 World Heritage Sites listed by UNESCO, of which 832 were cultural, 206 were natural, and 35 were mixed cultural-natural. The sites were located in 167 countries around the world. In 2016, Italy, China, Spain, France, Germany, Mexico, and India had the most UNESCO World Heritage Sites. By 2019, the number of sites had increased to 1,121.

It pays to examine the more restricted aspect of the heritage of history represented by World Heritage Sites in more detail in view of its importance, despite the fact that it is limited to the "crème de la crème," so to speak.

As far as the natural dimension of this heritage is concerned, this includes many places that are of great importance to the world and to humanity, most of which are now located in national parks throughout the world. Examples of UNESCO World Heritage Sites focused on the heritage of the natural world are the Los Glaciares National Park and Iguazú National Park in Argentina, Uluru and the Great Barrier Reef in Australia, Mount Kenya National Park/National Forest in Kenya, Dinosaur Provincial Park in Canada, Ilulissat Icefjord in Denmark, the Galápagos Islands off the coast of Equador, the Western Ghats in India, the Dolomites in Italy, Kinabalu Park in Malaysia, Monarch Butterfly Biosphere Reserve in Mexico, Sagarmatha National Park in Nepal, Jeju Volcanic Island and Lava Tubes in South Korea, the Danube Delta in Romania and Ukraine, the Central Highlands of Sri Lanka, Lake Baikal in Russia, Singapore Botanic Gardens in Singapore, the Grand Canyon and Yellowstone National Park in the United States, and many others.

World Heritage Sites recognized by UNESCO for their cultural significance include buildings of unusual historic significance and value, the centres of many well-known towns and cities, special monuments, historic sites, and venues, and such human-made creations as the Pyramids, famous forts and bridges, ancient ruins, and so forth. Examples of World Heritage sites in this realm include Angkor in Cambodia, the Pyramids of Egypt and related archeological sites, Persepolis in Iran, Chichen Itza in the Yucatán Peninsula in

Mexico, the centre of Saint Petersburg in Russia, the Lahore Fort in Pakistan, Samarkand in Uzbekistan, the Great Wall of China, the historic centre of Prague in the Czech Republic, the Acropolis in Greece, the Mayan archeological site of Copán in Honduras, Masada in Israel, historical monuments in ancient Kyoto in Japan, the ancient city of Petra in Jordan, and many others.

While there was a tendency in the early years to limit cultural sites of great international significance to those that were largely physical, material, and tangible in nature, pressure built rapidly throughout the world to extend this list to include many activities that are non-physical, non-material, and intangible in character, which is the case today. This List of the Intangible Cultural Heritage of Humanity includes such items and activities as dances, stories and story telling, athletic and recreational games, folk songs, embroidery, falconry, boat races, oral histories, theories, ideas, calligraphy, festivals, fairs, carnivals, tea ceremonies, throat singing, and a great deal else.

A number of specific examples of items and activities included on UNESCO's intangible heritage list should suffice to reveal the nature and extent of this heritage. Take coffee houses as one fascinating example. The origin of coffee houses dates back to a businessman from Damascus who opened one in Istanbul in 1540. The importance of such places was made clear in the following Arab poem written in the sixteenth century. It also helps explain why coffee houses remain so popular today:

Come into the coffee house
Where divine goodness favours those who share in its bounty.
The sweetness of life, the company of friends, the elegance of rugs,
These make it the abode of the blest.
For coffee is the source of our health,
The fire which consumes our grief,
And the stream which washes away our sorrow![2]

Coffee houses became extremely popular and fashionable in Europe after an Armenian businessman named Johannes Diodato opened a coffee house in Vienna in 1685. They enjoyed their heyday in this city in the nineteenth century when authors and artists would gather in coffee houses to discuss their work, converse, read newspapers attached to long wooden sticks, and exchange ideas. Famous Viennese coffee houses over the years have included Kaffee Alt Wein, Café Braünerhof, Café Griensteidl, Café Schwarzenberg, the Hotel Sacher (famous for its Sachertorte, a chocolate cake with apricot filling), and many others.

By the year 1700, coffee houses were popular not only in Vienna, but also in Venice, Paris, Amsterdam, London, and especially Leipzig, which was located at the intersection of the Via Regia and Via Imperii. This location was ideal since it was situated on the east-west route from Santiago de Compostela in Spain to Kiev in Ukraine and Moscow in Russia, as well as the north-south route from Rome and Venice to the Baltic Sea.

Small wonder that one of Johann Sebastian Bach's most well-known cantatas is his "Coffee Cantata" (BWV 211). This cantata is actually a short comic opera written about 1735 and inspired by Zimmerman's popular coffee house in Leipzig, Germany. The cantata is about an attractive young woman named Aria who loves and savours coffee. Her father is opposed to his daughter drinking coffee, so he bans her from doing so. Aria objects strongly, singing:

> Father sir, but do not be so harsh! If I couldn't, three times a day, be allowed to drink my little cup of coffee, in my anguish I will turn into a shriveled-up roast goat.
>
> Ah! How sweet coffee tastes, more delicious than a thousand kisses, milder than muscatel wine. Coffee, I have to have coffee, and, if someone wants to pamper me, ah, then bring me coffee as a gift!

Another excellent example of the intangible cultural heritage of humankind is the tango, which first became famous in Argentina. It originated in lower-class districts in the 1890s along the Rio de la Plata, the border between Uruguay and Argentina, and was made popular by Rudolph Valentino in the movie *The Four Horsemen of the Apocalypse* in 1921. It became even more popular through the music of Astor Piazzolla, which was played on a bandoneon, an instrument rather like an accordion. The origins and development of the tango have been traced still further back to country dances in England around 1650, the *danza* in Spain in the early part of the nineteenth century, and the Cuban *habanera* in the early twentieth century.

A third example of the intangible cultural heritage of humankind is traditional folk music of all types. A seminal step in preserving such music was taken when UNESCO collaborated with the International Music Council and especially musicologist Alain Daniélou to record the indigenous folk music of the world in its *Collection of Traditional Music* after World War II. This is one of the earliest and best examples of safeguarding and revitalizing an indispensable component of humanity's cultural heritage. It has recently been updated and expanded by Smithsonian Folkways Recordings in the United States to 125 albums documenting traditional music from all over the world and is now available in digital as well as analog form. This initiative followed on the heels of the growth in the popularity of folk music in many European countries, as well as its use by such well-known composers as Johannes Brahms in Germany, Franz Liszt, Béla Bartók and Zoltán Kodály in Hungary, and George Enescu in Romania. These and other composers recorded much of the folk music of Eastern Europe, especially Hungary and Romania, and used it frequently in their compositions.

Finally, the intangible cultural heritage of humankind includes its intellectual heritage, which is composed of all the thoughts, theories, ideas, ideals, and wisdom of thinkers and scholars in all disciplines and activities in the world over the centuries. This is a colossal heritage in its own right, one that is exceedingly important at a time when there are so many problems in the world and the need exists to tap into this remarkable treasure trove of intellectual creativity and mental ingenuity in every culture and country in the world.

These examples, and many others that might be cited, provide a sense of how certain elements in humanity's intangible cultural heritage have been created, cultivated, and sustained in specific parts of the world. In some cases, they have remained there. However, in many if not most cases, they have been transported or transmitted from one part of the world to another through cultural sharing, borrowing, imitation, interaction, and enrichment. This process is exceedingly important in improving conditions in all parts of the world.

It is also captivating and inspiring. Examples of this process abound throughout history, such as the transfer and spread of vital medical knowledge, crucial scientific inventions and technological discoveries, major developments in communications, different works and styles in music, painting, dance, drama, literature, cuisine, architecture, design, and the crafts, sports and games such as basketball, baseball, and badminton, sewing, embroidery, fashions, welding, construction, and countless others. The list is endless and the rewards that can be derived from tracking the international transmission of achievements such as these and countless others are extremely motivational, as trade routes such as the Silk Road connecting China and the Far East with the Middle East and Europe readily reveal and confirm.

In recent years, and particularly since the onset of the COVID-19 pandemic, the cultural, natural, tangible, and intangible heritage of humankind has been expanded exponentially in the "digital dimension." We are all the beneficiaries of new digital technologies, expanded Internet access, and the establishment of networking organizations such as the international association #DiCultHer, overseen and developed by Carmine Marinucci, which is committed to "the right of every citizen to be educated in the knowledge and responsible use of digital technology for the protection and enhancement of the cultural heritage and places of culture."

The sharing of important transformations and innovations means that various countries' specific heritages are now enjoyed by billions of people all over the world. Many traditions that people think are contemporary—coffee houses are a good example—were actually created many centuries ago and spread outward from their places of origin. This process of transference may well be one of the greatest achievements of all in the realm of culture.

It is also important to note that there exist threats to this incredible heritage that must be recognized, understood, and dealt with effectively. These threats result from a variety of sources and factors, such as looting, vandalism, terrorism, human indifference and neglect, tourist practices, corruption, violence, theft, war, the illegal sale of objects and artifacts, and a great deal else.

The list of these threats is long and the consequences great. During the last few decades, for instance, humanity has witnessed the destruction of the "Buddhas of Bamiyan." These two statues in Bamyan, Afghanistan dated back to the sixth century, and were destroyed because they were viewed as idols by the Taliban. Similarly, Afghan archaeological sites in Ai Khanoum, Bagram, and Hadda have been pillaged. Dubrovnik and other famous cities and historic sites in Croatia as well as in Bosnia, Serbia, and Herzegovina were attacked during the 1990s. Historical sites in Iraq, Syria, and other parts of the Middle East have been desecrated in recent years. While such attacks have occurred throughout history, they seem to be multiplying in recent years due to ethnic, racial, religious, political, tribal, and social unrest, increased violence, vandalism, terrorism, and especially war.

The same holds true for the natural heritage of humankind, primarily as a result of climate change, global warming, and rapid population growth. No doubt there will be much more devastation and disaster in the future if action is not taken to prevent it.

And this is only half the story. As atrocious as these developments have been, there is an even bleaker and more sinister side to these matters. While it is imperative to focus on the positive side of the cultural and natural heritage of humankind as much as possible, a great deal more attention will need to be given to the negative side of this heritage at present and in the future. Just as every person has a positive and negative side to his or her own individual cultural heritage, so every group, town, city, region, country, and the world also has a positive and negative side to their heritage.

The two world wars that dominated the first half of the twentieth century are only the most obvious examples of the dark heritage of humankind. Many other terrifying and vicious acts occurred before, during, and after these wars. To cite only a few well-known examples, there was the extermination of six millions Jews during the Holocaust, the slaughter of a million and a half Armenians during and after World War I, the deaths of millions of Russians, Ukrainians, and members of other ethnic groups in Stalinist Russia (as well as the imprisonment of many more), the killing and displacement of 40 to 70 million Chinese during the Great Leap Forward and the Cultural Revolution, the slaughter of more than a million people in Bosnia and Rwanda, the mass killings by Idi Amin's regime in Uganda, the adverse treatment of Indigenous peoples and Blacks in many parts of the world, and the ongoing physical and sexual abuse of millions of women and girls. And this is not all. There is also the slaughter of billions of animals for reasons that have little or nothing to do with human survival and well-being but a great deal to do with our cruelty and indifference towards other species.

These acts, and many others like them over the centuries, make it clear that forceful and deliberate actions must be taken by governments, international organizations, countries, and citizens in all parts of the world if humanity is to deal effectively with the negative side of the heritage of history. On the one hand, this means establishing legal and political institutions and mechanisms that are necessary to ferret out and punish terrorists, dictators, and perpetrators of reprehensible deeds. This necessitates the creation of war crimes and human rights tribunals, truth and reconciliation commissions, animal rights activism and legislation, and much else. On the other hand, it means dramatically and systematically improving educational practices, intercultural relations and exchanges, and especially "peace initiatives," such as the one commenced by Federico Mayor, former Director-General of UNESCO, when he created in Spain the Foundation for a Culture of Peace.

The heritage of history in general, and the cultural and natural heritage of humankind in particular, should serve as a vivid and perpetual reminder that the most brutal and despicable acts of humanity in the past and at present must not be repeated or tolerated in the future. A powerful statement attributed to Gandhi in the movie directed by Richard Attenborough provides a ray of hope in this regard: "When I despair, I remember that all through history the way of truth and love has won. There have been tyrants and murderers, and for a time, they can seem invincible, but in the end, they always fail. Think of it—**always**."

While truth and love must always prevail, so must all the safeguards and precautions required to ensure that the cultural and natural heritages of all people, all countries as well as humanity as a whole must prevail as well. Art galleries, museums, libraries, archives, and other custodial institutions, as well as educational systems at all levels, have an extremely important role to play in this regard. To do so, these institutions must be endowed with the necessary financial, operational, capital, and human resources. This will require the full support of municipal, regional, and national governments, international agencies and institutions, as well as corporations, foundations, and private benefactors.

This is particularly important with respect to international institutions and agencies such as UNESCO, the World Monuments Fund, the International Council on Monuments and Sites (ICOMOS), the World Wildlife Federation, and many other organizations that are working to ensure that the world's cultural treasures, landscapes, seascapes, historic sites, towns, cities, artifacts, intangible elements, other species, and so forth are preserved and protected for present and future generations.

We were presented in 2018 with a stark reminder of how imperative, precious, and precarious this task is when the National Museum of Brazil was gutted by a massive fire that resulted in the loss of more than 20 million outstanding artistic, scientific, and historic artifacts as well as the destruction of some of South America's greatest natural and anthropological treasures and assets. According to reports, the building and its holdings had been neglected for decades as a result of inadequate funding. Unfortunately, it is too late now to do anything about this, except to lament the fact that an indispensable part of Brazil's and South America's heritage has been lost forever and to ensure that this will never happen again.

There is another dimension to the cultural and natural heritage of history that must be considered as well. It is the need to protect, preserve, and perpetuate diversity in general and cultural and natural diversity in particular. This is required to prevent the homogenization of cultures, countries, and natural heritages, as well as to ensure that people have many different types of cultural and natural options and opportunities in their lives.

A key development in this regard took place in 2005 when UNESCO's *Convention on the Protection and Promotion of the Diversity of Cultural Expressions* was signed. This convention was initiated by Canada and France, approved by 148 nations throughout the world (as well as the European Union), and is designed to ensure that the cultural differences that exist throughout the world are not stamped out by the spread of a ubiquitous global culture, the coercive actions of governments and states, the commercial policies and practices of corporations, and the homogenization of societies through powerful developments in communications, technology, and social media. The significance of this should not be underestimated or ignored, given the necessity of achieving "unity in diversity" in the world of the future. And what is true for the diversity of cultural expression is also true for biodiversity. Constant care must be taken to ensure that all people and countries have access to a rich diversity of plants, animals, and other species, as well as a variety of landscapes, seascapes, parks, conservation areas, ecosystems, and so forth.

There is one final matter related to the heritage of history and historical manifestation of culture that needs to be addressed here because it has such a powerful effect on people, countries, the world, the world system, and humanity at present and going forward into the future. *It is the interpretation of history.*

Just as we inherit countless objects, artifacts, ideas, buildings, monuments, records, and so forth from the past, so we inherit interpretations of history. These interpretations can be, and often are, extremely powerful, since how we interpret history has a fundamental bearing on life, living, the world, global development, and human affairs in the present and the future. (We saw this earlier in connection with the economic interpretation of history.)

Prior to the nineteenth century, most interpretations of history were based on the belief that powerful people—usually rulers—as well as religions and religious institutions and leaders played the dominant role in determining the nature and direction of history and historical events. One need only think of figures such as Alexander the Great, Julius Caesar, Genghis Khan, Ashoka the Great, Charlemagne, Suleiman the Magnificent, Queen Elizabeth I, Peter the Great, Queen Victoria, and many others. This was also true—if not more so—for religions and religious institutions and leaders, such as Christianity and Christ, Buddhism and Buddha, Confucianism and Confucius, Judaism and Moses, Islam and Muhammad, and many others. This gave rise to interpretations of history which positioned prominent people and religions as central.

All this changed with Marx, who developed the economic interpretation of history, which positioned economics as the basis of historical reality. Although the economic interpretation of history has dominated the world for more than 150 years and is still deemed the most accurate view of history by most of the world's governments, corporations, and powerful leaders, there are three fundamental problems with this interpretation of history—and it is an *interpretation,* not a *fact*—that must be addressed rather than being ignored.

The first problem is that it neglects the natural environment as *the* most important factor in global development and human affairs. This has been a disastrous mistake. The second problem is that it treats economics as the whole and everything else as a part of this whole. This is not justified by reality, despite the extremely important role economics plays in our lives today and will likely play in the future. The third problem is that the economic interpretation of history is deterministic, something not warranted by examining history and historical developments and realities over a long period of time. The former Secretary-General of the United Nations and Chairman of the World Commission on Culture and Development from 1993 to 1995, Javier Pérez de Cuéllar, put his finger on the crux of this matter when he said:

> Today, rethinking development is necessary on a world scale.... It was believed, not so long ago, that the economy was the base, the infrastructure. That is wrong: the historians of the "long history" have shown that the decisive element is culture.... Without a large cultural transformation, development is doomed to the destiny of ghost towns.[3]

Despite the exceedingly important role economics and economies play in our lives, human beings have not always lived in an economic age. For instance, they lived in what might best be described as a religious age for many centuries prior to the commencement of the economic age in the eighteenth century. Moreover, human beings possess the freedom and independence to decide for themselves what direction the world and humanity should take in the future.

Since the economic interpretation of history is not consistent with the true nature of global development and human affairs over the centuries, a search must be commenced for a new and more accurate, objective, and impartial interpretation of history, especially in view of the fact that the past and the way it is interpreted have a quintessential bearing on the present and the future.

While there are many different views and opinions on this matter, clearly this search leads us to the realm of culture when culture is seen and dealt with in the all-encompassing, holistic sense. Raymond Williams affirms such an approach in his 1961 book *The Long Revolution.* About the same time that Marx was formulating and promoting his economic interpretation of history, several historians were formulating and promoting what eventually became known as the cultural interpretation of history. Most prominent among these historians was Jacob Burckhardt (1818–97), generally deemed to be the principal formulator of the cultural interpretation of history. Over the course of his life, Burckhardt developed a comprehensive understanding of culture and applied this to the cultures and civilizations of Greece and Rome, not only during the classical period but also, in the case of Rome and Italy, during the Renaissance.

Two of Burckhardt's most essential books on this subject are *The Civilization of the Renaissance in Italy*, published in 1860, and *The Greeks and Greek Civilization*, published in 1872. The breadth and depth of Burckhardt's knowledge and understanding of culture as a whole and individual cultures and civilizations as wholes or overall ways of life was immense and profound. This is confirmed by the organization of *The Civilization of the Renaissance in Italy*. The book is divided into six chapters dealing with the following matters: The State as a Work of Art; The Development of the Individual; The Revival of Antiquity; The Discovery of the World and of Man; Society and Festivals; and Morality and Religion. These headings speak volumes about matters that were of utmost importance during the Renaissance in Italy, as well as the crucial role that culture played in the development of the Renaissance in that country and eventually its flowering and flourishing in many other parts of the world.

Burckhardt's views on the nature, meaning, and importance of the cultural interpretation of history generated many studies on this subject by other cultural historians, most notably Karl Lamprecht, Johan Huizinga, Oswald Spengler, Arnold Toynbee, Raymond

Henry Williams, Will Durant, Thomas Berry, and others who have followed in Burckhardt's footsteps in one form or another. Studies of this type were also conducted by scholars who were interested in cultural history before Burckhardt, especially Voltaire, Herder, Vico, Gibbon, Möser, Macaulay, Adelung, and others. All these scholars were interested in culture, cultures, and civilizations in the broader and deeper holistic sense, and thus espoused a broader and holistic *cultural* interpretation of history rather than a narrower and more specific *economic* interpretation of history.

For cultural historians, scholars, and others interested in culture, cultures, and the cultural interpretation of history, the most fundamental question of all is: "How can a civilization or a culture be understood and presented in all its complexity and yet as an intelligible and structured whole?"[4] This question was posed by Karl J. Weintraub, another exceptional cultural scholar and historian, on the very first page of his book *Visions of Culture: Voltaire, Guizot, Burckhardt, Lamprecht, Huizinga, Ortega y Gasset.*

Weintraub answered this question by saying that the cultural historian is concerned with "the total way of life characteristic of a given social group at a given time," and therefore can only "give form to it by conceiving this totality as a structured whole."[5] He makes his case in no uncertain terms when he declares that "every cultural historian worth [their] salt will try to present the civilization [they have] selected for [their] investigation as a unity of interdependent parts, even if full of tension and contradiction. [They] therefore will search for a center, or a cluster of interrelated foci, from which the totality can be understood and presented as a *unified whole*."[6] And what is true for civilizations in this sense is also true for cultures.

Weintraub goes on to make the following statement about the functioning of cultures as wholes:

> Sheer scope and the esoteric subtlety of subject matter pose problems, but the historian of culture is in addition challenged by its complexity. He [she] sees a culture not as a mere aggregate of traits but as forming an intricately interrelated pattern. In this delicately fashioned network the arts may have their ties to religion and economic values, morality may

> affect the constitutional arrangements and in turn be affected by political realities, a mood reflected in literature may also come to the fore in a social custom, and a scientific insight may work back upon a religious belief.[7]

This view contrasts sharply with the conclusions arrived at by Marx. Whereas Marx claimed that there is a unilateral and largely irreversible relationship between the economic base and the non-economic superstructure—primarily for the purpose of making economics the root cause of everything in human society—Weintraub claims that there is an interactive and multilateral relationship among all activities in cultures, and that these interactions flow in both directions and not just one.[8]

This insight is of crucial importance. It pays, therefore, to persevere with Weintraub's keen observations into this matter for a moment longer. Here is what he had to say at greater length about this phenomenon, and consequently the work and interpretations of cultural historians:

> He [she] studies what a culture is and also how it develops. He [she] must be able to see a culture in the total, relatively static, configurations attained at a given time; but he [she] must trace as well its gradual transformation through time. This double concern ... implies, on the one hand, the study of connections between cultural factors in their structural relationship, and, on the other hand, the study of the gradual changes, either by the introduction of new factors or by a shift in emphasis among the existing relations, resulting in a modification of the cultural configuration. *In the world of the cultural historian all things touch one another. He [she] is compelled to keep track of a host of intricately interrelated matters simultaneously.*[9]

This statement has profound implications for the world of the present and the future. Whereas Marx's central conclusion was that economics must be given priority over everything else, the conclusion arrived at by Weintraub and many other cultural historians is that people are free to develop societies, countries, cultures, and civilizations *any way they see fit*. In other words, history is based on free will rather than determinism. Visualized in this way, history is always an open book to be written and charted in accordance with the circumstances people face.

There is something else of fundamental importance regarding the work of cultural historians and the cultural interpretation of history that must be dealt with here. It is the fact that the world is really composed of culture and cultures—and not economics and economies—at its core.

This has become steadily more apparent as a result of globalization, the migration and mingling of billions of people throughout the world, interactions among all the different cultures and civilizations of the world, the COVID-19 pandemic, and many other factors and developments. What is most significant is that cultures are total ways of life composed of countless interrelated parts that are weighed, prioritized, and valued differently by different people, groups, and countries. They are also constantly evolving and mutating. *This* is the reality of the world. While this reality has been ignored, especially over the last two centuries, it is of crucial importance. Attention must be focused first and foremost on culture and cultures in the holistic sense.

Seen from this perspective, the challenge of the future is clear and unequivocal. It is to develop culture and all the diverse cultures in the world in all their complexity and diversity, as well as to achieve balance and harmony among their many different parts and situate them effectively in the natural, historical, and global environment.

If sustainable development is to be achieved and the welfare and well-being of people, countries, and other species in all parts of the world is to be realized, this is a categorical imperative. Providing grounds for optimism in this regard is the fact that the cultural interpretation of history makes it possible to see the big picture, explain and interpret historical and contemporary developments and events more accurately, impartially, and fully, learn from the past and come to grips with the cultural baggage people and countries have inherited from it, and set the world and humanity on a different developmental path in the future.

The past has a prominent role to play in shaping the present and the future everywhere in the world, but in a free and open rather than deterministic and restricted manner. In this sense, no one recognized the importance of history in general and the heritage of history in particular better than the cultural historian Ernst Gombrich when he said:

> Our own past is moving away from us at frightening speed, and if we want to keep open the lines of communication which permit us to understand the greatest creations of [humankind] we must study and teach the history of culture more deeply and more intensely than was necessary a generation ago.... If cultural history did not exist, it would have to be invented now.[10]

What is true for the heritage of history is also true for the cultural interpretation of history and the historical manifestation of culture. We need to know a great deal more about the all-encompassing character of the cultural interpretation of history—as embodied in the research and writings of cultural historians—as well as to open up a commanding place for this interpretation of history and the historical manifestation of culture in the overall scheme of things. Doing so is key to unlocking the secrets of the past and crossing over the threshold to a more harmonious and sustainable period in the development of humanity.

Chapter Six

Personality Development

> The study of culture properly begins with the study of the cultural elements of the individual.
>
> —James Feibleman[1]

Given the escalating interest in culture and cultures in the nineteenth century, it was inevitable that sooner or later some scholars would turn their attention to the role that culture plays in the development of people and their personalities.

One of the first scholars to do this was the Scottish essayist, historian, mathematician, and educator Thomas Carlyle. Some claim that Carlyle's book *The French Revolution: A History*, published in 1837, provided the inspiration for Charles Dickens' popular novel *A Tale of Two Cities*. Others credit Carlyle with labelling economics "the dismal science" after reading Thomas Malthus' famous essay on population in which he predicted that population growth would eventually outstrip the means of subsistence.

However, Carlyle is best known for his "great law of culture." It states, "Let each [person] become all that he [she] was created capable of being; expand, if possible, to his [her] full growth; resisting all impediments, casting off all foreign, especially all noxious adhesions; and show himself [herself] at length in his [her] own shape and stature, be these what they may."[2] This law fit well with the conclusions Carlyle reached in his important book, *On Heroes, Hero-Worship, and the Heroic in History*. In this book, Carlyle contended that history results largely from the actions and achievements of "great" individuals such as Jesus, Muhammad, Genghis Khan, Napoleon, Shakespeare, Martin Luther, and so on.

Carlyle's great law of culture has important implications for the development of people's personalities. Many of these implications are positive, such as the belief that people can achieve authentic development by becoming what they ought to become, rather than failing to challenge themselves to do so. Thus they can resist the temptation to become imitative or conformist and instead realize their full potential, essence, and basic purpose in life. This idea is consistent with what John Calvin meant when he talked about people fulfilling their "calling," as well as what Joseph Campbell believed when he advised us to "follow your bliss" in order to achieve what you are intended to realize in life.

However, there are negative implications to Carlyle's great law of culture as well. They have to do with Carlyle's directive to show oneself in one's own "shape and substance, *be these what they may*." Doing so can obviously result in the emergence of heroes and great (and good) leaders, true enough, but it can also lead to the ascendancy of diabolical leaders and evil dictators like Hitler or Stalin. In other words, "great" individuals aren't always good. Once this was recognized, interest in Carlyle's great law of culture—as well as his overall interpretation of history—waned substantially. Nonetheless, it still serves a useful purpose in understanding the role of culture in the development of people's personalities and lives, because it makes clear that culture—like everything in life—has negative as well as positive implications, connotations, and consequences. As such, it acts as a constant reminder to exercise caution when dealing with culture by ensuring that its positive aspects prevail and negative aspects are minimized.

Thomas Carlyle was not the only scholar to write about the role of culture in the development of people and their personalities and lives in the nineteenth century. Matthew Arnold also did this. He was an English poet, cultural critic, and educator who served as an inspector of schools for many years and eventually became a Professor of Poetry at Oxford University.

For Arnold, culture was the pursuit of perfection, or, as he put it, "the cultivation of sweetness and light." Today we would likely say he meant the cultivation of the arts and education. Arnold advocated the relentless and lifelong pursuit of knowledge, wisdom, erudition, and learning. Such a quest is dynamic rather than static, a "growing and becoming" rather than "having and being." For Arnold, the quest to achieve perfection is best realized through the harmonious development of all the faculties that comprise human nature:

> Perfection—as culture, from a thoroughly disinterested study of human nature and human experience learns to conceive it—*is a harmonious expansion of all the powers which make the beauty and worth of human nature, and is not consistent with the over-development of any one power at the expense of the rest.* Here culture goes beyond religion, as religion is generally conceived by us.... It is in making endless additions to itself, in the endless expansion of its powers, in endless growth in wisdom and beauty, that the spirit of the human race finds its ideal. To reach this ideal, culture is an indispensable aid, and that is the true value of culture.[3]

Arnold also believed that culture should be dealt with in an *active* rather than *passive* manner, as well as in *altruistic* rather than *egotistic* terms. While the cultivation of sweetness and light tends to suggest a process that depends more on acquisition than action, taking rather than giving, Arnold was careful to point out that this should merely be the first step of many aimed at taking the arts and education out of the hands of the elite and sharing them with the whole of humanity. As an educator, Arnold felt strongly that society had an obligation to provide the best possible education for the greatest number of people:

> The moment this view of culture is seized ... and culture is considered not merely as the endeavour to *see* and *learn* this, but as the endeavour, also, to make it *prevail*, the moral, social, and beneficent character of culture becomes manifest... it knows that the sweetness and light of the few must be imperfect until the raw and unkindled masses of humanity are touched with sweetness and light....
>
> ....[M]en [women] of culture are the true apostles of equality. The great men [women] of culture are those who have had a passion for *diffusing*, for making prevail, for carrying from one end of society to the other, the best knowledge, the best ideas of their time; who have laboured

> to divest knowledge of all that was harsh, uncouth, difficult, abstract, professional, exclusive; to humanize it, to make it efficient outside the clique of the cultivated and learned, yet still remaining the *best* knowledge and thought of the time, and a true source, therefore, of sweetness and light.[4]

Arnold's views gave rise to one of the most valuable and worthwhile ideas about the contributions culture can make to people's lives and to the development of their personalities. It is the idea of the *whole person*. This idea remains highly relevant to all fields and all people today. For the whole person, the mind, body, senses, intellect, heart, spirit, and soul are indispensable elements in the overall composition, character, and functioning of their lives as well as the development of their personalities.

One person who was especially enamoured of the idea of the whole person was Jan Christiaan Smuts, who twice served as prime minister of South Africa. He is probably best known for his encounters with Mahatma Gandhi when Gandhi was a lawyer in South Africa. Smuts had to jail Gandhi on several occasions for civil disobedience. However, Smuts was a profound thinker. Here is what he had to say about the idea of the whole person:

> Personality then is a new whole, is the highest and completest of all wholes, is the most recent conspicuous mutation in the evolution of Holism.... [It is] the supreme embodiment of Holism both in its individual and its universal tendencies. It is the final synthesis of all the operative factors in the universe into unitary wholes, and both in its unity and its complexity it constitutes the great riddle of the universe.[5]

Smuts' contribution to the development of culture as personality does not end here. He also recommended that a new discipline called "Personology" be created to deal with all the problems that have to do with personality development, not just those related to the idea of the whole person. In doing so, he was decades ahead of his time. His proposed discipline possesses strong similarities with the discipline of psychology today. To quote Smuts once more:

> As the key to all the highest interests of the human race, Personality seems to be quite the most important and fruitful problem to which the thinkers of the coming generation could direct their attention. In Personality will probably be found the answer to some of the hardest and oldest questions that have troubled the heart as well as the head of man [woman]. The problem of Personality seems as hard as it is important. Not without reason have thinkers throughout the ages shied off from it. But it holds precious secrets for those who will seriously devote themselves to the new science or discipline of Personology.[6]

About the same time that Smuts was writing about the whole person and advocating the creation of the discipline of Personology, the anthropologist Bronisław Malinowski was focusing on people's "basic human needs" following his intensive investigations of numerous cultures throughout the world and especially those in the Trobriand Islands of eastern New Guinea. He identified these needs as nutrition, reproduction, bodily comfort, safety, relaxation, movement, and human growth.

Malinowski's pioneering work in this area eventually led to more detailed studies in the years to follow. One of the most active scholars in this area was Johan Galtung, a well-known peace activist and social theorist. He proposed as a working hypothesis the following set of basic human needs: security or survival needs (individual and collective protection again crime, violence, terrorism, and so forth); welfare and sufficiency needs (water, air, food, sleep, protection against climate and disease); identity or "closeness" needs (self-expression, self-actualization, roots, support systems, partnerships with nature, purpose in life, and so forth); and freedom or "choice" needs (choice of location, occupation, way of life, and the like).

For Galtung, these needs formed a holistic constellation rather than a pyramid, hierarchy, or ladder with the economic or material needs spread out across the lowest rung. As such, they differed from Abraham Maslow's "hierarchy of needs," which begins with satisfying people's basic material or economic needs and then moves progressively up the ladder or hierarchy to self-actualization or self-realization—the highest need of all according to Maslow, as set out in his popular book *Motivation and Personality*.

What these and many other studies have revealed is that people have a broad diversity of needs and wants that must be satisfied if they are to survive and live effectively in the world. These needs consist of many different requirements—economic, social, political, educational, artistic, scientific, religious, recreational, environmental, spiritual, and so forth—and they exist for every person in the world. While all of these requirements are important in their own right, what is especially important is the *process* whereby these requirements and the activities associated with them are woven together to form wholes composed of many parts. This provides a different way of looking at the whole person than the ideas of Arnold or Smuts. People must decide for themselves how their needs and activities will be woven together to yield a total and integrated spectrum of needs, wants, desires, and expectations.

Interest in these matters waned somewhat after Arnold, Smuts, Malinowski, Galtung, and others made their highly original contributions. However, shortly after the Second World War, Margaret Mead and Ruth Benedict became interested in this matter in connection with what was called "national character" or "national personality types and traits." Margaret Mead studied the development of the "collective national personality type" of people in England, while Ruth Benedict studied the national collective personality type of people in Japan, as described in detail in books such as *The Chrysanthemum and the Sword: Patterns of Japanese Culture*, published in 1946.[7] In retrospect, it is clear that these interests were intimately connected to developments during the Second World War and the quest to comprehend different national personality types in some of the major countries involved in that war.

Developments like these, along with the rapid growth of the discipline of psychology in the decades following the Second World War, led to a rapid escalation of interest in the important role culture played in personality development among cultural scholars, especially anthropologists. This interest was driven by such scholars as Abram Kardiner, Gordon Allport, Ralph Linton, Anthony F.C. Wallace, John Honigmann, Douglas Haring, Cora Du Bois, Robert V. LeVine,

Francis L.K. Hsu, and others. This led to the creation of a variety of approaches to the development of people's personalities, as well as the study of different personality types from a cultural perspective.

In terms of the concept of the whole person discussed earlier, the idea that culture plays a central role in personality development and the lives of people can and should be taken much further. In fact, it leads to the conclusion that people in all parts of the world live ***cultural lives*** in the sense that they combine all their various human faculties with all the different activities they are engaged in to form a dynamic and organic whole composed of countless parts. Whereas some people might place a higher priority on certain faculties and activities compared to others—such as the development of their minds, senses, or physical faculties and involvement in economic, social, religious, political, or technological activities—all people are compelled to combine all the faculties and activities they are engaged in to form integrated and holistic entities, although some people may be able to do this much better or more effectively than others.

Think about it for a moment. All people's lives, including our own, are made up of many different parts. Some of these parts are intellectual, emotional, physical, sensorial, and spiritual, whereas others are economic, religious, social, political, recreational, and so forth. Despite the fact that people may commit a great deal more time and place a much higher priority on some of these parts compared to others, they remain merely parts and not the whole. They only become the whole when all the aforementioned parts, and many others not mentioned here, are blended together to form holistic and all-inclusive entities. It was obviously this process that Ruth Benedict had in mind when she said that "cultures are really personalities writ large," since cultures are also wholes made up of many interacting and interrelated parts. We are not talking about how important or unimportant any given part is, or how much time people spend developing them. Rather, we are talking about how people weave all the parts together to form cultural wholes.

Every person in the world lives a *cultural life* in this all-inclusive, holistic sense. This is true regardless of whether they are rich or poor, where they live in the world, what socioeconomic class, race, or ethnic group they come from or belong to, what gender they are, what their ancestry is, or how they interact with other people, the natural environment, and other species.

This is a very different understanding of what it means to live a cultural life than the understanding that most people have today. Most people would probably say that living a cultural life means going to the theatre, attending concerts and plays, visiting art galleries and museums, enjoying operatic and dance performances, reading books, and being well-educated, informed, and refined. While these are all part of living a cultural life, living a cultural life *in the holistic sense* means something substantially broader, deeper, and more fundamental. It means combining all the various faculties one has with all the different activities one is engaged in to form a single and all-encompassing entity.

In today's world, the cultural life of most people is dominated by three powerful factors: economics, specialization, and technology. This is not surprising. Economics, specialization, and technology have dominated the world for more than two centuries and still dominate it today. Over the last two centuries, this domination has led to the creation of two very specific personality types, the economic personality and the specialist personality, which are the most prevalent personality types in the world at the present time.

The economic personality is grounded in the conviction that people should produce and consume as much as possible because this results in the creation of the maximum amount of material and monetary wealth, allowing people to maximize their consumer satisfaction in the marketplace. The specialist personality is based on the conviction that acquiring a specific skill or technological ability and working in a particular occupation or profession is the best way for people to fulfill both their economic and non-economic needs. This conviction can be traced back to Adam Smith and *The Wealth of Nations*, since Smith believed that every person should be engaged in a specific production function and focus their energy and attention on cultivating highly specialized skills and abilities. Doing so produces the most income and wealth as well as yielding the highest standard of living and quality of life.

The problem is that these two personality types are breaking down—and breaking down very rapidly—in most parts of the world today. The economic personality is breaking down because people are seen and treated largely as producers and consumers of goods and services and maximizers of their consumer satisfaction. While this may provide an accurate description of the way most people fit into modern economic systems, this description relates to only one dimension of their personalities and lives, albeit an extremely important one. This view also tends to treat people as objects to be exploited and manipulated in the interests of the marketplace and economic growth. Among the results has been a great deal more part-time, seasonal, contractual, and precarious work. This way of thinking also has a devastating effect on the natural environment because of the colossal demands it makes on the world's scarce resources.

The specialist personality is breaking down because modern economic systems are changing so rapidly that people's skills and technological capabilities are often out of date or redundant soon after they are acquired, causing them to lose their jobs and making it difficult for them to find new employment opportunities. To this should be added the fact that this specific personality type produces a perception of people that is one-dimensional, fragmented, and incomplete rather than multi-dimensional, integrated, and comprehensive.

It wasn't very long ago that most people held only one or two jobs over the course of their lives, usually in the same or a very similar field. Today, however, people often hold ten to fifteen jobs throughout their lives, in very different fields and professions. This means they must be retrained for these new jobs, actively search for them, go back to school to acquire the skills, expertise, and technological abilities that are required, or become unemployed. This doesn't auger well for most people in the future, since it makes their employment situation precarious, vulnerable, and unpredictable.

Technological change is exerting a powerful and profound effect on all this. Despite the fact that many people in the world are much more technologically literate than they were in the past, digital technologies are changing the nature of work and the workplace so quickly that it is difficult if not impossible to keep up. Moreover, major developments in artificial intelligence, robotics, and so forth are eliminating millions of jobs at present and likely many more in the future. In these conditions, the relevant and pressing question for most people in the world today is: Where will the jobs and income opportunities come from in the future that will be necessary to feed, clothe, and house myself and my family, as well as look after all our other needs?

These technological changes are accompanied by numerous social changes. People are becoming more self-absorbed, largely because of the rapid expansion of social media networks such as Facebook, Twitter, Instagram, and so forth. These platforms tend to have an isolating rather than unifying effect on people.

This is all occurring at a time when profound changes are taking place in the natural environment. People in all parts of the world are being challenged to live a way of life that is much more compatible with present and future ecological requirements by diminishing the demands they are making on the world's resources.

Given these and many other changes taking place in the world today, more and more people are being thrown back on their own resources, forced to take control of their own destinies and lives to a much greater extent. This raises a series of fundamental questions about people's lives and the development of their personalities, as well as the need to create new ways of life that are consistent with their physical, emotional, intellectual, and spiritual requirements.

These developments pave the way for the emergence of a new type of human personality in the future—the *cultural personality*. To be effective and in tune with reality, present circumstances, and future needs, the cultural personality should be *holistic*, *centred*, *creative*, *altruistic*, *idealistic*, and *humane*.

When Goethe said, "he who wills the highest, must will the whole," he put his finger on the crux of what it means for the cultural personality to be holistic. For in the process of "willing the highest," the cultural personality comes face to face with the need to live a cultural life in the all-inclusive holistic sense as fully as possible, as well as to unite all the different faculties and activities of life in such a way that they create a harmonious whole made up of many different parts. The senses, body, mind, intellect, heart, spirit, and soul combine with all the other human activities to become one, so to speak, indispensable elements in the overall composition and character of this specific personality type. This is what Smuts had in mind when he wrote:

> The great practical problem before the Personality is thus to effectuate and preserve its wholeness through the harmonizing of its several activities, and the prevention among them of any random discord or sedition, whereby one or other might be enabled to assume ascendancy over the rest and so prepare the way for the disintegration and destruction of the whole....
>
> In proportion as a personality really becomes such, it acquires more of the character of wholeness; body and mind, intellect and heart, will and emotions, while not separately repressed but on the contrary fostered and developed, are yet all collectively harmonized and blended into one integral whole; the character becomes more massive, the entire man [woman] becomes more of a piece; and the will or conscious rational direction, which is not a separate agency hostile to these individual factors, but the very root and expression of their joint and harmonious action, becomes more silently and smoothly powerful; the wear and tear of internal struggle disappears; the friction and waste which accompany the warfare in the soul are replaced by peace and unity and strength; till at last Personality stands forth in its ideal purity, integrity and wholeness.[8]

It matters little that holism in some ultimate, metaphysical, or idealistic sense is unattainable, since it is always possible to add new information, insights, and ideas to the ever-expanding dimensions of the whole. What is most important for the cultural personality is to be constantly and systematically *striving* to achieve this end, and, as such, relentlessly endeavouring to fuse all aspects of being and living together to form a seamless web. This requires perpetual acts of integration, synthesis, and symbiosis aimed at melding all the different and diverse fragments of being and becoming together—internal and external, subjective and objective, material and non-material, self and other—to form a unitary entity. John Cowper Powys recognized the crucial importance of this when he said:

> The whole purpose and end of culture is a thrilling happiness of a particular sort—of the sort, in fact, that is caused by a response to life made by a harmony of the intellect, the imagination, and the senses.[9]

Since holism is "the tendency in nature to form wholes that are more than the sum of the parts by creative evolution,"[10] it is appropriate to ask what it is that makes the whole greater than the parts and the sum of its parts in the case of the cultural personality. This "extra something" has been variously described as a value system, spirit, soul, or philosophy of life. Since it is through this process that the cultural personality becomes *centred* in the self as well as in the world, it requires some explanation.

As with personality development of any type, the starting point for the cultural personality is with life's everyday experiences and multifarious needs and activities. These experiences, needs, and activities are not only exceedingly diverse, but also largely undifferentiated. They invade the individual at all times, as well as from all sides and places. With the passing of time, however, the cultural personality begins to make connections and associations between the myriad experiences, needs, and activities that are encountered in everyday life. These connections and associations provide the basis for the formation of values, since they involve comparisons between one type of experience, need, or activity and another. This is where assessments are made of life's many different encounters in the world and priorities are established between and among them, thereby making it possible to rank them all in the overall scheme of things. Just how important culture is in this process of value formation was revealed by Mircea Malitza when he said that "culture is the crucible from which values emerge, where preferences are formed and the hierarchy among them is established."[11]

Just as there are collective values in the larger and more impersonal cultural sense, so there are individual values in the smaller and more intimate cultural sense. These values give centredness, rootedness, substance, character, and integrity to the cultural personality. They make it possible for the cultural personality to differentiate between what is relevant and irrelevant, valuable and valueless, and meaningful and meaningless. Without values, there is no way of separating truth from falsehood or fiction, good from evil, justice from injustice, and morality from immorality. In the process of cultivating a viable set of values in the individual sense, the cultural personality becomes aware that values are not only essential ingredients in a fully developed person, but also sources of integrity and inspiration. As a result, they should be savoured at all times:

> There is a sense in which the whole of human culture is a struggle towards the higher values. Can there be any greater expression of culture than art? Art surely lifts us up, although it would not be likely to exist without it.... We were meant to actualize the higher values, and incidental to this task is the privilege of enjoying them.[12]

It is through the process of struggling to formulate and refine values that the cultural personality becomes aware of a deeper development that begins to take place in the fertile soil of the self, the spirit, the mind, and the soul. It is the creation of a set of central organizing principles and practices around which personal values are galvanized, coalesced, and understood. These central organizing principles and practices may be predicated on love, beauty, truth, integrity, compassion, caring, sharing, creativity, productivity, or any other worthwhile human asset or combination of them. Since they are finely honed over a long period of time, they have a seasoned quality, stability, and solidarity about them that is difficult to describe but easy to appreciate.

No greater mistake could be made than to assume that values are fixed, immutable, and unchanging. On the contrary, they are flexible and constantly being broadened, deepened, and intensified in order to remain in tune with the dynamic nature of external reality and the internal needs of the self. For just as the world is constantly producing new problems, challenges, and possibilities, so the cultural personality is constantly refining its central organizing principles and practices in order to bring them into line with reality as well as the ever-evolving requirements of society, humanity, the world, and the self.

It is important to emphasize that these central organizing principles and practices are what make it possible for the cultural personality to feel centred and rooted in the self, as well as fluid, adaptable, and responsive to the never-ending changes that are taking place in the world. By providing the fundamental focal point around which values are organized, arranged, and coalesced, these central organizing principles and practices provide connectedness, continuity, and coherence in space and time. While they mature and ripen over a long period of time depending on people's individual needs and preferences, they nevertheless remain the benchmarks and touchstones that are needed for the effective functioning of the cultural personality in the world. It is through the progressive refinement of these central organizing principles and practices—or what some people prefer to call the creation of a viable *value system*—that the cultural personality begins to fashion a very distinct philosophy of life. In his book *Cosmic Understanding: Philosophy and Science of the Universe*, Milton K. Munitz explains why it is so essential to have a philosophy of this type:

> When acquired, such a philosophy provides a framework of basic principles that helps guide a person's reactions to the crises and opportunities of life, to the universal facts of human existence—being born and dying, being a member of society, being part of a wider universe. To have a set of basic guiding principles, whether accepted from some external source or worked out for oneself, is an inescapable requirement for a human being.[13]

What is significant about this philosophy for the cultural personality is how unique it is. Having taken the time and trouble to wrestle with all the diverse elements that go into making up this philosophy, it could hardly be otherwise:

> A philosophy of one's own, grown tough and flexible amid the shocks of the world, is a far more important achievement than the ability to expound the precise differences between the great philosophic schools of thought....

> The art of self-culture begins with a deeper awareness, borne in upon us either by some sharp emotional shock or little by little like an insidious rarefied air, of the marvel of our being alive at all; alive in a world as startling and mysterious, as lovely and horrible, as the one we live in. Self culture without some kind of *integrated* habitual manner of thinking is apt to fail us just when it is wanted the most. *To be a cultured person is to be a person with some kind of original philosophy.*[14]

It is through hammering out this philosophy that the cultural personality begins to comprehend what it means to be totally centred in the self as well as in the world. This is because there is a growing realization that a central rudder has been created that provides strength, durability, and a clear sense of purpose, direction, and vision for the future life course. John Cowper Powys used a botanical illustration to drive this point home with great clarity and conviction:

> Slowly, as life tightens the knot of our inner being, our outer leaves, like those of a floating water-plant, expand in the sunshine and in the rain of pure chance; but we still are aware of the single stalk under the surface, of the single root that gives meaning to all.[15]

As profuse and unpredictable as life's events and experiences are, it is not the events and experiences themselves—or the values, value system, and philosophy of life that emanate from them—that make the cultural personality *creative*, yet another basic characteristic of this personality type. Rather, it is the way these events and experiences are woven together to produce a unique way of life. In the process of creating this way of life, the cultural personality is compelled to exercise a great deal of creativity. It is creativity that derives from the inalienable right of all people to fashion a way of life that is consistent with the demands and dictates of their own internal needs, values, and experiences as well as their external circumstances and realities. Every person, regardless of his or her background, financial situation, social circumstances, religious persuasion, or spiritual requirements has the right to fashion this way of life in such a way that it is highly inventive and distinct in its design, development, evolution, and execution.

The type of creativity we are talking about here is not the kind that is often found in or associated with artists, scientists, and scholars. However, it is creativity nonetheless. It will probably never manifest itself in the creation of great paintings, rare books, superb musical masterpieces, or famous inventions—that is to say, in the production of works of art, science, and scholarship that can withstand the test of time. But it is still creativity because it involves taking the infinite building blocks of life and arranging them in such a way that the result is a cultural life that is without duplication in the world. It follows from this that life is dynamic and organic rather than static and fixed when this occurs. It is in a constant state of evolution, change, and flux, not only in the way values and experiences are constantly being arranged and rearranged, but also in the way in which the central organizing principles and practices and underlying philosophy of life are being constantly enlarged, reformulated, refined, and revitalized. Ralph Linton, writing about the relationship between culture and personality, refers to this dynamic and organic property this way:

> Personalities are dynamic continuums, and although it is important to discover their content, organization and performance at a given point in time, it is still more important to discover the processes by which they develop, grow and change.[16]
>
> Each individual is born with a unique configuration of physical and psychological potentialities, and from the moment of birth finds himself [herself] in interaction with his [her] environment. The process of personality development is one of continual assimilation and organization of the experiences which he [she] derives from this interaction. As each new item of experience is integrated it becomes a factor in later interactions with the environment, and consequently in the production of new experiences.[17]

It is this dynamic and organic quality that renders to the cultural personality the ability to adjust to a world that is in perpetual motion and state of flux, as well as to confront and overcome whatever problems, challenges, and obstacles stand in the way. This is especially important today with respect to all the major changes that are taking place in the world, such as the COVID-19 pandemic, racial protests, technological change, and many other factors indicated earlier. Not only will this require transformations in people's education, training, and learning, but also it will require the development of the entrepreneurial skills and abilities that are necessary to make ends meet and live a full and fulfilling cultural life in the future. This will necessitate the cultivation of creativity, excellence, ingenuity, and entrepreneurship to a much greatest extent. It will also require people who are more innovative and inventive than people were in the past, thereby making the creative dimension of the cultural personality one of the most essential characteristics of personality development of all.

While it is important to develop creativity in the short run, it is even more essential to develop it in the long run. Every person in the world must confront and come to grips with the fact that a kind of "static malaise" or "psychological death" can set in at any stage or age in life if the necessary precautions are not taken to prevent it. Regardless of whether a person is in the prime of life, mid-career, early retirement, or the final stages of life, there is the perpetual risk of becoming so mired in the muck of reality and contemporary problems that it is impossible to extricate oneself and get back on track. If the creative, entrepreneurial, and dynamic spirit and capabilities of the personality are not swung into action at this time and brought to the fore, what may result is a kind of deadening process that slowly but surely wraps itself around everything and sucks every ounce of energy and enthusiasm out of the life process. The cultural personality is always aware of this and constantly taking steps to prevent it. It does this by drawing on its own inner reserves and innovative abilities and creating new challenges and opportunities. No sooner is one challenge met or opportunity achieved than new ones are put in their place.

It is unlikely that the cultural personality can do this without acquiring one of the highest and noblest human qualities of all. I am referring here to *altruism*, or the ability to give to others and make commitments to causes and missions that are greater than the self. It was altruism that Matthew Arnold had in mind when he talked about the need to take the arts and education out of the hands of elites and share them with the whole of humanity. It was also altruism that Picasso had in mind when he said, "Your challenge in life is to find your gift; your purpose in life is to give it away." Pitirim Sorokin had something similar to say about this matter—but for humanity as a whole and not just the individual—when he penned the following passage:

> If humanity mobilizes all its wisdom, knowledge, beauty, and especially the all-giving and all-forgiving love and reverence for life, and if a strenuous and sustaining effort of this kind is made by everyone—an effort deriving its strength from love and reverence for life—then the crisis will certainly be ended and a most magnificent new era in human history ushered in. It is up to mankind [humankind] to decide what it will do with its future life course.[18]

For the cultural personality, altruism is not an alternative to egoism. Rather, both are part of a single reality. While the cultural personality is interested in the development of the self, this is not seen as an end in itself but rather as a means to serving broader and deeper interests and objectives for humanity, as well as helping other people and those in need. Why is this so necessary? It is necessary because, as Samuel Butler said, "the works of all people, regardless of whether they are in literature, music, pictures, paintings, architecture, or anything else, are always portraits of the self. And the more people try to conceal it, the more clearly their characters will appear and assert themselves in spite of this."

While altruism is a fundamental characteristic worthy of a great deal of commitment, devotion, and pursuit, it is not sufficient in and of itself to ensure that the cultural personality is *idealistic*. The two are intimately connected, needless to say, because doing good deeds for others or humanity as a whole usually results from having an idealistic rather than realistic, egocentric, or pessimistic personality and outlook on life and the world.

Surely it was idealism like this that Herman Hesse had in mind in the following passage in his book *The Glass Bead Game*:

> World history is a race with time, a scramble for profit, for power, for treasures. What counts is who has the strength, luck, or vulgarity not to miss the opportunity. The achievements of thought, of culture, of the arts are just the opposite. They are always an escape from the serfdom of time, man [woman] crawling out of the muck of his [her] instinct and out of his [her] sluggishness and climbing to a higher plane, to timelessness, liberation from time, divinity.[19]

It is impossible to do this without having a positive outlook on life and the world, as well as looking for the best rather than the worse in human affairs and everything else. For the cultural personality, this is also true for humanity's highest, wisest, and most valuable ideals, including the pursuit of beauty and truth, the need for justice, order, stability, and security, commitment to freedom of movement, speech, ideas, and expression, the quest for equality, identity, and spirituality, the desire to live a full, upright, and meaningful life, and the search for ecstasy and the sublime. While the cultural personality is fully aware of the fact that history is filled with exploitation, greed, hate, genocide, racism, violence, oppression, and war, it never permits the negative dimensions of history or of life to stand in the way of believing that there is an ascendency about history, humanity, life, the life force, and the world that indicates that things are getting better rather than worse. It is this assessment that always causes the cultural personality to move forwards and upwards rather than backwards and downwards in life.

And this brings us to the final characteristic of the cultural personality, namely the need to be *humane*. It is not difficult to determine how this final characteristic should be played out and addressed, since the cultural personality will have to provide a good example for others if this is to be achieved. Such an example must flow from the highest forms of conduct and character as well as inspire the noblest forms of action and behaviour. This will not be an easy task. Indeed, it will probably be the most difficult task of all, since the temptations of living in a materialistic, secular, and technologically dominated world are so great that exemplary conduct will be difficult to achieve and may be confined to people who are most committed, dedicated, and courageous.

Surely the best place to start in this respect is to return to the idea of the harmonious development of all the faculties, activities, and factors that are combined together to form the cultural personality. In the process of uniting all these faculties, factors, and activities, the cultural personality is compelled to develop many of the sensitivities, sensibilities, and convictions that are needed to become fully human and truly humane. It is here that the heart, spirit, senses, and soul are fused with the mind, body, and intellect; egoism is tempered by altruism and gives way to it; and truth, beauty, justice, equality, and the sublime assert themselves frequently. The result is an individual who is more in tune with the self, compassionate and respectful of other people's needs, requirements, and differences, as well as being more settled in the self and in the world.

Strong leadership skills are required for this. They grow out of the realization that values and ideals have great importance for our lives as well as for communities, societies, countries, and the world at large, and therefore demand our highest priorities and fullest attention. Albert Schweitzer explains why this is so important:

> We may take as the essential element in civilization the ethical perfecting of the individual and of society as well. But at the same time, every spiritual and every material step in advance has a significance for civilization. The will to civilization is then the universal will to progress which is conscious of the ethical as the highest value for all. In spite of the great importance we attach to the triumphs of knowledge and achievement, it is nevertheless obvious that only a humanity which is striving after ethical ends can in full measure share in the blessings brought by material progress and become master of the dangers which accompany it. To the generation which had adopted a belief in an immanent power of progress realizing itself, in some measure, naturally and automatically, and which thought that it no longer needed any ethical ideals but could advance to its goal by means of knowledge and achievement alone, terrible proof was being given by its

> present position of the error into which it had sunk.... But what is the nature of the attitude toward life in which the will to general progress and to ethical progress are alike founded and in which they are bound together? It consists in an ethical affirmation of the world and of life.[20]

For the cultural personality, human conduct requires not only recognition of the fundamental foundations of human existence in general and human behaviour and actions in particular, but also acceptance of the fact there are implications and consequences for all things as indicated earlier, regardless of whether it is confronting the self, dealing with others, making consumer choices, participating in political causes, or interacting with the natural environment and other species. Commitment to the existential belief that in committing ourselves we are committing the whole of humanity provides the logical point of departure for this. Adherence to this belief requires the cultural personality to think long and hard about the implications, consequences, and outcomes of all forms of behaviour. This necessitates a kind of "reverential thinking," a willingness to consider the impact of behaviour not only on the self, but also on other people, all forms of plant, animal, and mineral life, and the planet.

Reverential thinking is not an end in itself, but rather the logical and necessary step towards reverential action. If consumption practices have an inimical effect on the natural environment or are wasteful of natural resources, they are not condoned and perpetrated regardless of how much they satisfy personal needs, wants, aspirations, or desires. If success means running roughshod over the needs, rights, and lives of others, it is not pursued regardless of how much this might advance personal interests. If standards of living in one part of the world are enjoyed at the expense of people living in other parts of the world, they are not condoned regardless of how fulfilling they are or might be. In each of these cases, and others too numerous to mention, the cultural personality is careful to choose a course of action that does not involve exploiting others or the natural environment in order to satisfy the interests and concerns of the self.

It is important to emphasize that the cultural personality is not a tower of strength, virtue, or perfection in this sense. Like all people, it makes mistakes and errors. However, what it is always *striving* to do is to live a way of life that is based on achieving personal aspirations and standards without injuring others. If this cannot be achieved with one mode of behaviour, the cultural personality sets in motion other modes of behaviour that are capable of accomplishing this.

In attempts to glean a clearer impression and understanding of the nature of conduct that lies at the core of the cultural personality, it may be helpful to consider the two Chinese notions of "face." The first is *mien-tzu*; and the second is *lien*. Here is how Hu Hsien-Chin describes and elaborates on these two notions. Their relevance for the conduct of the cultural personality is readily apparent:

> [*M*]*ien-tzu* ... is a reputation achieved through getting on in life, through success and ostentation. This is prestige that is accumulated by means of personal effort or clever maneuvering. For this kind of recognition, ego is dependent at all times on the external environment. The other kind of "face," *lien* ... is the respect of the group for a man [woman] with a good moral reputation: the man [woman] who will fulfil his [her] obligations regardless of the hardships involved, who under all circumstances shows himself [herself] a decent human being. It represents the confidence of society in the integrity of ego's moral character, the loss of which makes it impossible for him [her] to function properly within the community. *Lien* is both a social sanction for enforcing moral standards and an internalized sanction.[21]

While the cultural personality is obviously an admixture of both forms of conduct and behaviour, it is clear where the real emphasis lies. It lies with *lien*. While the cultural personality is concerned with success in an external sense, this is not achieved at the expense of others. What can be accomplished by maintaining integrity is accomplished; what cannot be accomplished by maintaining integrity is discarded or rejected. It is through commitment to ideals—rather than adherence to the norms and mores of a specific group, community, government, corporation, society, or culture—that the cultural personality seeks to fashion its conduct in the world. The goal is always to work out for oneself the type of behavior that is most appropriate under the circumstances, rather than following a predetermined course of action, prescribed set of rules, or what is in vogue at a particular time. Commitment to this goal causes the cultural personality to transcend the limitations and shortcomings of cultures whenever it is necessary to do this, thereby making the cultural personality a "culture-maker" rather than a "culture-taker."

Whenever the norms, ideological beliefs, and systems of a culture are based on unacceptable assumptions or conflict with the interests of culture as a whole, the cultural personality is anxious to contest, challenge, confront, and change them. Whether or not it is possible to do this depends on a variety of factors. As Goethe said in a letter to Schiller: "Your own epoch you cannot change. You can, however, oppose its trends and lay the groundwork for auspicious developments." In the process of doing this, the cultural personality is compelled to become extremely "cause-oriented" and "culturally conscious." Rather than calculating everything in terms of how it advances personal interests or career aspirations, the cultural personality evaluates everything in terms of how it advances causes and consciousness. If something doesn't advance a cause and consciousness to which the cultural personality is committed, it is not pursued regardless of how it satisfies personal ambitions or career aspirations. To do this is to "be the change you want in the world," as Gandhi put it.

What are some of the causes to which the cultural personality is deeply wedded and irrefutably committed? Invariably, they are causes that are concerned with environmental sustainability, resource conservation, freedom, independence, human dignity, truth, justice, and equality regardless of social status, religious persuasion, economic or financial circumstances, gender, geographical location, or any other factor. Here, as well, Schweitzer has something very meaningful, powerful, and profound to say:

> The ripeness that our development must aim at is one which makes us simpler, more truthful, purer, more peace loving, meeker, kinder, more sympathetic. That is the only way in which we are to sober down with age. That is the process in

> which the soft iron of youthful idealism hardens into the steel of a full-grown idealism which can never be lost.[22]

Sorokin was equally aware of the importance of this type of personality development, as well as the need to ensure that it is situated in a much broader and deeper societal, cultural, environmental, and cosmic context. Speaking of the need for a heightened sense of human consciousness in order to achieve this, he said:

> The most urgent need of our time is the man [woman] who can control himself [herself] and his [her] lusts, who is compassionate to all his [her] fellow men [women], who can see and seek for the eternal values of culture and society, and who deeply feels his [her] unique responsibility to the universe.[23]

Foremost in this commitment to "see and seek for the eternal values of culture and society" is a commitment to respecting and disseminating the tangible and intangible cultural heritage of humankind. The more the cultural personality transcends the limits of his or her own culture and cultural conditioning, the more it gains insight into and understanding of the vast reservoir of knowledge, wisdom, artifacts, objects, and ideas that constitute the universal achievements and legacy of humanity. In much the same way that the cultural personality is anxious to gain access to this indispensable treasure trove to educate, enlighten, and improve the self, so he or she is equally anxious to share this precious gift with all members of the human family.

It is here that the cultural personality parts company with cultural purists and imperialists. Whereas the latter are concerned with asserting the superiority of one culture over another—largely for the purpose of imposing the values and ideals of one culture on another culture or on many other cultures—the former is concerned with sharing the fruits of all the diverse cultures and civilizations in the world with all members of the human family. In short, the cultural personality is concerned with those acts of kindness, generosity, and benevolence that promote trust, reciprocity, sharing, and peace in the world. The great Indian sage and poet, Rabindranath Tagore, foresaw this day when he said, "We must prepare the field for the co-operation of all the cultures of the world where all will give and take from each other. This is the keynote of the coming age."[24] Mahatma Gandhi reinforced this conviction when he said, "I do not want my house to be walled in on all sides and my windows to be stuffed. I want the culture of all the lands to be blown about my house as freely as possible. But I refuse to be blown off my feet by any."[25]

The objective here is intimately connected to laying the foundations and creating the conditions for a better world—a world characterized by more justice, equality, harmony, happiness, freedom, and peace for all members of the human family and humanity as a whole. Such a world requires a continuous outpouring of those qualities that are most deeply entrenched in the conduct of the cultural personality: concern for others; empathy; and most of all, love and compassion. Without this, the cultural personality is a pale shadow of what it could and should be.

There is one final matter that remains to be dealt with in this chapter. It is how the cultural personality is positioned in the world. For, as noted earlier, where and how the individual positions himself or herself in the world is of fundamental importance in determining the ultimate outcome of events and developments. Presumably this is what Kant had in mind when he said:

> If there is any science man [humanity] really needs, it is the one I teach, of how to occupy properly that place in creation that is assigned to [it], and how to learn from it what one must learn in order to be a man [woman].[26]

There is much to be learned about the importance of positioning oneself in the world from people such as Mahatma Gandhi, Mother Teresa, and Martin Luther King, Jr., as well as from many others who have had a profound effect on the world. Whether any of these people set out to change the world is impossible to say. What it *is* possible to say is that they had an incredible impact on world events and the course of history by deliberately positioning themselves in a very specific place in the world, working and interacting with local people. They did not go racing around the world attempting to make the world a better place for all. On the contrary, they stayed largely where they were situated and allowed the force of their personalities and passion of their convictions and commitments to speak for them.

Much can be learned from remarkable people like this that is germane to the cultural personality. Rather than setting out to influence the course of global history or world events, the cultural personality is constantly striving to put into practice in everyday life those spiritual qualities and human ideals that are required to inspire others and produce concrete results. The focus is not so much on "thinking globally but acting locally"—although this is undoubtedly a very important aspect of this—but rather, and more fundamentally, "thinking cosmically but acting personally." To do so is to allow the individual to discover within the self and the other the "reflection of the cosmos and its supreme unifying principle." Surely this is what Goethe had in mind when he said, "Live in the whole, in the good, in the beautiful." It is also what Joseph Campbell meant when he declared, "Follow your bliss and the universe will open doors where there are only walls." For the cultural personality, this is what life and living in the world are really all about.

Chapter Seven

The Complex Whole or Total Way of Life

> All people adopt or inherit a culture, an integral whole of accumulated resources, both material and non-material, which they utilize, transform, and transmit in order to satisfy their needs, assert their identity, and give meaning to their lives.
>
> —Awori Achoka[1]

A remarkable transformation took place in the way culture was visualized and defined in the middle and latter part of the nineteenth century. While most people continued to understand culture in terms of the arts, humanities, heritage of history, and personality development, a number of cultural scholars were beginning to think of it in far more expansive terms.

What makes this transformation so remarkable is the fact that virtually all manifestations of culture before the mid-nineteenth century were "partial manifestations"—they were a part or parts of something much larger. However, most of the manifestations of culture that have appeared in the world since then have been "holistic manifestations," concerned with "the whole" in terms of cultures, societies, and the human species, all the other species in the world, all the countless interactions that go on between all the many different species in the world and the natural environment, and mythology, worldview, and cosmology. As we will discover in this chapter and those to follow, these manifestations are known generally as the anthropological, sociological, biological, ecological, and cosmological manifestations of culture.

The anthropological manifestation of culture, the subject of this chapter, serves as a major watershed in the historical evolution of culture as an idea and a reality by setting this expansive process in motion. It became popular as a result of the work of cultural scholars such as Paul Broca, Theodor Waitz, Richard Francis Burton, and especially Sir Edward Burnett Tylor. In fact, Tylor is usually credited with being the world's first anthropologist, as well as the first scholar to define culture in holistic terms, as noted earlier. He did this on the very first page of his book *The Origins of Culture*, published in 1871:

> Culture ... taken in its wide ethnographic sense, is that *complex whole* which includes knowledge, belief, art, morals, law, customs, and *any other capabilities and habits acquired by man* [*woman*] *as a member of society*.[2]

What caused Tylor to define culture in this all-encompassing, holistic sense? He did so because this is what he and many other anthropologists discovered when they travelled to different parts of the world to study human cultures in depth and on the ground. While people in the various parts of the world to which Tylor and his fellow anthropologists travelled had words to describe all the specific activities they were engaged in as they went about the process of living their lives, what they did not have—and needed desperately—was a word that described how all these activities—economic, social, political, educational, religious, recreational, spiritual, and so forth—were woven together in different combinations and arrangements to form complex wholes or total ways of life made up of many distinct and interrelated parts.

Culture was the word anthropologists came to use to designate this all-inclusive process and all-encompassing phenomenon. Thus anthropologists who followed in Tylor's footsteps, including Lewis Henry Morgan, Augustus Henry Lane Fox Pitt Rivers, James George Frazer, Franz Boas, Alfred Radcliffe-Brown, E. E. Evans-Pritchard, Bronisław Malinowski, Alfred Louis Kroeber, Clyde Kluckhohn, Ruth Benedict, Margaret Mead, Ralph Linton, and many others visualized culture as "the *sum* of *all* activities in society," "*all* manifestations of a community," "the *totality* of material and non-material traits," "the *sum total* of ideas," "conditioned emotional responses and patterns of habitual behaviour," and the "*total* body of beliefs, behaviour, knowledge, sanctions, values, and goals that mark the way of life of any people."

Conceived, defined, and dealt with in this holistic sense, culture is concerned with the way people combine all the diverse activities they are involved in to form a complex whole or total way of life that is greater than the parts and the sum of the parts. This is because new properties are brought into existence when the complex whole or total way of life is created that are not in the parts taken separately or by themselves. Ruth Benedict, the American anthropologist, described this holistic process, using the example of making gunpowder:

> The whole, as modern science is insisting in many fields, is not merely the sum of all its parts, but the result of a unique arrangement and inter-relation of the parts that has brought about a new entity. Gunpowder is not merely the sum of sulphur and charcoal and saltpetre, and no amount of knowledge even of all three of its elements in all the forms they take in the natural world will demonstrate the nature of gunpowder. New potentialities have come into being in the resulting compound that were not present in its elements, and its mode of behaviour is indefinitely changed from that of any of its elements in other combinations.[3]

Understood in this way, culture as a whole or total way of life is concerned with all aspects of life and not just some aspects. It runs the gamut of possibilities, from the way people visualize the world, organize themselves, conduct their affairs, and act in the world to the way they elevate and embellish life, interact with each other, the natural environment, and other species, interpret history and the past, comprehend and assess the present, plan and prepare for the future, and position themselves in the world. While anthropology as a discipline has been subdivided into many different sub-fields since the time of Tylor and other early anthropologists—most notably into cultural, physical, archeological, and linguistic anthropology—it is important to emphasize that our concern in this chapter as well as throughout this book is with anthropology and culture as a whole.

There are many advantages to defining culture in holistic terms.

Most importantly, it makes it possible to see "the big picture" as well as the complex relationships that exist—or do not exist—between the component parts of the big picture, as noted earlier. This capacity has been lacking in the world for a long time and unfortunately is still lacking today. Humanity has been so caught up with specialization and specific parts of the whole over the last few centuries—including economics but also many other activities such as technology, science, politics, and so forth—that attention has been deflected away from the whole, and with it, the big picture in the all-inclusive sense. This makes it difficult to create the changes that are needed to ensure the survival of human beings and other species in the world.

This is not the only advantage to be realized from visualizing, defining, and dealing with culture in holistic terms. As a descriptive and all-encompassing concept, culture exposes both the positive and negative sides of the big picture—both the things human beings have done and are doing well as well as those they have done and are doing badly. It is only when attention is focused on the whole—and therefore on culture in the all-inclusive sense—that it is possible to deal with the negative as well as positive aspects of human behaviour and to understand the relationships between these different elements of human life. Raymond Williams emphasized the quintessential importance of the study of these relationships when he said:

> I would then define the theory of culture as the study of relationships between elements in a whole way of life. The analysis of culture is the attempt to discover the nature of the organization which is the complex of these relationships. Analysis of particular works or institutions is, in this context, analysis of their essential kind of organization, the relationship which works or institutions embody as parts of the organization as a whole.[4]

What is true for culture is equally true for cultures. Since cultures derive their existence, content, character, substance, and essence from culture, cultures are the manifestations in the real world of the concept of culture in the holistic sense. As such, they are complex wholes or total ways of life that are made up of many distinct and interrelated parts. Like culture, they also run the gamut of possibilities, from worldviews, values, value systems, beliefs, and organizational principles and practices to activities, customs, traditions, traits, religions, languages, habits, behaviours, and virtually everything else.

Most conspicuous in this respect are all the activities that people are engaged in, as well as all the different groups, organizations, and so forth that are created in relation to these activities. This includes all economic, social, political, agricultural, industrial, technological, and medical activities and organizations, as well as all social, educational, artistic, scientific, recreational, religious, spiritual, environmental, and other activities and organizations.

This explains why we have terms in our vocabulary such as economic culture, social culture, agricultural culture, industrial culture, technological culture, gay culture, elite culture, popular culture, technological culture, digital culture, ecological culture, and so forth. They are all specific parts of cultures as wholes that share the underlying holistic nature of culture in common. This also explains something else—something often ignored but extremely important. *It cannot be emphasized too strongly or too often that economics and economies are really part of culture and cultures—rather than culture and cultures being part of economics and economics—when culture and cultures are visualized, defined, and dealt with in holistic terms.* When culture and cultures are viewed in this way, they constitute "the context" or "container" within which economics, economies, and all other human activities are situated and take place.

This point also makes clear why Tylor's holistic perception and definition of culture marked a real watershed in the historical evolution of culture as an idea and cultures as realities. Whereas ideas of culture and cultures before Tylor's time were partial and incomplete—parts of the whole or notes in the melody, so to speak—here at last was a perception and definition of culture and cultures that was holistic and total. Understood in these terms, culture and cultures are concerned with virtually everything that exists in the world.

This is why it is so imperative at the present stage in history to move from viewing the world as economics to the world as culture. Doing so is consistent with the real nature of the world. Only by changing our way of looking at the world can we come to grips with its problems.

Interestingly, culture and cultures as ideas and realities can be classified in many different ways. One of culture's greatest strengths is that culture and cultures are not confined to the human species but include other species, the entire realm of nature, and the cosmos as a whole. This is especially true for the broadest and most all-encompassing manifestations of culture that are discussed in the final chapters of this book. In this chapter, however, the objective is to deal with culture and cultures as they relate to the human species and its activities.

When it comes to human cultures as the most obvious and essential manifestations of culture in the world, people are probably most familiar with cultures in the geographical sense, whether the cultures of individual streets and neighbourhoods, municipalities, regions, and nations, as well as what seems to be an emerging, all-embracing "global culture."

Added to all these geographically based cultures are the cultures of different genders, groups, organizations, associations, and so forth. There are countless cultures throughout the world grounded in the realities of specific groups of people, including family, ethnic, racial, religious, linguistic, popular, and elite cultures to name just a few. This is also true for the cultures of organizations and associations, which today are attracting an incredible amount of attention, particularly the cultures of corporations, police forces, sports teams and leagues, hospitals, and the like. All these cultures, and countless others, are structured differently depending on their specific worldviews, values, value systems, organizational features, and behavioural practices, as well as the many different activities, goals, objectives, and ideals that underlie, motivate, drive, and comprise them. How often have we heard it said in the last few years that it is necessary to *change* the cultures of organizations and associations? When people talk today about changing the culture of an organization, they don't just mean changing one or two elements of that culture. Rather, they mean changing the *entire* culture—the fundamental way an organization functions in the world.

These are not the only ways to understand and classify cultures.

Far from it. Cultures can also be understood and classified according to the different technological and communications devices and systems that underlie and dominate them as well as determine their content, composition, and character. Consider the findings of two Canadian communications experts and cultural scholars in this particular area. Harold Innis and Marshall McLuhan argued that different technological devices produce different types of cultures. We will discuss this idea in more detail in the next chapter of this book. We are also now discovering that a major distinction is being made throughout the world between "actual cultures" and "virtual cultures," the latter having come to the fore as a result of the COVID-19 pandemic and remarkable changes in communications and technology over the last few decades.

And this is not all. Another way to understand and classify cultures is through their genetic roots, underpinnings, and characteristics. Mira Sartika, founder and director of the Chakra Cultural Foundation in Indonesia, has carried out pioneering work on the complex connection between genetics, environments, societies, and cultures, thereby resulting in some fundamental differences between maternal, paternal, land, and sea cultures and environments.

One can also understand and classify cultures through their most significant achievements, their most important contributions to the world, their food, drink, and cuisines, and their music, dances, forms of dress, customs, and celebrations. On and on the list goes. What we can learn from culture and cultures is both limitless and profound. Cultures are without doubt the most captivating creations in the world despite their complexity and diversity. That is why many people want to travel to other countries and parts of the world to explore and discover different cultures firsthand. It is also why cultures should be studied and examined in detail and in depth.

When all the different ways of understanding, classifying, and experiencing the countless diverse cultures of the world are considered in totality, it is obvious that there is very little in the world that is not concerned with or connected to culture in general and cultures in particular in one form or another. Acceptance of this fact makes it clear why it is so essential to place a high priority on knowing, understanding, classifying, experiencing, and dealing with cultures in the holistic sense at this particular juncture in human history as well as in the future.

Edward T. Hall, an American cultural scholar, put his finger on the crux of this matter when he said:

> One cannot normally transcend one's culture without first exposing its major hidden axioms and unstated assumptions concerning what life is all about—how it is lived, viewed, analysed, talked about, described, and changed. Because cultures are wholes, and systematic (composed of inter-related systems in which each aspect is functionally interrelated with all other parts), and are highly contexted as well, it is hard to described them from the outside. *A given culture cannot be understood simply in terms of content or parts. One has to know how the whole system is put together, how the major systems and dynamisms function, and how they are interrelated.*[5]

There is another equally compelling reason for dealing with cultures in this holistic and systemic sense. It is because the whole is greater than the parts and the sum of the parts. Ruth Benedict confirmed this most emphatically in her book *Patterns of Culture* when she said, "The whole *determines* its parts, not only their relation but their very nature."[6]

Accepting this fundamental fact about culture in general and cultures in particular is the key to breaking out of the present ways of thinking and creating new ones. Focusing on culture and cultures as wholes or total ways of life makes it possible to "change the context" within which all human activities and developments take place. This is imperative because changing the context changes the contents, as Benedict argued.

At this crucial time in the history of the world, we must persevere with the quest to know and understand far more about culture and cultures in the holistic sense than we do today. This is not an easy task. It is not possible to *see* culture and cultures as wholes or total ways of life because they are composed of far too many parts and it is impossible to discern all the organizational principles, processes, and practices that combine all those parts to form wholes or total ways of life.

How, then, is it even possible to know, understand, and deal with culture and cultures as wholes or total ways of life? A clue to this was provided by Giles Gunn in his book *The Culture of Criticism and the Criticism of Culture* when he said:

> We cannot understand the parts of anything without some sense of the whole to which they belong, just as we cannot comprehend the whole to which they belong until we have grasped the parts that make it up. Thus we are constantly obliged to move back and forth in our effort to understand something "between the whole conceived through the parts which actualize it and the parts conceived through the whole which motivates them" in an effort "to turn them, by a sort of intellectual perpetual motion, into explication of one another."[7]

To achieve this, it is necessary to take the next logical step in this fascinating process. It is to select parts of cultures that are *symbolic* or *representative* of cultures as wholes or the total ways of life, and therefore *epitomize* these wholes or total ways of life in many fundamental ways.

Take food, cuisine, and the culinary arts as one of the most symbolic, representative, and obvious examples of this. While they constitute only one of the many different parts that make up the diverse cultures of the world, they are extremely important. People must eat in order to survive. As a result, food, foodstuffs, cuisine, and the culinary arts reveal a great deal about the holistic nature of cultures, probably more than any other part. They bring a great deal of joy into people's lives and reveal much about the nature of cultures in every part of the world. This was illustrated very effectively by Anthony Bourdain in his popular television series *Anthony Bourdain: Parts Unknown*. Bourdain visited different countries and communities to experience and comment on their food, foodstuffs, and cuisine, thereby providing an effective "gateway" to understanding their cultures.

Consider the culture of China as an example of the way food, foodstuffs, cuisine, and the culinary arts can serve as a symbolic representation of a country's culture as a whole and consequently a gateway to it. One of the most important aspects of the culture of China is the principle of yin and yang or of opposites: male and female, light and dark; positive and negative; strength and weakness; and so forth. Success comes from how well Chinese people are able to deal with these and other opposites and create balance, harmony, and synergy between and among them. It is no coincidence in this regard that Chinese cuisine is also based on opposites—hot and cold, sweet and sour, spicy and mild, and so forth—and on how well these opposites are blended together to form integrated and harmonious entities.

Japanese culture provides another excellent illustration of the same principle, but in a very different way. It is a well-known fact that "simplicity" is a fundamental aspect of Japanese culture. Japanese cuisine also epitomizes this quality, since the challenge is to create outstanding gastronomic experiences with the least amount of complexity and complication. Hence the emphasis on meals that are aesthetically pleasing, exquisitely served, delicious to eat, and yet incredibly simple.

Food and the culinary arts are only one example among many of how symbolic or representative parts of cultures can and do shed a great deal of light on cultures as wholes and total ways of life. There are many others. The material arts or crafts do this extremely well, which is why many people want to decorate their homes with craft objects or artifacts from their own culture or others.

I discovered this many years ago when I was scouring Toronto looking for craft objects to beautify our home. I learned very quickly that there are many areas in this rapidly expanding multicultural city where exquisite craft objects from the different cultures of the world can be found. Roncesvalles Avenue, for example, was ideal for Polish crafts, most notably table runners and beautiful hand-carved wooden plates with scenes of the Tatra Mountains on them. Bloor Street West, in an area known as "The Village," was ideal for Ukrainian crafts, everything from exquisite pots and bowls to table runners and tablecloths decorated with colourful geometric designs, shapes, patterns, and motifs. College Street, between Bathurst and Spadina, was superb for South American and especially Spanish crafts—everything from outstanding leatherwork to replicas of famous Spanish heroes such as El Cid, Don Quixote, King Ferdinand and Queen Isabella, as well as exquisitely painted plates with swords, armour, or beautiful landscapes on them.

And what about carpets? Is there anything more symbolic or representative of the culture of Iran and other Middle Eastern countries and their cultures than their carpets? The very names of the cities that have made carpets rightly famous—such as Tabriz, Qom, Kashan, Bakhtiari, Shiraz, Kerman, Mashhad, Bukhara, and so forth—are legendary and conjure up images of Arabian nights, religious motifs, mythological themes, and a great deal else. Does anything say more about the cultures of Iran and other Middle Eastern countries in the all-encompassing sense than their carpets?

Architectural buildings and religious edifices do this, too, and do it very well. There is a great deal to be learned about the culture of France, for instance, through its cathedrals as well as the response to the 2019 fire in the Notre-Dame Cathedral in Paris. These and other internationally famous religious buildings, monuments, and sites in other parts of the world say a great deal about their country's cultures, whether it be the Taj Mahal in India, the Blue Mosque in Turkey, the Jameh Mosque in Iran, or many others.

The same is true for many other art forms. Indeed, all art forms are effective gateways to cultures in the symbolic sense. The old adage "a picture is worth a thousand words" is a cliché, but it speaks volumes about the capacity of visual images to convey an incredible amount of information about the holistic character of cultures that cannot be communicated in any other way.

This is a subject that Robert Redfield, the American anthropologist, studied in great detail. Here is what Redfield had to say about the ability of artists of all types to help us glean a clearer, cleaner, and more comprehensive impression and understanding of the all-encompassing character of culture in general and all the various cultures in the world in particular:

> The characterisations of the artist ... are of course not precise at all; but very much of the whole is communicated to us. We might call them all portraits. They communicate the nature of the whole by attending to the uniqueness of each part, by

> choosing from among the parts certain of them for emphasis, and by modifying them and rearranging them in ways that satisfy the "feeling of the portrayer."[8]

Let us return for a moment to the cultures of regions, towns, and cities to illustrate this essential phenomenon. Think of how Joseph Canteloube's *Songs of the Auvergne* give us a sense of the holistic character of the culture of the Auvergne region of France. Sibelius's *Karelia Suite* gives us a similar sense of Viipuri Province, while the paintings of Van Gogh and Monet provide an all-embracing sense of different regional cultures in France and the literary works of George Eliot, the Brontë sisters, Mark Twain, William Faulkner, and Alice Munro help us understand such regional cultures as the Midlands and Yorkshire in England, rural Mississippi in the United States, and the cultures of small towns and rural areas in southwestern Ontario, Canada.

What is true for the cultures of regions, towns, and cities is also true for the cultures of countries. This struck home with startling clarity for me when I took several trips to many different countries in Europe when I was younger. What I found especially symbolic about the cultures of these countries as wholes was their music. English music, for instance, was very regal and majestic, most notably the music of Edward Elgar and his *Pomp and Circumstance* marches. Interestingly, many other aspects of English culture were also regal and majestic, such as the monarchy, which is so deeply entrenched in English culture, as well as the nature, customs, and lives of the English citizenry. German music, on the other hand, seemed much more ponderous, pensive, and heavy compared to English music, most notably the music of Beethoven, Brahms, and Wagner. But then, so, too, is German food, cuisine, philosophy, architecture, and the German language itself. Then there is French music. It was much lighter, delicate, and more impressionistic than English or German music, especially the music of François Couperin, Rameau, Lully, Debussy, Ravel, Chaminade, and others. But this was also true for many other aspects of French culture, such as cuisine, language, architecture, and so forth. And finally, there is Italian music. It was very lively, gay, and concerned with people and their various lives, loves, and personal affairs compared to English, German, and French music, especially the music of Vivaldi, Puccini, Verdi, and Rossini.

But it was Spain that provided the best example of all of how a country's music, paintings, and artistic activities symbolize its culture as a whole and act as gateways to broadening and deepening one's knowledge, understanding, and "feeling" for Spanish culture. Through the music of Joaquín Rodrigo, Manuel de Falla, Isaac Albéniz, and Enrique Granados, musical styles such as flamenco, the lyric-dramatic genre zarzuela, the paintings of Pablo Picasso, Salvador Dali, El Greco, Diego Velázquez, Francisco Goya, and Joan Miró, the writings of Miguel de Cervantes, Federico García Lorca, Lope de Vega, dances like the sardana and the bolero, and the remarkable architectural accomplishments of Antoni Gaudi, a very strong impression and feeling for one of the most distinctive national cultures I have ever experienced emerged and took shape. It is a culture that is characterized by hot days, cool nights, festivals, fairs, a great deal of historical and contemporary creativity, a distinctive cultural identity and legacy, and a great deal of contemporary innovation. Whenever I hear Mahatma's Gandhi's saying that "a nation's culture resides in the hearts and in the soul of its people" and Churchill's famous remark that "a nation that forgets its past has no future," I immediately think of the culture of Spain and especially the works of Spanish artists who provide such a remarkable gateway to that culture.

The more I reflected on this, the more I became convinced that the arts play a major role as "gateways" to cultures in the all-inclusive, holistic sense. It is not just a case of understanding the intimate connection between music, painting, dramas, dances, literature, architecture and cultures, but also understanding the fundamental role that all the arts play in revealing the overall ways of life and holistic character of cultures and especially their similarities and differences. The more I listen to music, watch plays, enjoy dances, read stories, and see paintings, craft objects, and architectural masterpieces, the more my knowledge and understanding of the different cultures of Europe as wholes or total ways of life are broadened, deepened, and intensified. And what was true for these and other national cultures in Europe is also true for many other national cultures and their artistic symbols in other parts of the world.

Similarly, in the same way that the arts act as gateways to cultures, so do many other activities, such as sports, celebrations, and so forth. It is through symbolic or representative parts such as these—and many others—that strong impressions of all the different cultures in the world as complex wholes or total ways of life can be created, especially if enough of these parts—and especially highly symbolic parts—are examined and explored in detail and depth. The culture of United States provides another excellent example of this general phenomenon—one that is likely much better known to people and countries in other parts of the world than most other cultures in the world. It is through the works of composers such as George Gershwin, Richard Rodgers, Irving Berlin, Aaron Copland, and Samuel Barber, authors such as Mark Twain, Henry David Thoreau, Robert Frost, Virginia Woolf, Harriet Beecher Stowe, Arthur Miller, and Alice Walker, painters such as Georgia O'Keeffe, Andy Warhol, Norman Rockwell, and Jackson Pollock, architects such as Frank Lloyd Wright, musicians such as Louis Armstrong, Aretha Franklin, and Leonard Bernstein, dancers such as Fred Astaire, Michael Jackson, Ginger Rogers, and Martha Graham, athletes such as Michael Jordan and Serena Williams, scientists such as Linus Pauling, Jonas Salk, and Alfred Kinsey, and inventors such as Thomas Edison, that a strong impression of American culture as a complex whole crystalizes and takes concrete form.

No person has contributed more to our individual and collective understanding of American culture as a complex whole or total way of life as well as in the symbolic, representative, and pictorial sense than the documentary filmmaker Ken Burns. He has demonstrated an uncanny knack for selecting specific people, places, events, achievements, and artistic works that are not only highly symbolic and significant in their own right, but also representative of American culture and the American way of life. This is apparent in all of his films, but especially in such documentaries as *Country Music*, *Jazz*, *Baseball*, *The Civil War*, *Jackie Robinson*, *The Roosevelts: An Intimate History*, *The Statue of Liberty*, and *The National Parks: America's Best Idea*. It is impossible to watch these films, and others like them, without learning a great deal about American culture as a whole made up of countless parts.

In order to progress further in this area, it is necessary to delve into a country's or culture's legal systems, economic practices, political policies, social customs, worldviews, values, value systems, ideals, traditions, traits, behavioural characteristics, and beliefs. This is consistent with the conviction of Clifford Geertz that *thick description* is necessary to get to know cultures in the holistic sense in any systematic and realistic way. In his book, *The Interpretation of Cultures*, he states:

> As interworked systems of construable signs (what I ... would call symbols), culture is not a power, something to which social events, behaviors, institutions, or processes can be casually attributed; it is a context, something within which they can be intelligibly—that is thickly—described.[9]

Surely Edward Burnett Tylor had it right when he visualized and defined cultures in the formal sense as "complex wholes" made up of many interacting and interrelated parts. While it is not possible to know, understand, or see any culture in the world as a complex whole or way of life in all its diverse aspects and forms, it is possible to achieve a "reasonable approximation" of this by constantly and progressively broadening and deepening our knowledge, understanding, and awareness of all the different cultures in the world though this symbolic or representative process, going backward and forward between the parts and the whole as Giles Gunn advised.

This is where the sciences in general, and the social sciences in particular, are extremely helpful and have a prominent role to play by creating the methods, techniques, developments, and initiatives that are needed to expand the world's collective knowledge and understanding of the holistic character of all the diverse cultures in the world. This will likely be enhanced substantially in the years and decades ahead through major breakthroughs in artificial intelligence, computer systems, virtual reality, and digital devices that make it possible to deal with the vast array of parts that exist in all cultures, and especially the way these parts are combined together to form wholes or overall ways of life.

As indicated earlier, this is what makes studying, exploring, and experiencing the many different cultures of the world so exciting, fascinating, enriching, and rewarding. Not only are there significant differences in the parts of all cultures—especially the symbolic parts—but there are also substantial differences in their origins, structures, histories, traditions, composition, and in the complex relationships between and among their parts. No two cultures are the same. Every culture in the world is unique, even if they all share certain similarities with other cultures due to similar origins, historical roots, contemporary experiences, the forces that impact and impinge on them, their geographical location, or a host of other factors.

Some cultures are best known for their mythological beliefs and environmental convictions, particularly Indigenous cultures; others are best known for their food, drink, and cuisines, most notably the cultures of France, Italy, Japan, India, South Korea, Thailand, Turkey, and Mexico; and still others are known most for their architectural accomplishments, athletic capabilities, or national celebrations, such as many European and South Asia cultures as well as the cultures of the United States and most South American and Caribbean countries. This is why more and more people in the world are anxious to learn more about these and other cultures. This can be achieved in many different ways, including watching videos, reading books and undertaking research studies, and especially visiting them (if this is possible) since cultures are incredibly stimulating and inspiring when people take the time and trouble to get to know them in intimate ways.

Few subjects are more important in the world these days than learning about all the different cultures in the world and their many similarities and differences. On the one hand, a great deal of knowledge, wisdom, information, and fulfilment, as well as numerous benefits and opportunities, can and are being derived from learning about the diverse cultures of the world. It is amazing, for instance, what can be learned about maintaining good health and physical fitness from Chinese and Japanese cultures, experiencing *joie de vivre* and *la dolce vita* from French and Italian cultures, and cultivating good manners and acting in an orderly and civilized fashion from English and Scottish cultures, to cite only a few examples from literally millions. On the other hand, it is possible to understand why there are tensions and clashes between cultures, since this results from differences in the diverse elements and parts that comprise them as well as the principles, priorities, and processes that are used to combine all the elements. These tensions and clashes can erupt at any time and escalate into major conflicts if the necessary precautions are not taken to prevent this. This makes learning about and experiencing the different cultures of the world one of the most essential, worthwhile, and urgent tasks in the world today, as well as going forward into the future.

These reasons, and many others, confirm why it is so essential to bring the world as culture into existence and enable it to flourish, as well as to make the development of culture and all the different cultures in the world in breadth as well as in depth the centrepiece of the world system and principal preoccupation of municipal, regional, national, and international development in the years, decades, and centuries ahead.

Developing culture in breadth and depth means learning about all the major manifestations of culture and all the disciplines that are most concerned with this, such as the arts, humanities, cultural studies, history, sociology, anthropology, ecology, biology, cosmology, philosophy, and so forth. It also means according these manifestations and disciplines a very high priority in the overall scheme of things. This will make it possible to extend these manifestations and disciplines in all directions, as well as intensify their cultivation, impact, characteristics, and effectiveness. Developments like this are essential to ensure that all the various aspects and dimensions of culture are attended to properly and advanced accordingly throughout the world, as well as ensuring that much more emphasis is placed on many of humanity's and culture's most essential and worthwhile ideals, such as peace, harmony, happiness, order, security, and equality as well as freedom, trust, truth, compassion, and cooperation since these are all essential elements in culture.

Developing cultures in breadth and depth means ensuring that all the different parts of cultures are taken fully into account in this process. This may sound similar to developing economies but on a substantially larger and more expansive scale. In some ways it is; however, there is one very significant and important difference here, since cultures are wholes and economies are parts of wholes.

Whereas the principal objective and priority in the case of economies is to develop economies in breadth and depth, the principal objective and priority in the case of cultures is to develop cultures in breadth and depth, true enough, but also, and much more fundamentally and essentially, *to ensure that **balanced** and **harmonious** relationships are established between all the diverse parts of cultures.* This is what developing the whole and wholes—as opposed to a part or the parts—really means and is most concerned with. This additional requirement is what differentiates economics and economies as well as world as economics from culture and cultures and the world as culture.

This need for balance and harmony is essential with respect to the relationship between people, the natural environment, and other species. But it is especially pressing at this difficult time in history when it comes to the relationship between the material and non-material dimensions of development, the quantitative and qualitative components of life, rich and poor people and rich and poor countries, different genders, races, and religions, the arts and the sciences, the public sector and the private sector, people's rights and responsibilities, and technology and society. We urgently need a judicious balance and harmony in these relationships if we are to be successful in coming to grips with the problems of the present and the future. Imbalances and disharmonies have sprung up and intensified in all these relationships during the development of the world as economics that must be addressed at present and rectified in the future because they are having a disastrous and debilitating effect on the natural environment and global situation. The reasons for these imbalances and disharmonies are vast, varied, complex, and multidimensional. In fundamental terms, however, they have resulted from the adoption historically of partial rather than holistic worldviews as well as partisan rather than all-inclusive policies, perceptions, and perspectives.

The Dutch cultural scholar and historian Johan Huizinga gave us a profound insight into how adverse imbalances and detrimental disharmonies like these can be dealt with and overcome:

> The realities of economic life, of power, of technology, of everything conducive to man's [people's] material well-being,

> must be balanced by strongly developed spiritual, intellectual, moral, and aesthetic values. The balance exists above all in the fact that each of the various cultural activities enjoys as vital a function as is possible in the context of the whole. If such harmony of cultural functions is present, it will reveal itself as order, strong structure, style, and rhythmic life of the society in question.[10]

In order to achieve this, Huizinga felt strongly that power and preoccupation with materialism and monetary wealth must be accompanied by an equally powerful commitment to "service" as well as the aforementioned values and ideals:

> A community is in the state of culture when the domination of nature in the material, moral, and spiritual realms permits a state of existence which is *higher* and *better* than the given natural conditions; and when this state of existence is furthermore characterized by a harmonious balance of material and spiritual values and is guided by an ideal ... toward which the different activities of the community are directed.[11]

When this is not the case, Huizinga provided the solution for coming to grips with adverse imbalances and detrimental disharmonies such as these as well as others when he said:

> A culture which no longer can integrate the diverse pursuits of men [people] into a whole, which cannot restrain men [people] through a guiding set of norms, has lost its center and has lost its style. It is threatened by the exuberant overgrowth of its separate components. It then needs a pruning knife, a human decision to focus once again on the essentials of culture and cut back the luxuriant but dispensable.[12]

Huizinga's insights in this matter provide the paths and approaches that are imperative to coming to grips with and achieving a great deal more harmony, happiness, and well-being in life and the world, as well as to establishing the arts, humanities, spirituality, learning, ethics, and so forth as fundamental necessities and high priorities in the development of cultures in the future. Many benefits and opportunities can and will arise from this. Most importantly, a better balance will be achieved between the material and non-material dimensions of development and the quantitative and qualitative aspects of life. This will result in a great deal more caring, sharing, compassion, and cooperation between all the diverse peoples, cultures, countries, and civilizations of the world because income and wealth will be shared more equally, fairly, and fully. It will also result in more policies, practices, and funding being directed towards building up public-sector institutions, overcoming major disparities in the funding of artistic activities, programs, courses, and research compared to the scientific and technological fields, closing the gender gap in income and employment realities and prospects, and coming to grips with the inequalities, inequities, and injustices suffered by different racial, ethnic, minority, marginalized, and oppressed groups, cultures, and countries.

What is true with respect to achieving a better balance and harmony between all the activities that constitute cultures is also true for situating cultures effectively in the natural, historical, and global environment.

This is especially important with respect to positioning cultures properly in the natural environment and reducing the demands human beings are making on this environment. This is because many spiritual, humanistic, intellectual, moral, and aesthetic activities make far fewer demands on the resources of nature than most industrial, commercial, and technological activities. Failure to do this will result in much more serious and frequent environmental difficulties, disasters, and upheavals.

What is desperately needed here is a dramatic shift in direction with respect to the total way of life of people. Such a shift must include *all* aspects of the environmental crisis, such as growing shortages of natural resources and higher prices for basic foodstuffs, and not only climate change and global warming. People, countries, and the world at large will have to undergo a profound change in their directions, values, lifestyles, behaviour, and thought processes if this crisis is to be averted. This will require a major transformation in cultures as complex wholes and total ways of life and not just changes in a few specific parts or activities.

The same holds true for situating cultures effectively in the historical environment. As noted earlier, it is necessary to learn from our mistakes in the past and correct them in the present and the future, as well as to deal effectively with all the cultural baggage we inherit from the past. Problems like these can only be dealt with effectively through cultural education and intercultural dialogues and exchanges that connect people from different countries, cultures, and parts of the world in a more humane, compassionate, equitable, and cooperative way.

Added to this is the need to situate cultures effectively in the global environment. Here, it is necessary to recognize that international relations in the future should be conducted on the basis of what is in the best *cultural* interests of people, countries, and cultures and not what is in their best *economic* interests, especially whenever there is a discrepancy between these two sets of interests.

Acting on what is in the best *cultural* interests of people, countries, and cultures will produce major changes and transformations in international relations. This is because decisions will be made according to balancing qualitative and quantitative factors more effectively and efficiently, as well as not favouring economic and quantitative factors and solutions over all others. This, in itself, will transform international relations very significantly since what is in the best cultural interests of people, countries, and cultures will be decided by considering the full range of factors, consequences, and activities and not just economic factors.

This will open the doors to more interactions between people, countries, and cultures in the arts, humanities, social affairs, education and academic affairs. This is especially important for cultures that are experiencing open hostilities and severe conflicts with others, such as those that exist between Israel and Palestine, Turkey, Armenia, and Syria, China, Hong Kong, Taiwan, and Japan, Iraq, Iran, Saudi Arabia, and Egypt, and others.

In order to be successful in developing cultures in these many different ways, it will be necessary to develop a set of *comprehensive cultural indicators* that are consistent with culture and cultures as wholes and total ways of life. These indicators will provide more effective and accurate ways of assessing the real cultural state of countries and cultures and improving people's cultural lives and well-being than do existing economic indicators such as gross national product, per capita income, and the rate of economic growth. Unfortunately, these are still the main forms of measurement that are used by most countries, governments, and people in the world today, despite concerted attempts by the United Nations and other international agencies and institutions to broaden these forms of measurement to include such indicators as education, health care, longevity, and, in the case of the government of Bhutan, "gross national happiness." This latter form of measurement is seen by many to be a considerable improvement on per capita income, the rate of economic growth, and other economic indicators of this type, despite the fact that it is not recognized or used by the large majority of countries or governments in the world at present. It may well take root in the world of the future.

Shifting attention from economic wealth to cultural well-being is the key to developing and using these new forms of measurement. This requires developing indicators that are capable of measuring cultural well-being in *qualitative* as well as quantitative terms. In the development of these indicators, four matters are essential. First, the indicators must come from many different disciplines and policy fields—such as the arts, sciences, humanities, health, the environment, religion, education, and politics, and not just economics, business, commerce, and technology—and be capable of being combined together and compared. Second, the *best* indicators in each discipline and policy field will have to be selected for inclusion in the final set of indicators. Third, the final indicators will have to be refined in order to improve their effectiveness, coverage, and application. And fourth, but most essential, the final set of indictors will have to reflect and be consistent with the changes in values, lifestyles, and the ways of life that are needed to deal effectively with humanity's and the world's most difficult, dangerous, and debilitating problems. This requires putting much more emphasis on the qualitative dimensions of development and life and less emphasis on the quantitative dimensions of development and life.

It will take time to develop this set of comprehensive cultural indicators. However, many of the most important of these indicators already exist and therefore only need to be pulled together and refined rather than created from scratch. Among others, these indicators include *environmental indicators* such as the quality of water and air and levels of toxicity, pollution, and waste; *health indicators*, such as longevity, the availability of health care services and institutions such as hospitals as well as disease and virus control and prevention centres as well as substance abuse; *economic indicators*, such as material standards of living and income and employment rates, prospects, and opportunities; *social indicators*, such as participation rates in community, regional, national, and international affairs as well as welfare rates and levels of violence and crime; *educational indicators*, such as student-to-teacher ratios, access to elementary, secondary, and post-secondary education for different racial, gender, and income groups, educational costs and requirements, student drop-out rates and debt loads, the availability of qualitied teachers, and lifelong learning possibilities; *recreational indicators*, such as the availability of parks, conservation areas, and leisure-time facilities and activities; and *aesthetic, political, spiritual, scientific, and technological indicators*, such as the quantity and quality of artistic offerings, the stability of political institutions and systems, the provision and state of safety and security measures, the diversity of religions and religious and spiritual options, and the availability of scientific and technological opportunities and techniques. Needless to say, the development of this set of comprehensive cultural indicators will require a great deal of collaboration, consultation, compromise, and expertise on the parts of policymakers, planners, and scholars from a variety of fields and professions in all countries, as well as all the different international institutions and agencies that exist in the world.

Concrete and forceful actions like this are necessary if we want to capitalize on the profuse panorama of benefits and possibilities that can be derived from creation and development of the world as culture. As Wade Davis, the noted anthropologist, said in his book *The Wayfinders*, the myriad cultures that make up our world today are "humanity's greatest legacy ... the product of our dreams, the symbols of all we are and all that we have created as a wildly imaginative and astonishingly adaptive species."[13]

This is probably what the celebrated cultural scholar, cherished poet, and former president of Senegal, Léopold Sédar Senghor, also had in mind when he said, "Culture is the alpha and omega of any sound development policy."[14] Such a policy must be based on achieving balance and harmony between all the different factors, forces, and activities that constitute culture and development in general and situating cultures effectively in the natural, historical, and global environment in particular. This is ultimately the key to the world of the future as well as making the world as culture a concrete realty rather than just a theoretical ideal.

Chapter Eight

Societies, Social Systems, Communications, and Technology

> Culture, a word of varied meanings, is here used in the more inclusive sociological sense, that is, to designate the artefacts, goods, technical processes, ideas, habits, and values, which are the social heritage of a people. Thus, culture includes all learned behaviour, intellectual knowledge, social organization and language, systems of value—economic, moral or spiritual. Fundamental to a particular culture are its law, economic structure, magic, religion, art, knowledge and education.
>
> —Paul J. Braisted[1]

About the same time that interest in anthropology was beginning to take shape and take off in the middle half of the nineteenth century, so, too, was interest in sociology. While the origins of both fields in one form or another can be traced back many centuries, it was not until the middle decades of the nineteenth century that they became recognized as formal disciplines and subjects of intellectual interest, scrutiny, and concern.

Some scholars claim that Ibn Khaldun, the fourteenth century Arab-Islamic scholar from Tunis, was the actual "founder of sociology" because his *Al-Muqaddimah* ("The Introduction"), which was published in Arabic in 1396, marked the first real effort to assert the need for social-scientific thinking, reasoning, and objectivity with respect to social cohesion, conflict, and many other social requirements and activities. Since this happened in isolation and was not picked up by other scholars, the emergence of sociology had to wait several more centuries and it is now generally accepted that the principal founders of sociology were Auguste Comte, Herbert Spencer, Karl Marx, Max Weber, Émile Durkheim, and Georg Simmel.

Although there were many similarities between anthropology and sociology at the beginning, there were also some significant differences. Whereas the principal concern of anthropology as a discipline was culture and cultures as wholes or total ways of life—largely because anthropology as a formal discipline was defined as the study of human beings and their actions and behaviour in holistic rather than partial terms—the principal concern of sociology as a discipline was deemed to be societies, social systems, the behaviour and traits of different individuals, groups and classes, and especially the diverse signs, signals, traits, patterns, customs, and technological devices and communications vehicles that manifested themselves in society.

Many scholars believe August Comte was the real father of sociology. He used the term "sociology" for the first time to describe the scientific study of societies in general and of social systems, groups, classes, individuals, and their actions, behaviour, and interactions in particular. According to Comte, all societies go through three distinct stages of development: *religious*; *metaphysical*; and *scientific*. Whereas the first two stages were to a large extent grounded (in Comte's opinion) in superstition and speculation, the third stage was grounded for the most part in facts, empirical evidence, and intensive analysis. Comte also felt that the science or discipline of sociology should be divided into two distinct parts or components: *dynamics*, or the study of the processes whereby societies and social systems change; and *statics*, or the study of the processes whereby societies and social systems endure. Through the use of scientific methods and techniques, Comte believed it is possible for societies and social systems to progress in positive directions even if they have experienced many ups and downs along the way.

In contrast to Comte, Herbert Spencer tended to see societies as living organisms made up of many interdependent parts. According to Spencer, a change in any one of these parts of society will cause changes in all other parts. Every part had an important role to play in contributing to the stability and survival of societies and social systems. A strong believer in Darwin's theory of evolution—it was he, not Darwin, who coined the phrase "the survival of the fittest"—Spencer was convinced that all societal systems tend towards equilibrium, social harmony, and stability over time.

Karl Marx, another founder of sociology in the eyes of many, disagreed strongly with Spencer's ideas on this matter. He believed that conflict was inevitable between the different classes and interest groups in society. Whereas the classical economists believed there were three principal classes in society—landlords, labourers, and capitalists—Marx believed there were really only two classes (labourers and capitalists) because landlords possessed a great deal of wealth and were really capitalists at heart. Whereas capitalists owned the means of production and therefore the bulk of the income, wealth, capital, and status in societies, the proletariat or labouring class owned nothing but their own labour and were compelled to sell their labour to the capitalists, who exploited them ruthlessly. This led to constant tensions, pressures, and conflicts between these two classes, as was apparent in Britain and continental Europe during the Industrial Revolution. Marx's theories of class struggle and conflict were so compelling that they eventually gave rise to the whole world being divided into capitalist and communist components with constant conflicts going on between them throughout most of the twentieth century.

Émile Durkheim came later than Marx and Spencer. His major contributions to sociology involved theories related to the social structure of societies, the division of labour, the nature of specialization, and a condition that he called *anomie*, which led to the breakdown of social norms. He was interested in how traditional and modern societies evolve over time, as well as in "social facts" that were defined largely in terms of values, norms, and societal structures, that were largely external rather than internal in nature, and that therefore were intimately connected to people's needs, wants, motivations, and desires. If something occurred to create societal disequilibrium, Durkheim believed that societies would adjust to this disequilibrium and return to a stable state, since societies were really social systems composed of many interrelated parts and no individual part could function independently of the others. Durkheim also believed that traditional societies were primarily homogeneous because people shared similarities in dress, customs, traditions, and values. Modern societies, however, were much more heterogeneous because people had different customs, habits, traditions, values, and so forth, and consequently such societies were far more complex and difficult to manage. This caused more anomie and alienation in modern societies compared to traditional societies.

Max Weber disagreed with the "objective evidence only" beliefs of Durkheim and others. He was convinced that sociologists must consider people's interpretations of events and not just the events themselves, since people act on those interpretations. Like Marx, Weber was interested in the nature, functioning, and shortcomings of capitalism, especially as it evolved rapidly in the final decades of the nineteenth century and first decades of the twentieth. This led him to undertake intensive studies of this basic phenomenon, especially the relationship between capitalism and religion in Europe. He concluded from these studies that the growth of capitalism was more compatible with the beliefs and practices of Protestants in northern Europe than with those of Catholics in southern Europe. In his book *The Protestant Ethic and the Spirit of Capitalism*, Weber argued that Protestants had a greater tendency to work hard and save money, leading to greater levels of capital accumulation and investment.

Finally, there is Georg Simmel. He was more interested in the nature, well-being, and cultivation of people as individuals than the functioning of societies, groups, and classes. According to Simmel, the biggest problem in modern societies is the need of every person to preserve their identity, autonomy, independence, and individuality in the face of powerful social and societal forces. This led Simmel to develop a theory of *cultural tragedy*, which had its origins in Marx's theory of *commodity fetishism*.

For Simmel, cultural tragedy occurs when societies modernize and produce massive amounts of goods and services—what he called "objective culture"—that eventually overshadow, overwhelm, and subdue "subjective culture," or the culture of the individual. Presented with more choices than a person could reasonably cope with (according to Simmel something that happened more often in urban than in rural areas), individuals run the risk of becoming stifled and thwarted in their psychological growth as well as in their social and cultural development. These goods and services become so fetishized that they acquire a power over people that they do not possess inherently.

The thoughts and theories of these principal founders and pioneers in sociology, as well as others who might be included in this list, make it clear that there were some major differences between anthropology and sociology as they evolved as disciples and therefore between the work of anthropologists and sociologists. While there are many exceptions to the rule, generally speaking anthropology and anthropologists tend to be more concerned with culture and cultures as wholes or total ways of life. In contrast, sociology and sociologists tend to be more concerned with society, societies, and social systems—also wholes, true enough—but much more fundamentally, with the *specific parts, elements*, and *relationships* in society, societies, and social systems. This includes all the different individuals, groups, classes, customs, fads, fashions, traditions, traits, memes, and behaviours that constitute and characterize society, societies, and social systems, as well as the complex interactions, interconnections, and interrelationships that go on between and among these complicated entities. This led to countless debates, discussions, and disagreements between anthropologists and sociologists over the real character, meaning, methods, objectives, and techniques of anthropology and sociology in general and anthropologists and sociologists in particular.

This situation came to a head in the middle half of the twentieth century in a dialogue between Talcott Parsons, one of the United States' most prolific sociologists, and Alfred Kroeber, one of its most prominent anthropologists. In 1958, they co-authored an article titled "The Concepts of Culture and of Social System" in the *American Sociological Review* that was designed to examine similarities and differences between anthropology and sociology. They concluded that these two disciplines share many similarities but also have such significant differences that they should be developed separately rather than together, but with a great deal more cooperation, interaction, and collaboration between them.

Parsons and Kroeber pointed out that considerable confusion existed among scholars in both disciplines about the ideas of *culture* and *society* (or "social systems"). This confusion had actually slowed progress in understanding how the two concepts are interrelated. On the one hand, sociologists considered "cultural systems as a sort of outgrowth or spontaneous development, derivative from social systems." For their part, "[a]nthropologists are more given to being holistic and therefore often begin with total systems of culture and then proceed to subsume social structure as merely a part of culture."

As a result, Kroeber and Parsons argued, one ended up with "distinct systems," with sociologists and anthropologists "abstract[ing] or select[ing] two analytically distinct sets of components from the same concerete phenomena":

> Statements made about relationships within a cultural pattern are thus of a different order from those within a system of societal relationships. Neither can be directly reduced to terms of the other; that is to say, the order of relationships within one is independent from that in the other....
>
> To speak, then, of the analytical independence between culture and social system is, of course, not to say that the two systems are not related, or that various approaches to the analysis of the relationship may not be used. It is often profitable to hold constant either cultural or societal aspects of the same concrete phenomena while addressing attention to the other. Provided that the analytical distinction between them is maintained, it is therefore idle to quarrel over the rightness of either approach. Important work has been prosecuted under both of them. It will undoubtedly be most profitable to develop both lines of thinking and to judge them by how much each increases understanding....

Rather than arguing about whether scholars can best understand culture from "the perspective of society or society from that of culture," Parsons and Kroeber "propose[d] a truce." They likened the situation to debates among biologists about whether heredity or environment plays the greater role in shaping an organism. Just as in that instance, sociologists and anthropologists must realize it is no longer a matter of which discipline is "right," but of how the key concepts of culture and society function in the world and "how they are interwoven with each other." The most productive way for both disciplines to move forward is for the "traditional perspectives of anthropology and sociology" to "merge into a temporary condominium." By doing so, anthropologists and sociologists could achieve "a differentiated but ultimately collaborative attack on problems in intermediate areas with which both are concerned."[2]

There is another dimension to this argument that should be identified and addressed here. Anthropologists tend to put more emphasis on culture and cultures in general and worldviews, values, value systems, ideals, and ways of life in particular because these matters are quintessential parts of the "big picture" and of culture and cultures as "complex wholes" or "total ways of life." This is why these matters are often referred to as *universals*. In contrast to this, sociologists tend to put much more emphasis on society and societies in general and social systems, groups, classes, individuals, customs, behaviour, beliefs, traditions, signs, signals, symbols, and the myriad interactions that are constantly going on between these and other entities in particular. Indeed, these elements and components are often referred to as *particulars* because they are more specific and concentrated in character.

Looked at from afar and in very general terms, these two disciplines do indeed share a great deal in common, something which is helpful in broadening and deepening our knowledge and understanding of the composition, nature, and ingredients of all the diverse cultures and societies in the world. And, too, cultures and societies look very similar when viewed from a distance; they are made up of many of the same (or similar) parts, such as agriculture, industry, education, value systems, classes, and many others. However, viewed from the inside, up close, or in very specific terms, it quickly becomes apparent that the nature, content, and substance of cultures and societies can be, and often are, very different.

This results largely from the fact that sociologists tend to look at their discipline and its subject matter in more concentrated, concrete, detailed, and specific ways, and therefore tend to be more preoccupied with and aware of the parts of societies, as well as analysis of these parts and the interactions that are constantly going on between and among them. This differs from the work of many anthropologists, who tend to be much more concerned with looking at cultures and examining their nature, character, meaning, and functioning as complex wholes or total ways of life, and consequently from a substantially broader and more all-encompassing perspective.

Interestingly, the work of sociologists over the last two centuries has made us more aware of why there are so many disagreements, misunderstandings, conflicts, clashes, and wars in the world. This is because (as the old saying goes) "the devil is in the details." This fact is revealed much more often through the study of parts and particulars than of wholes and universals. The work of sociologists has also made us much more aware of the fact that cultures, like societies, have their weaknesses, problems, and negative features when examined up close and in detail.

This is true for all of humanity's disciplines and activities, not just cultures, societies, and social systems. Think, for instance, of the negative as well as positive features, effects, and consequences of science, economics, and religion as specific examples of this observation. Science has expanded humanity's knowledge of the universe and the laws of nature immensely. However, it has also made it possible to create weapons of war that possess the capability of killing millions of people and ending civilization. Economics has improved the standard of living and quality of life of billions of people, but it has had a devastating effect on the natural environment. Religion has enhanced people's spirituality in myriad ways. Nevertheless, it has also pitted one religion against another, causing numerous tensions and conflicts.

So, too, do societies, social systems, and cultures have their negative as well as their positive features, consequences, and effects. Without a willingness to admit this and come to grips with it, humanity will be in for a rocky ride.

These negative features cause numerous conflicts and hostilities around the world because societies and social systems as well as cultures are becoming more heterogeneous, multidimensional, and complex due to the migrations of millions of people, new developments in transportation and communications, as well as countless other changes. This is causing a great deal of stress, anxiety, and apprehension; many people find it increasingly difficult to identify with their own societies, countries, and cultures, much less those of others. This makes it imperative to be ever mindful of the many problems that exist within and between different cultures, societies, and social systems. It is doubtful we would be as aware of the negative side of societies, social systems, and even cultures had it not been for the research and writings of sociologists.

The most obvious example of this is *genocide*. Over the course of history, millions of people have been killed for reasons having to do with fundamental differences in societies and cultures and their diverse worldviews, values, customs, beliefs, traditions, and ways of life. According to the United Nations Genocide Convention, genocide involves "acts committed with intent to destroy, in whole or in part, a national, ethnic, racial, or religious group, including the systematic harm or killing of its members, imposing living conditions that seek to bring about physical destruction in whole or in part, preventing births, or forcibly transferring children from one group to another group."

The Political Instability Task Force estimates that between 1956 and 2016, a total of 43 genocides took place in the world causing the death of more than 50 million people. Since then, more than half-a-million Rohingya people in Myanmar, formerly Burma, have been displaced in what some observers warn is an impending or current genocide.

Closely connected to such actions is what is called "cultural genocide," "cultural cleansing," or "ethnic cleansing." While there is little agreement on the specific nature and meaning of these terms throughout the world today, it is generally agreed that they denote the effort to oppress and destroy the most important parts of people's lives, culture, society, identity, and sense of belonging, and, along with this, their worldviews, values, value systems, customs, traditions, beliefs, languages, dress, and ways of life.

Examples of this abound as well, such as the persecution of the Bahais and the Bahai religion in Iran; Nazi Germany's attempt to erase Polish culture; the "retraining" or "re-education" of members of China's Muslin Uyghur minority; efforts to wipe out Armenia's cultural heritage in Turkey; the destruction of famous architectural sites by the Taliban in the Middle East and the desecration of manuscripts and kidnapping of young girls by the Boko Haram in Nigeria; the creation of residential schools in Canada that were designed to suppress or eliminate the cultures of Indigenous peoples; and many others.

On a lesser scale, there are also all the culture clashes and social wars that go on in many if not all societies, cultures, and countries. Areas of dispute include gender, abortion, sexuality, race, ethnicity, religion, the right to bear arms—the list seems endless.

Many of these clashes and wars have become highly politicized. This trend became more apparent after governments in many countries attempted to develop policies and practices that are more equitable and just, something opponents of those policies have denounced as "political correctness." Many of these policies are designed to give minority groups more control over their own cultures and ways of life. At the same time, inequality and discrimination persist.

Developments like these led to the publication of many books on this and related subjects, especially in the United States. This includes, for example, Samuel P. Huntington's *The Clash of Civilizations*, Adam Kempton Webb's *Beyond the Global Culture War*, Curran, Gaber, and Petley's *Culture Wars: The Media and the British Left*, Morris P. Fiorina's *Culture War?: The Myth of a Polarized America*, and James Davison Hunter's *Culture Wars: The Struggle to Define America*. This last book, which was published in 1991, set off a major dispute over whether a "culture war" existed in the United States, and if so, how pronounced and dangerous it might be.

Such concerns are not unrelated to the battles that are currently going on in the United States and many other parts of the world over a series of demographic shifts and their impact on the preservation of national identities and cultures. The most obvious example of this involves the composition and character of the population of the United States and a number of western European countries, such as Greece, Italy, and Hungary. This has resulted from major influxes of immigrants and refugees over the last few decades.

When Donald Trump talked about "making America great again" during the many speeches he gave prior to becoming president in 2016, it sounded like he was calling for a return to the "old days" when the population of the United States was more homogeneous and white. This perception was intensified when potential immigrants from a number of Middle Eastern countries, Mexico, and other parts of the world were prevented from entering the United States, as well as when many illegal immigrants were compelled to return to their countries of origin. What makes problems like this difficult to deal with is the fact that people from other cultures and societies see the world differently, act in the world differently, and assign different weights, priorities, and values to the component parts of their lives, societies, social systems, and cultures. This creates a situation that is ripe for conflict and confrontation.

Developments like these, and others, help to explain why sociology as a disciple became very prominent in the twentieth century. As well as Comte, Marx, Spencer, Weber, and Durkheim, important scholars in the field included Harriet Martineau in the nineteenth century—often heralded as the first female sociologist—as well as Beatrice and Sidney Webb, Thorstein Veblen, Charles Beard, and John Dewey in the early decades of the twentieth century, C. Wright Mills, Theodor Adorno, Hannah Arendt, and Herbert Marcuse in mid-century, and Jürgen Habermas, Immanuel Wallerstein, and Pierre Bourdieu later in the twentieth century. (Some of these scholars were actually trained and worked as historians or philosophers, but made important contributions to sociology.) Well-known institutions included the Institute for Social Research (founded in 1918), hub for the Frankfurt School of critical theory—now part of Goethe University Frankfurt though earlier affiliated with New York's Columbia University—and the New School for Social Research, created in New York City in 1919.

Many of the aforementioned sociologists were strongly committed to the creation and development of these institutions and schools because they were disillusioned with the prevalent socioeconomic practices and systems—whether capitalism, fascism, or communism—and hoped to establish new and alternative paths to the development of societies, social systems, classes, and countries through the creation of new social, philosophical, and critical theories with strong social, cultural, and artistic implications. Included among scholars taking such an approach were Theodor Adorno, a critic of the cultural industries of the period as well as a musician and author of such works as *Aesthetic Theory;* Pierre Bourdieu, a leading thinker in media studies and the study of popular culture; Immanuel Wallerstein, who studied global economic and social systems; Michel Foucault, author of *Madness and Civilization* and many other books on social issues and cultural matters; and Herbert Marcuse, who was interested in human development and wrote *Eros and Civilization*, an effort to bring together the ideas of Marx and Freud. Some of these scholars and schools were criticized, especially in the 1920s and 1930s, for misreading political developments in Europe that saw powerful dictators such as Hitler, Mussolini, and Stalin twist existing social systems and practices to oppressive purposes rather than attempting to alleviate social problems. However, there is no doubt that these and other sociologists were striving the improve society through their research and writing.

Meanwhile, other thinkers, such as Hannah Arendt, C. Wright Mills, and Thorstein Veblen were more interested in the effect of specific groups and classes on the development and functioning of social systems. This eventually gave rise to the development of a field called *cultural studies*, which came into existence in the latter part of the twentieth century and remains prominent in many institutions of higher learning throughout the world today. These studies were spearheaded initially by a group of Marxist scholars and educators in the late 1960s and 1970s in the UK. Among them were Richard Hoggart, Raymond Williams, and Stuart Hall, who were involved in the creation and development of the Centre for Contemporary Cultural Studies at the University of Birmingham in 1964. Hoggart was the author of a popular book called *The Uses of Literacy*, Williams was well known for his books on culture such as *Culture and Society* and *The Long Revolution*, and Hall wrote numerous important journal articles and books as well as presenting a television series on Caribbean culture and history. The Birmingham Centre expanded rapidly after Stuart Hall took over as director in 1968 and awareness of his writings and ideas spread quickly to other parts of the world.

Central to this scholarly work was examining the complex connection between societies, cultures, politics, conflict, and power, and consequently the political dynamics of contemporary cultures and social systems. A particular concern at that time—and still today—is how cultural and social practices relate to systems of corporate, elite, and especially governmental and political power, authority, and control, as well as how all this is associated with, and operates through, such mechanisms as ideologies, class struggles and structures, and so forth. Since that time, there has been an explosion of interest in cultural studies. This has resulted in linking together such diverse pursuits as political theory and ideology, media studies, the arts and humanities, aesthetics, philosophy, and much else. How "meaning" is generated, disseminated, contested, and bound up with systems of control, dominance, power, gender identities and realities is also very much part of this work.

Another development that is assuming greater prominence throughout the world today is what is called *cultural appropriation.* This occurs when people in the dominant culture of a country, society, or social system exploit minority, oppressed, and marginalized peoples by using those people's cultural symbols and practices for their own purposes. A good example is the cultural appropriation of Indigenous peoples' customs, artwork, and identities.

In an informative article entitled "What's Wrong with Cultural Appropriation?" Maisha A. Johnson identified nine major reasons for cultural appropriation. These reasons include trivializing historical oppression, enabling the privileged to profit from oppressed people's culture and labour, and perpetuating racial and racial stereotypes. Criticisms have been levelled against some of the world's top fashion designers for appropriating the cultural symbols of minority groups, and there have been demands to eliminate scenes in well-known and respected works of art that are deemed to be racist, such as the Chinese dance in Tchaikovsky's *The Nutcracker* and "La danse des négrillons" in the ballet *La Bayadère.* Many protests like these, including the Woke movement, cancel culture, and call-out culture, are going on in different parts of the world today. They are designed to correct economic injustices, as well as to eliminate cultural practices and political policies that have adverse psychological, social, spiritual, and cultural implications and consequences for various ethnic, racial, and societal groups.

In recent years, these activist and protest activities have resulted in the tearing down or defacing of specific flags as well as the statues of major historical figures who were involved historically in adverse practices of one type or another. The most obvious examples of such actions have occurred in the United States, where Confederate flags and statues of such famous people as Jefferson Davis, president of the Confederacy, and Robert E. Lee, its leading general, have been defaced or toppled. According to the Southern Poverty Law Center, more than 100 Confederate monuments have been removed from public places, squares, and other locations in order to protest the role of such individuals in maintaining slavery and systemic racism.

These developments are not limited to the United States. Similar actions have taken place in Canada and other countries, such as England and Belgium. In Canada, for instance, statues of different public figures have been torn down, removed, or defaced, including those of Sir John A. Macdonald, the country's first prime minister, and Egerton Ryerson, who played a prominent role in educational development, because of their racist views and leading role in creating residential schools for Indigenous children.

And this is not all. Protests erupted around the world following the killing by police of George Floyd, a Black American, in Minneapolis. These protests were spearheaded by activist groups like Black Lives Matter. They called for major changes in policing and society generally. The fact that the police officer who kneeled on George Floyd's neck, causing his death, was convicted in a jury trial in April 2021 helped provide a ray of hope that matters might improve in the future.

Another recent development with strong social and cultural implications is the collection and selling of information about people's lives, lifestyles, habits, and ways of life for commercial or political purposes. In George Orwell's novel *Nineteen Eighty-Four* (published in 1949), governments kept tab on their citizens through constant intrusive monitoring.

Big Brother—Orwell's totalitarian dictator—may not yet exist, but over the past several decades organizations such as Facebook, Google, YouTube, Twitter, and other social media giants created platforms that allow people to share information free of charge, supported by the revenue these companies collect from advertisers. But then it was discovered that people's personal data was being sold for commercial use and other purposes. Matters became even more alarming when it was revealed that a British political consulting firm was using confidential information acquired by Facebook about its members to intervene in election campaigns.

Great concern now exists about the use of private information by tech companies and whether it violates basic privacy rights. As a result, tremendous pressures are now being exerted on governments to restrict such developments and protect people's fundamental rights.

Shoshana Zuboff's recent book *The Age of Surveillance Capitalism* provides additional insight into how companies collect and use people's personal data for financial gain. Information about what people look for on search engines and social media platforms and their online habits is very valuable to companies selling products and services.

It is clear from the foregoing that societies and social systems and all the diverse developments that occur in them are strongly influenced by, and intimately connected to, communications technology in deep, diverse, complex, and dynamic ways. While this is a vast issue that extends well beyond the compass of this book, suffice it to say that such issues are likely to loom even larger in the future.

Many of these problems and possibilities were foreseen more than half a century ago by Harold Innis and Marshall McLuhan, two prominent Canadian scholars mentioned briefly in the last chapter. Both Innis and McLuhan believed that communications technology—*and especially the changes that take place in the nature of that technology*—affect virtually every aspect of individual, institutional, social, societal, and cultural life, from habits, traditions, customs, fashions, memes, and relationships to worldviews, values, value systems, and overall ways of life. Here is what Harold Innis had to say on this subject:

> A medium of communication has an important influence on the dissemination of knowledge over space and over time and it becomes necessary to study its characteristics in order to appraise its influences on its cultural setting. According to its characteristics it may be better suited to the dissemination of knowledge over time than over space, particularly if the medium is heavy and durable and not suited to transportation, or to the dissemination of knowledge over space than over time, particularly if the medium is light and easily transported. The relative emphasis on time or space will imply *a bias of significance to the culture in which it is imbedded.*[3]

McLuhan expanded on this general principle and remarkable insight when he claimed that the means or modes by or through which people communicate in a society, social system, or culture can be more important than the information transmitted in the communication:

> In a culture like ours, long accustomed to splitting and dividing all things as a means of control, it is sometimes a bit of a shock to be reminded that, in operational and practical fact, *the medium is the message*. This is merely to say that the personnel consequences of any medium—that is, of any extension of ourselves—result from the new scale that is introduced into our affairs by each extension of ourselves, or by any new technology.[4]

McLuhan went on to say that "[i]t is the medium that shapes and controls the scale and form of human association and action."[5]

For McLuhan, history in general and western history in particular can be divided into three distinct, basic, and overlapping periods: *oral*, *print*, and *electric*. McLuhan also used the terms *pre-literate, literate,* and *post-literate* and *tribal*, *individualist*, and *global* to describe these stages. Each era has its own specific features and special characteristics, as well as communications vehicles and technological devices that are reflective of it. McLuhan was especially fond of illustrating this general phenomenon and basic principle by using the example of "print society or culture," which resulted from the introduction of printing presses using mobile type into Europe in the 1440s by Johannes Gutenberg of Germany. In McLuhan's view, Gutenberg's work not only made the Renaissance possible, but also led to the rise of individualism and nationalism, the Protestant Reformation, the French and American revolutions, scientific rationalism, and the expansion of individual rights including property, voting, and free speech. All these ideas are spelled out in detail in McLuhan's book *The Gutenberg Galaxy*.[6]

According to McLuhan, the introduction of electronic communications devices has had a similarly profound impact on the modern world. Everything is turned topsy turvy as a result of the creation of an "environmental surround" that is instantaneous and generates an all-out assault on the values of the literary society and culture. These new communications technologies obliterate space, time, and national boundaries, according to McLuhan, because we are constantly being bombarded with information, ideas, and images from all directions. This produces a sense of "all-in-oneness." This massive shift in how we receive and process information has brought with it equally massive problems. Many contend that it is creating numerous health problems for people, such as mental health issues and addictions. It also seems to be producing a great deal more chaos and disorder and a "global village" filled with countless difficulties and problems, not just possibilities and opportunities.

Accompanying the rise of such communications technologies has been the phenomenal growth of giant tech companies such as Meta (Facebook's parent company), Amazon, Apple, and Alphabet (Google's parent company). Many of these developments and institutions have become so colossal and are expanding so rapidly that they have taken on a character and life all their own, and are no longer accountable to government or the general public. This explains why so many demands are being made in many countries in the world today to rein in these powerful institutions and make them accountable.

Problems like these—especially those mentioned earlier that involve complex interactions and the intermingling of people with very different worldviews, values, customs, traditions, beliefs, and ways of life—will always be with us to a certain extent, even if ways are devised to deal with them. On the one hand, this means learning a great deal about the real nature of our own cultures—*including societies and social systems as a very fundamental component of culture*—since, as Mary E. Clark explained in her book *Ariadne's Thread: The Search for New Modes of Thinking*, "Culture is learned as a child, and as children we each learned from those around us a particular set of rules, beliefs, priorities, and expectations that moulded our world into a meaningful whole. *That is our culture.*"[7] On the other hand, it means learning a great deal about the cultures of others. This is especially important because it is difficult for people who are born and grow up in one culture to fully comprehend, appreciate, and accept or understand the cultures and cultural practices of others due to of the limits of our cultural conditioning. Antonio Alonso-Concheiro, the

Mexican cultural scholar, explained why it is so difficult for people to acquire knowledge and understanding of other cultures:

> [W]e generally assume that cultures are simply different modes of adaptation to nature, different codes for the same fundamental purposes.... We seldom recognize that in this manner we are only studying and classifying cultures which we invent through our own cultural framework and not the cultures themselves. In other words, we generally reach for and obtain only ethnocentric visions of other cultures.[8]

Despite such difficulties, it is imperative to persevere with the *quest* to understand, appreciate, and respect other cultures, societies, and social systems, as well as their worldviews, values, value systems, customs, and beliefs. This is necessary not only to diffuse cultural conflicts, tensions, pressures, and clashes as much as possible, but also to learn from other cultures, societies, and social systems. Needless to say, there is an incredible amount to be learned if we are wise enough to realize that no one culture, society, or social system has all the answers. People in other cultures and parts of the world see matters differently than we do, largely because their ways of life are different. As a result, they can—and often do—see things that we cannot see or understand in our own cultures, societies, and social systems, either because we are too close to them, we take them for granted, or we are so deeply immersed in them that we are unable to see their shortcomings and not just their strengths.

No subject is more important at present and going forward into the future than learning about the many diverse cultures in the world. While this is an exceedingly difficult task—cultures as wholes and total ways of life are immensely complex—a great deal can and will be accomplished when a much higher priority is placed on education in culture and cultures at all stages and ages in life. This education should start very early in life and end very late, be fully incorporated into children's early development, continued throughout their elementary, secondary, and post-secondary education, sustained later in life through adult education courses and lifelong learning capabilities, and, equally important, maintained into the final stages of life.

Unfortunately, few educational institutions in the world are in a position to provide the kind of holistic or comprehensive cultural education that is required at the present time. This is due to the lack of qualified and well-trained teachers in cultures, as well as the fact that there are very few learning and teaching materials available at present dealing with culture and cultures in the all-encompassing sense. While some schools provide "multicultural days" that are designed to introduce students to different cultures in the world through their food, foodstuffs, dances, customs, traditions, costumes, and so forth, and others celebrate specific ethnic holidays and other special cultural occasions and social events for similar purposes, these activities are usually extracurricular rather than curricular in nature and therefore fall short of the type of all-embracing and lifelong cultural education that is required.

To be effective, a comprehensive and lifelong cultural education should include four major components. The first should be learning about *the nature and meaning of culture in general and cultures in particular in all their main manifestations*. This is necessary because there is a great deal of confusion at present over the nature and meaning of culture and cultures that needs to be overcome. In order for education of this type to be successful, it should show that perceiving and defining culture in terms of the arts, humanities, and heritage of history—a perspective still popular in most educational systems, institutions, and countries today—is only one of a number of manifestations of culture and cultures that exist. As we have seen, there are many other manifestations—such as the anthropological, sociological, ecological, biological, and cosmological ones—that are becoming more widely accepted in the world because they are very relevant to the problems confronting humanity at present and the need to find effective solutions to these problems in the future.

The second component should be learning about *the basics of culture and cultures*. This is necessary because all cultures are based on certain underlying assumptions, axioms, worldviews, values, values systems, principles, ideals, and so forth that shed a great deal of light on how they are structured as dynamic and organic wholes, as well as how they function in the world in both the theoretical and practical sense.

The third component should be learning about *the contents and parts of culture and cultures*, such as the different activities that comprise them, as well as how some activities and parts are much more important than others because they possess the potential to act as symbols, signs, and gateways to culture and cultures as wholes through this symbolic or representative process. This is of crucial importance for cultural education since it is not possible to see or know culture and cultures as wholes or total ways of life without selecting certain parts to represent and symbolize them as wholes. It doesn't take a great deal of imagination to visualize how it is possible to create portraits, images, and visions of all the diverse cultures in the world though this miraculous, symbolic, and all-encompassing process.

Finally, the fourth component of a comprehensive cultural education should deal with the *context of cultures as well as culture and cultures as contexts*. This involves studying how culture and cultures are situated in space and time, how they are affected by a variety of factors such as myths, legends, cosmologies, worldviews, globalization, and so forth, and especially how effective culture and cultures can be as ideal contexts for situating virtually all activities, disciplines, and institutions, regardless of whether we are considering economics, politics, science, the arts, technology, communications, the world system, or governments and international agencies. This is one of the most crucial elements in this type of education because "context determines contents," as Ruth Benedict reminded us. A change in the context of disciplines, activities, and institutions will instantly cause a change in the contents of these disciplines, activities, and institutions.

Initially, cultural education should focus on the cultures of the countries people and students are living in at present. However, later this should be complemented by courses that juxtapose, compare, and contrast the different cultures and civilizations of the world. There is a vast reservoir of knowledge here that needs to be pulled together, classified, assessed, and compared in a systemic, methodical, and sustained fashion.

A very important initiative in this regard occurred in 2020 when Olimpia Niglio, a distinguished professor of architecture, founded Reconnecting With Your Culture (RWYC). She is the driving force behind this remarkable organization, which seeks to provide opportunities for children and young people ages 5 to 17 in primary and secondary schools around the world to explore their cultures and heritages in their own localities and communities and document their experiences by drawing pictures, making maps, creating exhibitions, and through other means. This organization and its program and methodology are spreading rapidly throughout the world, confirming the fundamental need for opportunities of this type.

A similar development has been taking place in Ukraine at Volodymyr Dahl East Ukrainian National University, where Galyna Shevchenko, director of the Research Institute of Spiritual Development of Man and UNESCO chair in spiritual and cultural values of upbringing and education has been preparing students and young people for living in a cultural age for more than a decade.

A third such development is the O-City project, which is financed by the European Commission within the Erasmus Plus (Knowledge Alliances) program. Firstly, this project develops an online application to visualize the natural and cultural heritage of towns and cities around the world. On this platform, cities can represent not only their monuments and natural spaces, but also their culture and traditions through videos, photographs, animations, and other multimedia elements developed as educational projects in the classrooms of training centres and institutions. Secondly, it facilitates the work of teachers in the classroom in the development of these projects, such as an educational platform aimed at teachers that offers courses distributed in four training modules in business, technical (multimedia), cultural, and soft skills. The combination of these two developments is a powerful motivational tool for students in the classroom as they can see their work published in an online application. Participation helps them improve their digital skills and awareness of the importance of the culture and nature of their villages, towns, and cities as symbols of identity and also contributes to the economic promotion of the community.

Just as it is possible to learn a great deal about all the different religions of the world through courses in comparative religions, so it is possible to learn a great deal about all the diverse cultures in the world through comparable courses in cultures. If, as the Russian proverb states, "all is known by comparison," then it follows from this that comparisons between cultures are essential and extremely valuable because they reveal an enormous amount about the diverse cultures in the world and their origins, evolution, layers, societal and social systems, customs, traits, behavioural characteristics, fundamental features, and the overall ways of life they encompass.

Education of this type will also make it possible for people to understand and appreciate all the various cultures in the world including civilizations as wholes or total ways of life. This will enrich and enhance their lives in numerous ways. They will be able to cultivate more effective ways of seeing, thinking, feeling, acting, behaving, believing, and valuing things. The door will be opened to accepting, appreciating, and respecting other cultures and other peoples, expanding consciousness and mindfulness, improving welfare and well-being, broadening and deepening individual and collective well-being and lifestyles, increasing job opportunities and employment possibilities, and experiencing a great deal more fulfillment, happiness, and spirituality in life.

No one is more conscious of these benefits or writes more convincingly about this than Brian Holihan. His extensive travels in many different countries and cultures have provided him and his readers with rare insights into how much can be learned that will improve and enhance our lives. This is documented in detail in his book *Thinking in a New Light: How to Boost Your Creativity and Live More Fully by Exploring World Cultures*. In Chapter 13, Holihan provides a useful method for finding "paradise on earth" by "looking at, with, and beyond cultures," or what he calls "the AWB circle."[9] Through this method, people can learn not only an incredible amount about other cultures and civilizations but also a great deal about their own culture and cultural conditioning. An additional advantage of this book is that it is premised on developing these capabilities through intensive analysis and assessments of the historical and contemporary development and achievements of cultures in Southeast Asia that are rapidly gaining prominence in the world as well as garnering much more respect, recognition, attention, and interest.

What is slowly but surely emerging as this examination of the main manifestations of culture unfolds and takes shape is the realization that such an examination must alert us to the shortcomings of cultures as well as their benefits, strengths, and opportunities. Over the last century, and especially over the last few decades, the sociological manifestation of culture has played a major role in this by analyzing specific aspects of cultures, societies, social systems, and civilizations, as well as emphasizing the need to create the capabilities required to deal with these aspects and dimensions of culture and cultures effectively.

It is impossible to achieve the "dual capacity" inherent in culture in this sense without taking full advantage of science in general and the social sciences in particular. A major advantage of the social sciences in this regard—and especially such social sciences as anthropology and sociology in this specific case—is their ability to hold things at "arm's length" and examine them with a critical eye as well as from an objective and impartial perspective. If this dual capacity had been utilized in the development of the world as economics—and consequently consideration had been given to the devastating effects economic growth would have on the natural environment—it is quite possible that humanity would not be confronted with an environmental crisis today and would be on a much better, safer, and more favourable path to the future.

Let's not make this mistake a second time. In order to avoid doing so, it is essential to deal with culture, cultures, societies, and social systems in specific terms as well as in breadth and depth, taking full advantage of their incredible strengths as well as dealing with their fundamental shortcomings. This is what makes the sociological manifestation of culture so relevant and timely at this time.

Chapter Nine

Behaviour and Ways of Life of Other Species

> Culture consists of certain biological activities, neither more or less biological than digestion or locomotion.... Culture is merely a special direction which we give to the cultivation of our animal potencies.
>
> —José Ortega y Gasset[1]

In much the same way that the idea of culture went through a profound transformation in the latter part of the nineteenth century when anthropologists and sociologists began to apply the concept of culture as a complex whole to human beings, so it has gone through another profound transformation in the latter decades of the twentieth century and first two decades of the twenty-first. This has resulted largely from research by biologists, zoologists, botanists, and horticulturalists who see and deal with culture in even more expansive terms by including other species, not just humans.

Like the earlier transformation, the present broadening of the concept of culture has not replaced the traditional manifestations of culture as the cultivation of the soul, the arts, humanities, and the heritage of history. Most people in the world as well as governments, corporations, foundations, international organizations, and even many educational institutions remain committed to dealing with culture in this way, as are many cultural organizations as well. Despite this, UNESCO did recognize and endorse the anthropological manifestation of culture as a complex whole or total way of life at its Second World Conference on Cultural Policies in Mexico City in 1982.[2] This confirmed that the anthropological manifestation of culture was gaining traction.

This is also true for the much more recent and expansive biological manifestation of culture. It has not replaced earlier holistic manifestations of culture, such as the anthropological and sociological conceptions, or the more traditional definitions. What it did do, however, was to expand the holistic understanding of culture to include other species in a far broader conception of culture and cultures. This has powerful implications and consequences for human beings and other species in the years and decades ahead.

The origins of this biological manifestation of culture can be traced back more than a century and a half ago. Most prominent in this regard is the work of Charles Darwin, Gregor Mendel, Louis Pasteur, Carl Linnaeus, and George Washington Carver in earlier times, and Rachel Carson, Beatrix Potter, Desmond Morris, Jane Goodall, Dian Fossey, Anne Dagg, and many others more recently.

While anthropologists and sociologists were among the first scholars to make the case that cultures and societies are wholes and not just parts of wholes, their studies in this area were limited to human beings and did not focus a great deal on other species or the natural environment. These disciplines are still largely concerned with humans, despite the fact that more attention is now being accorded to the natural environment.

It took the work of biologists, zoologists, botanists, horticulturalists, and others to expand this domain by focusing on other species and specifically the similarities and differences among all the diverse species in the world. Very early in their studies they raised the question of whether all species have culture and create cultures, or are culture and cultures confined to human beings?

It wasn't long before the answer to this question emerged, since it was apparent that human beings and other species shared an enormous amount in common. Humans, like other species, are living organisms, and members of an order of animals called *primates*. Other primates include gorillas, chimpanzees, and gibbons. Like other living things, human beings need water, air, and food to survive. They also go through similar stages in their development and functioning over the course of their lives, such as birth, growth, decline, and death. Bodily functions like consumption and elimination, procreation, and communications and bonding are shared with other living organisms as such. Moreover, humans and other species have similar techniques of organization, social interaction, community development, and so forth.

Of course, there are many differences between species as well as similarities. This is especially true of the differences between human beings and other species. In fact, many people believe that culture in general—and the ability to create cultures, societies, social systems, and so forth in particular—is predominantly, if not exclusively, a human ability and therefore the sole preserve of human beings. Even if other species have the capacity to create cultures, societies, social systems, and the like, advocates of this belief contend that this capacity is so elementary compared to human beings that it is not worth thinking about. For such people, culture and the ability to create cultures, societies, social systems, and other human collectives is *the* principal difference between human beings and other species.

For centuries, it was assumed that only human beings possessed the ability to think, reason, and, perhaps most important of all, engage in self-reflection. This led to the conclusion that most human actions were grounded in intelligence—the ability to think things out and act in a logical, rational, and consistent manner. This contrasted fundamentally, as advocates of this belief were quick to point out, with the behaviour of animals, which was based largely on instinct.

Other people have a different take on this matter, although it boils down to much the same thing in the end. They tend to see all the different species as living organisms in the world as forming a gigantic pyramid or hierarchy with human beings at the top of the hierarchy, animals beneath, plants much farther down than animals, and all other living organisms—for instance, protozoa and bacteria—at the bottom.

Views like this were often condoned by religions such as Christianity that were based on the belief that human beings were created in the image of God, granted "domination over the earth" by God, and therefore occupy a privileged position at the very apex of the pyramid. This was often interpreted to mean that people could act in any way they liked towards other species since those species had been placed on the earth to serve human beings.

Beliefs like this made it possible for human beings to create a huge divide between themselves and other species. This helped to mitigate the sense of guilt they felt from the way they treated other species, especially animals. As a result, they dominated animals, subordinated them to their will, killed them for their meat, used their hides and fur to make clothes and create shelters to provide warmth, put them to work carrying heavy loads or lifting awkward objects, displayed them in circuses and caged them in zoos, and so forth. Whatever the explanation, attitudes like these were prevalent at one time and used to justify the separation of the human realm from the realm of other organisms. Consequently, not a great deal of research was undertaken about other species except as sparked by the curiosity of various scholars. This was especially true for animals' basic behaviour, capabilities, organizational forms, structures, activities, and traits, as well as for their overall ways of life. It was decided that such things were not all that important in the larger scheme of things.

These beliefs have changed dramatically over the last few decades. There is today a remarkable amount of interest in the ways of life of other species. This interest has grown substantially, so much so that research into the nature, behaviour, traits, sensory abilities, cognitive capabilities, and organizational forms, structures, and ways of life of other species is compounding rapidly. With this has come growing awareness and acceptance of the fact that other living organisms have culture and create cultures, just as humans do. Moreover, the similarities between human beings and animals and plants are now deemed to be far greater than was assumed earlier. This has led to the conclusion that the differences among all the diverse species in the world are largely differences in degree and magnitude and not in substance or kind. Every species in the world has its own forms of culture that are manifested in its way of life.

There is a vast number of living organisms and different species in the world. This includes not only animals (including humans) and plants, but also micro-organisms such as bacteria, archaea, protozoa, algae, and fungi. Viruses are often included in the list as well, but most scientists do not consider them living organisms because they cannot reproduce themselves outside a host cell. Interestingly, the biggest living organism that has ever existed in the world is not a blue whale or giant redwood tree, as most people would think, but rather a colossal honey fungus that exists in the Blue Mountains of Oregon and measures more than three kilometres across. All these species create cultures in one form or another, even if they may be very different than the ones created by human beings.

Consider bees and their culture as one of the best illustrations of this. Without the capabilities of bees, it is very likely that human beings and many other species might not exist today.

Like human beings and human cultures, bees create highly complex and intricately designed cultures that are concerned with their survival, habitation, community development, solidarity, communication, interaction, and well-being. These cultures, with their queen, drone, and worker bees, rigid hierarchies and divisions of labour, finely tuned communications systems, sensing capacities, and productive capabilities, structure how bees live as well as ensuring their survival. Like human beings, bees create a continuous flow of products. These products, such as honey, wax, beehives, and honeycombs, are much in demand in the human realm and have both a functional and aesthetic significance. Beehives and honeycombs, for instance, are remarkable creations, comparable in their style, design, function, and complexity to many of the cultural creations of human beings, though on a much smaller scale.

Just as bees prefer certain types of habitats and create their homes, so all animal species have habitats and homes of one kind or another. These homes or habitats may be in a city, forest, dessert, grassland, wetlands, tundra, or mountainous area, or, in the case of fish, oceans, lakes, streams, and rivers. Animals live in a variety of accommodations, such as dens, lairs, holes, tree trunks, hollow branches, caves, nests, hills, woods, ponds, and so forth. We now know that octopuses are capable of using clam and coconut shells to create their homes on the ocean floor. Moreover, the homes of some animals can be very elaborate and ornate, such as bird nests, beaver dams, and ant hills.

Interestingly, contemporary research is revealing that ants are much better traffic engineers than people because they never have to endure traffic jams and gridlock. Investigations into this matter at the University of Potsdam and the Martin Luther University in Germany revealed that a nest of black meadow ants had four main trunk lines leading to their foraging area in a forested region of Saxony. The ants treated each track to and from the art hill like a three-lane highway: when traffic volume was low they travelled down the centre of the track, whereas when it was high they spread out. Similar arrangements were made with respect to leaving and returning to their ant hills; ants searching for food went out on one side of the line or track and returned with food on the other side. There were also strict rules with respect to how and when to pass, deal with obstacles and encumbrances, and speed up or slow down depending on the density of the traffic.

In order to compete for survival and ensure their well-being, many animals have been compelled to develop, adopt, and cultivate very specific traits, attributes, and sensory capabilities that may not only be on a par with those of human beings, but actually in many cases are far superior. This is especially true with respect to the different senses. Elephants, bears, and sharks, for example, are said to have the strongest sense of smell. Bears can detect a dead carcass some 20 miles away; elephants can detect water 30 miles away; and dogs can sniff out drugs and other items in densely packed suitcases, as well as detect illnesses in people, through their highly cultivated sense of smell. When it comes to sight, hawks can see far better than people, even though their eyes are substantially smaller than those of humans. Apparently, moths have the best sense of hearing in the world, largely as a result of having to evade their most dreaded predator, the bat. Moreover, catfish have the best sense of taste, primarily because they have more than 100,000 taste buds situated in their mouths and other parts of their bodies whereas humans have only about 10,000 taste buds.

And this isn't all. Recent research is revealing that animals have many different ways of communicating in general and communicating information related to their survival and well-being in particular. When bees leave the hive to hunt for flowers in order to extract their nectar to produce honey, they dance when they return to their hives in order to communicate this information to other bees. This tells the bees in the hive what direction to fly by following the position of the sun in the sky, how far away the flowers are from the hive, and how large the food supply is at this specific location.

Communication of this type—as well as language in general—is not restricted to bees. Every animal species has its own form of language and communication that enables members of that species to communicate with other members of the species and even members of other species on occasion. Birds, for instance, have different dialects in song that enable them to communicate information about who they are, where they are, what their territories are, whether or not they want to copulate, and a great deal else. The master at this is without doubt the mockingbird. It was made famous as the principal symbol or metaphor in Harper Lee's novel *To Kill a Mockingbird*. Interestingly, T. Gilbert Pearson called the mockingbird "the song-king of the lawn," and, as far back as 1929, the noted ornithologist E. H. Forbush wrote that the mockingbird equals and even exceeds "the whole feathered choir." These birds are renowned for their ability to mimic the sounds of dogs, cats, trucks, and people. They are said to have over 200 songs, tunes, and words in their vocabularies and repertoires, which is why their scientific name—*mimus polyglottos*—means "many-tongued mimic." This description might be contested by lyre birds and parrots: lyre birds are able to mimic the sounds of chainsaws, heavy trucks, and so forth; and parrots are able to mimic or duplicate the voices and words of human beings and even talk or sing to them on some occasions. Small wonder a bird was Mozart's favourite companion, in this case a starling that he loved and was attached to so much that he wrote a musical work—*A Musical Joke*—in its honour.

When it comes to intelligence, certain types of animals are no slouches. There are many examples of this. It is a well-known fact that chimpanzees are very smart, and why not in view of the fact that they share 98 percent of their DNA with human beings. Chimps can easily recognize and remember changing signs and flashing images on computer screens when they are taught to do so. Dolphins can identify themselves in mirrors when specific markings are made on them, which they immediately try to rub off or remove. Elephants can tell whether it is a man, woman, or child talking, and some crows, which have long been recognized as being very intelligent and incredibly creative and crafty, were able during one experiment to get a toy floating on top of the water under a tall, narrow glass by dropping pebbles into the glass until enough water was displaced that the toy rose to the top of the glass where it was quickly grabbed by the crow in its beak. But perhaps the most intelligent feat of all performed by animals may be reserved for raccoons and their ability to figure out how to open garbage cans, bins, and other containers! For years, they have been waging a war with humans and outsmarting designers by opening ever more complicated and sophisticated garbage cans, bins, and containers that have been specifically designed to keep them out.

And there is more. Much more. Modern advances in biology and zoology are revealing that animals possess many other capabilities, traits, and characteristics similar to those of human beings. These includes the capacity to experience joy, happiness, pain, sorrow, and suffering, protect their young, respect their elders, and assist other animals that have disabilities or are handicapped or distressed in some way. They also have feelings and emotions such as sympathy, empathy, love, and compassion, engage in acts of kindness, generosity, and reconciliation as well as retaliation and vengeance, make concessions and compromises, seek and extend forgiveness, and cooperate when needed. They make aesthetic judgements and choices, especially during the courting and mating season, as well as appreciate beauty and beautiful things, indulge in play and recreation, recognize and follow rules, act morally in certain situations, have memories and—consistent with the finding of Anne Dagg, Jane Goodall, and others—have personalities and personality traits much like human beings, such as agreeableness, aggression, extroversion, introversion, depression, anxiety, and self control.

It is impossible to think about the personalities of animals and their various traits and characteristics without mentioning Camille Saint-Saëns' famous musical work *Carnival of the Animals* and the wonderful description of this evocative composition and the animals in it written by Ogden Nash. While not all animal species may display human characteristics, many do. And why not? Other animals are just like people in many ways, and people like animals in numerous ways as well. If they didn't possess similar qualities, characteristics, and abilities as humans, their lives would be very different from ours, and ours from theirs. However, we are similar because humans are animals themselves—we evolved from a common ancestor we share with chimpanzees.

Much like humans, animals have many different mating customs, habits, and rituals. These can be very elaborate and even ceremonial in certain situations, extending all the way from puffing up their chests and ruffling their feathers in the case of birds to many different types of dances, hoots, and calls for other animals. Interesting, when swans court and date, they curve their necks towards each other in the shape of a heart, lift their wings, and bow, a reason why swans are regarded as genuine courtiers in the animal realm.

Just as it is for courting, dating, and mating habits, so it is for "hiving off," procreation, and sexual practices. Some animals spend their entire lives together while others only come together during mating season, some of these reuniting with the same partner year after year, others taking a new partner each year. Animals who remain together for life or rejoin the same partner every mating season include gibbons, macaroni penguins, sandhill cranes, seahorses, grey wolves, barn owls, bald eagles, beavers, and doves. Of course, sexual practices of animals vary greatly from one species to another. One of the most fascinating species in this regard is corals, which are giant colonies of very tiny creatures. Their sexual practices result from mass spawns tied to seasonally warming water and lunar cycles. They ejaculate collectively in the sense that when one ejaculates all the others follow suit immediately afterward, creating a wave-like effect similar to the types of waves in crowds that are often seen at sporting events.[3]

Similarly, how animals look after their offspring after birth can vary significantly. Animals that stay together tend to assume parental responsibilities together, except that it seems to be more commonplace among many animal species for the male to remain in the home while the female goes out foraging for food. Interestingly, this seems to be happening more frequently in the human domain as well in recent years, due to all the changes that have occurred in the workforce and the fact that more women are now working outside the home.

In a study conducted recently by Paul Zak at Claremont Graduate University, it was found that the feeling of attachment can be very strong in animals, in much the same way as it is for human beings. According to Zak, the hormone oxytocin is as strong a bonding agent in other animals' relationships as it is for humans, and "animals are capable of falling in love the same way humans are." And much like humans, this love can extend well beyond one's own species to members of other species. There are numerous cases of an animal of one species becoming strongly attached to a member of a different species. Moreover, everyone knows that humans have great affection and an incredible amount of love for their pets and these pets have an incredible amount of love and affection for their owners as well. This may be especially true for dogs and dog owners. Many dogs have lamented the loss of their owners for a very long time after their deaths and have gone to the grave sites of their owners every day for years and sometimes for decades to show their love, affection, devotion, and remorse. The same is true for animal owners, who often show the same feelings and emotions when they lose their cherished pets. It often takes years to recover from tragedies such as this if at all.

Given all the individual traits, attributes, and capabilities of animals, it is not surprising that animals and animal species have culture and create cultures much like humans. In addition, their culture and cultures can be highly developed and very sophisticated wholes or total ways of life. Take the culture of elephants as a well-known example of this. Elephants have been known and appreciated for centuries for their symbolism in the human domain, and are greatly admired for such qualities as sensitivity, wisdom, stability, loyalty, intelligence, reliability, peacefulness, and determination. Often called "gentle giants," these remarkable animals show a great deal of affection, care, and compassion towards each other, including toward their offspring and elders, thereby acting as excellent role models for other animals and humans, too. Not only do elephants bond with each other in much the same way that human beings bond, but also they are each other's keepers. They are very attentive when other elephants are sick, elderly, in distress, or threatened in some way. They also form circles to protect themselves from other animals when they are being attacked, just as humans "circle the wagons" and "have each others' backs."

Elephants also look after their young in much the same way that humans do, often doting over them and actively participating in their upbringing, education, and development. It is not surprising in this regard that mother elephants and their children often live together for decades. Elephants mourn the deaths of loved ones, return to the bodies and bones of deceased elephants, and often leave sticks, stones, or leaves on their grave sites. Perhaps more than any other group of animals, elephants have many different ways of communicating, such as trumpeting and creating low and deep sounds that cannot be detected by humans. They also have many different types of gestures, taps, nudges, kicks, grunts, the caressing of trunks, the flapping of ears, and a variety of head movements to convey their feelings. Living in groups of up to 400 members, they can be very sensitive as well, consoling other elephants in distress by sticking close together and putting their trunks in the mouths of other elephants as a sign of friendship, love, trust, companionship, and devotion.

This contrasts sharply with the culture of meerkats, who gorge themselves during mating season in order to be and remain dominant. While they live in one of the animal kingdom's most cooperative cultures, the offspring of meerkats are usually raised communally rather than by a single mother (as is the case with elephants and most other animal species), since only one "alpha pair" of parents is permitted to breed. This makes the competition for alpha status fierce, often causing the dominant females to eat the siblings of other meerkats in order to ensure that only their own descendants survive. They may also exile offending meerkats from their colony. Since only the largest and heaviest female meerkats have the right to reproduce, all other meerkats must resign themselves to spending their lifetimes as babysitters since the alpha mothers may give birth to as many as fifty babies during their lives. This seems a much better system of reproduction, however, than is employed by guinea hens, mother pandas, and African black eagles, which are known to eat some of their siblings, or permit their healthier siblings to feed on less physically endowed and weaker ones in order to survive. They also kick some siblings out of their homes if they are not likely to make it in the "dog eat dog" world of animal survival.

Another good example of animal culture and cultures, and one that has always generated a remarkable amount of interest, curiosity, fascination, and attention among humans, involves wolves. In many ways, it bears the closest resemblance to human culture and cultures. Wolves also have well-organized social structures, obey strict rules of conduct and behaviour, and are playful when they are well-fed but ferocious and vicious when they are hungry. They live in packs ranging from two to 36, usually averaging about six per pack, which consists generally of a single family with possibly one or two additional members. The one exception to this general rule is the lone wolf, which decides to go it alone.

Wolf packs generally consist of an alpha male and alpha female, usually the father and mother, but not always the strongest male and female in the pack. Siblings and offspring are organized and ranked in descending order of importance as far as the pack is concerned, and especially in terms of hunting and attacking other packs or animals. This includes beta members—next in line in the hierarchy to the alpha male and alpha female—and zeta members, who are usually the "war generals" of the pack and organize an attack after the alpha male or alpha female has provided the plan and gives the command. Interestingly, the rank of wolves in the pack is often revealed through how they hold their tails. If their tails are held high, they are usually alpha wolves; if the hold their tails lower or halfway down, they are likely to be in the middle of the pack; and if they hold their tails between their legs or drag them on the ground, they are likely to be the lowest members in the pack.

Recent research into wolf packs has revealed that older wolves often share their knowledge, experience, and hunting strategies and techniques with younger wolves, maintain lifelong friendships and bonds with them, and often pass on special cultural habits, characteristics, and secrets from one generation to the next, thereby creating a cultural legacy or heritage for the pack that is not unlike the cultural legacies and heritages of human beings. Moreover, what neighbourhoods, communities, legacies, and heritages are to humans is also true for wolves. It is matters like this that caused Rudyard Kipling to claim that "the strength of the pack is the wolf, and the strength of the wolf is the pack."

This is by no means the end of the story, or why wolves and wolf packs are especially captivating for human beings. In recent years, there has been a tendency in the world and especially in some Asian countries to talk about "wolf cultures" and "lamb cultures," as well as to compare and contrast these two cultures in business circles, corporations, politics, and diplomatic affairs. The wolf culture is usually depicted as using any means possible to achieve a specified goal, disregarding or setting aside ethics and morality in order to achieve it, eliminate competitors, and reign supreme. Many of these characteristics were set out in a book called *Wolf Totem* and an eight-disc DVD set called *Wolf-like Managers* that were and still are extremely popular, especially in China.

This is often contrasted with lambs and the "lamb culture." Whereas wolves and the wolf culture represent ruthlessness, lambs and the lamb culture represent kindness, meekness, gentleness, obedience, trust, serenity, and goodness. These dichotomous and very different types of animal cultures are sometimes used to describe or advocate for different forms of behaviour among humans, especially corporations and business but also governments and entire countries. In order to even odds between these two very distinct types of behaviour and cultures, some people contend that while the wolf culture might be more successful *in the short run* in business and government, the lamb culture might be most successful *in the long run*. However, the problem here, as John Maynard Keynes, the British economist, pointed out many years ago, is that "in the long run we are all dead!"

Finally, and perhaps most interesting of all in terms of animals' abilities that have a great relevance for human beings and their development, is the capacity that some sea creatures have to regrow hearts and even whole new bodies, just as some lizards can lose their tails to get away from predators when necessary.[4] When sea creatures eat a certain type of algae, they can photosynthesize their food from oxygen and sunlight, much like plants do. This "regenerative capacity," which makes it possible for some sea creatures to create new organs, may perform a very valuable function in the future by enhancing our knowledge of how the molecular mechanisms in human cells and tissues can be used to repair damage to certain organs or possibly even replace them.

One person who has done a great deal of empirical research on animals and especially the similarities and differences between animals and humans in general—and animal brains, behaviour, characteristics, traits, capabilities, and cultures in particular—is Georges Chapouthier, a neuroscientist, philosopher, and emeritus research director at the French National Centre for Scientific Research (CNRS). According to Chapouthier, most of the differences between human beings and animals can be explained by differences in the size, strength, and capabilities of their brains. Since humans have more powerful brains than other animals, they are able to create and produce many more sophisticated things and deal with more complex problems and situational difficulties.

This is particularly evident in the ability human beings have to create "super tools" such as computers and complicated machines and technological devices that are becoming more and more complex and sophisticated all the time. It is also evident in the development of languages and techniques that enable people to transmit information from one person or group to another, one generation or century to the next, and one country or part of the world to others. Humans also possess the ability to be inventive and innovative, the capacity to discuss ethics, morality, ideas, and philosophy, and the capacity to have visions and discuss these visions with other people as well as to create highly complex works of art, science, and scholarship, and a great deal else. Chapouthier believes the gap between other animals' and humans' brain capabilities is widening rapidly and will probably widen even more in the future.

Nevertheless, there is a great deal to be learned from animals and animal behaviour as well as their cultures and ways of life. As Frans de Wahl said in his book *Are We Smart Enough to Know How Smart Animals Are?*:

> Animals should be given a chance to express their natural behaviour. We are developing a greater interest in their variable lifestyles. Our challenge is to think more like them, so we can open up our minds to their specific circumstances and goals and observe and understand them *on their own terms.*[5]

This is true for plants as well, although perhaps not to the same extent or on the same scale. Plants are also living organisms and as such they share many needs and wants in common with humans and other animals, such as the need for food, water, air, sunlight, and other nutrients. They share life stages and processes like birth, development, and death, consumption and elimination, the ability to communicate with one another, and a great deal else with other living beings. In fact, recent research is revealing that the gap between plants and animals (including humans) is not as great as was once assumed.

Nevertheless, there are some basic differences between plants and animals. Plants are able to create their own food using water, sunlight, and carbon dioxide through a process called photosynthesis, while animals must eat other animals or plants to survive. There is another key difference between plants and animals that turns out to be a real advantage for animals and disadvantage for plants. Since animals have specialized nervous and muscular systems, most of them are able to move and travel from place and place. Lacking this ability, plants are confined to a specific location. As a result, animals can flee when they are in danger or are attacked, whereas plants remain in one place.

Despite these differences, do plants experience pleasure, pain, emotions, love, and affection much as animals and humans can? In his book *The Secret Lives of Plants,* Cleve Backster claims that some of these things can be experienced by plants, although this has been disputed by many natural scientists. All the same, Susan Dudley, a professor of biology at McMaster University in Hamilton, Ontario, did recently discover that plants prefer to be near their offspring rather than other plants that are not related to them. She concluded that "the ability to recognize and favour kin is common in animals, but this is the first time it has been shown to exist in plants." Her research on this matter revealed that plants become competitive when they share pots with other types of plants by growing more roots that enable them to suck up more moisture and mineral ingredients. However, they don't do this when they are sharing pots with members of their own species or family.

Then there are trees. They are undoubtedly in a class by themselves. In their book *Tree Cultures: The Place of Trees and Trees in Their Place*, authors Paul Cloke and Owain Jones confirm the fact that trees have many practical uses as well as an incredible amount of symbolic significance. Not only do trees provide us with wood, bark, fruit, and other types of materials and ingredients that are required to create specific types of products and certain kinds of chemicals, but they also draw carbon dioxide out of the air and consequently are one of the best assets of all in fighting climate change.

Trees have served as cultural symbols for centuries. There are many examples of this, such as maple trees in Canadian history and culture, as well as the "mighty oak" in British history, culture, and folklore. Among other things, the ancient Druids in England worshipped oak trees and groves, as well as burning yule logs made of oak at the time of the winter solstice. Moreover, many people have carried the fruit of the oak tree—acorns—with them for good luck and good health for centuries; "Heart of Oak" is the official march of the Royal Navy; and the composer Charles Dibdin wrote a piece about the oak as "England's Tree of Liberty" in 1795. To this list should be added fig tress, which are cherished in African culture and history. This fact came to light recently when a revered 100-year-old, four-storey-high fig tree situated in a prominent square in Nairobi, Kenya was saved after it was about to be chopped down and removed to make way for the construction of a superhighway. Protestors reacted so vigorously and forcefully to this that the president of Kenya, Uhura Kenyatta, was compelled to step in and to save this special tree by declaring that it is a real "beacon of Kenya's cultural and ecological heritage."

And this is not all. Peter Wohlleben, who has spent the bulk of his life studying tress in general and forests in particular, revealed recently that decades of empirical research show that trees like to stand close together, enjoy each other's company, feel pain, have emotions, and experience "fear." In his recently published book *The Hidden Life of Trees*, Wohlleben states that there is a great deal of friendship among trees. They can "bond like an old couple, where one looks after the other," are not competitive, are incredibly social, and have memories. Trees also exchange a great deal of chemical information, not only among their own types but also among other types of trees as well as other plants and shrubs. When dangers occur or they are threatened by other species, some trees will immediately alert other trees, shrubs, and plants in the vicinity to this threat through the sense of smell, primarily by emitting volatile and often bitter organic compounds which boost the tannin levels in their trunks, branches, and leaves.

This makes them less attractive to animals and herbivores as well as alerting other plants in the area.

Trees also create cultures, especially when they grow close together and interact constantly with each other through their root systems. This is especially true in forests, where submerged underground exist massive root systems not unlike icebergs in the ocean. As Wohlleben explains in his book:

> If you look at roadside embankments, you might be able to see how trees connect with each other through their root systems. On these slopes, rain often washes away the soil, leaving the underground networks exposed. Scientists in the Harz mountains in Germany have discovered that this really is a case of interdependence, and most individual trees of the same species growing in the same stand are connected to each other through their root systems. It appears that nutrient exchange and helping neighbors in times of need is the rule, and this leads to the conclusion that forests are superorganisms with interconnections much like ant colonies.[6]

The roots systems of trees are really quite remarkable. They are not unlike cultures in many ways because they are composed of many elements that are constantly interacting with each other and impinging on one another. Tim Flannery, in the introduction to Wohlleben's book, writes:

> A tree's most important means of staying connected to other trees is a "*wood wide web*" (this is a phrase created by Suzanne Simard, a forest ecology professor at the University of British Columbia in Canada in talking about the "language of trees") of soil fungi that connects vegetation in an intimate network that allows the sharing of an enormous amount of information and goods. Scientific research aimed at understanding the astonishing abilities of this partnership between fungi and plant has only just begun.[7]

The fact that trees and other plants share much in common with human beings and can create cultures and benefit from them in much the same way is exceedingly important, especially as far as the future of humanity and life in general is concerned. Unlike many other disciplines that are focused primarily or entirely on human beings and their cultures, the biological manifestation of culture does not confine culture to the human realm but includes many other types of living organisms as well.

There is no doubt that this is one of culture's greatest assets and foremost capabilities. Culture is both partial and holistic because it is perceived and defined in many different ways and not just in one way. This makes it possible for culture to move backward and forward as well as horizontally and vertically across a vast array of different disciplines and diverse fields.

As a result, culture is an ideal discipline in coming to grips with climate change, global warming, and the environmental crisis since it encompasses all these different areas. We urgently need an activity or discipline of this type if we are to be successful in preserving the natural environment, protecting the biosphere and vulnerable ecosystems, improving the well-being of humans and other species, achieving sustainable, self-sustaining, and regenerative development, dealing effectively with infectious diseases, and overcoming the biggest threat to humanity and the planet of all, namely a universal environmental catastrophe.

Frans de Waal summed this up best when he said:

> Instead of making humanity the measure of all things, we need to evaluate other species by what *they* are. In so doing, I am sure we will discover many magic wells, including some as yet beyond our imagination.[8]

Perhaps this is what caused Alfred Kroeber and Clyde Kluckhohn to highlight the centrality and quintessential importance of culture and its remarkable potential in both the human and natural realms:

> Culture constitutes the topmost phenomenal level yet recognized—or for that matter, now imaginable—in the realm of nature. This of course does not compel the prediction that

> emergence into our consciousness of a new and higher plane is precluded.[9]

Whether this new and higher plane ever emerges, there is no doubt that the biological manifestation of culture possesses a remarkable potential to contribute to the world of the future in all areas of life and among all the different species in the world.

Chapter Ten

Interactions with the Natural Environment

> The major problems in the world are the result of differences between how nature works and how we think.
>
> —Gregory Bateson[1]

If over the past seven or eight decades a profound transformation has taken place in the world from seeing the whole in terms of the human species to seeing the whole in terms of all the different species that exist in the world, this is now accompanied by an even larger transformation—one that sees the whole in terms of all the interactions that go on every second of every day between *everything* that exists in the natural world. This is often described as the *ecological manifestation of culture.*

This transformation might have occurred much sooner had anthropology and anthropologists focused more attention on the role that the natural environment and other species play in the idea and reality of culture. However, anthropology as a discipline was defined largely in terms of human beings and their cultures, so this did not occur. This problem was compounded by the fact that most anthropologists directed the bulk of their attention to the study of "culture traits" rather than the study of culture and cultures as complex wholes or total ways of life, as Ruth Benedict pointed out in her book *Patterns of Culture*:

> Anthropological work has been overwhelmingly devoted to the analysis of culture traits, however, rather than to the study of cultures as articulated wholes. This has been due in great measure to the nature of earlier ethnological descriptions.[2]

One of the first individuals to demonstrate a keen interest in the ecological way of perceiving and understanding culture was Gregory Bateson. He was viewed by many in the anthropological domain as a renegade because his thoughts and ideas roamed far and wide across many different disciplines including psychiatry, philosophy, cybernetics, and epistemology, in addition to anthropology. Despite this, Bateson was keenly interested in—and very committed to and concerned about—the relationship between nature, the natural environment, other species, culture, cultures, the human species, and especially the character and functioning of the human mind. His interest in these matters was set out in two of his most important books—*Steps to an Ecology of Mind* and *Mind and Nature: A Necessary Unity*—that were published in the 1970s.

With the passage of time, it became evident that Bateson had made major contributions not only to the development of ecology as a discipline but also to the creation of what is now called the "information era," what is known in psychiatry as the "double bind" theory of schizophrenia, and epistemology. He also contributed a great deal to postmodernist thought, primarily by writing about the human mind as a major factor in the development of culture, cultures, and ecology. We have Bateson to thank as well for such phrases as "all experience is subjective," which in many ways lies at the heart of the postmodernist movement.

Bateson's contributions, the development of ecology as an academic discipline, and the rise of the environmental movement led to the emergence of the concept of *ecological culture*. Many believe the origins of this idea can be traced back to 1984, when a number of Soviet environmental experts proposed the term for the first time in an article titled "Ways of Fostering Ecological Culture in Individuals under the Conditions of Mature Socialism" that was published in the second volume of *Scientific Communism* in Moscow. Interestingly, a summary of this article was published in a Chinese newspaper, the *Guangming Daily*, where the term "ecological *culture*" was translated into Chinese as "ecological *civilization*" because the Chinese didn't have a comparable word for "culture." However, some scholars maintain that this is not really the same thing as ecological culture because the word "civilization" is more confined in scope and implies a more advanced state of affairs than the term culture.

In 1987, the concept of an ecological civilization was picked up and promoted in earnest in China by Ye Quianji, an agricultural economist. It was promoted even more forcefully by Pan Yue, deputy vice minister of the China State Environmental Protection Administration (SEPA) when he recommended a comprehensive and sustainable change in politics, economics, society, culture, and theory as a way of bringing about a major transformation in civilization. Then, in 2007, the idea of an ecological civilization was raised for the first time in the political domain at the 17th National Party Congress in China. This indicated that this idea was going to be incorporated into the political, developmental, and diplomatic activities and plans of the Chinese government and China as a country. This caused what was called "ecologically civilized development" to be taken more seriously as a means of integrating ecology into China's economic development plans and policies so that environmental conservation, the creation of a low-carbon economy, and the like could take on a higher priority. This idea of an ecological civilization was also promoted in China and among Chinese scholars and diplomats about this time, if not before, by Roy Morrison, an American ecologist, as well by Arran Gare, who defended the idea of an ecological civilization as the ultimate goal for humanity in his book *The Philosophical Foundations of Ecological Civilization: A Manifesto for the Future* (2016).

These developments received a far more powerful endorsement a year later when Xi Jinping, president of China, addressed the 19th National Congress of the Communist Party in Beijing in October 2017. He stated that "what we are doing today" was not just talking about an ecological civilization but building "an ecological civilization that will benefit generations to come." This idea was not confined to China but included other countries as well, as Jinping made apparent in his address in the following statement: "Taking a driving seat in international cooperation to respond to climate change, China has become an important participant, contributor, and torchbearer in the global endeavor for ecological civilization." As a result, China is now seen by many as the first country in the world to officially endorse the idea of an ecological civilization, as well as to commit to a national developmental plan, policy, and strategy predicated on this idea.

Like many developments in the world, China's commitment to an ecological civilization—as well as the commitment of other countries to this idea—had a number of important antecedents and can be traced back to earlier developments on the ecological and environmental front. One of the earliest and most influential of these developments was the publication of Rachel Carson's book *Silent Spring* in 1962. In this book, Carson brought the ecological devastation that was going on in the world to widespread attention through her research and writing on the deadly effects of pesticides and other chemicals generated by industry. Her book helped to activate and accelerate the environmental movement.

Also making an important contribution was Eugene Odum, who is considered by many to be the founder of the discipline of ecology because of the courses he created and taught on these subjects and the pioneering book he co-authored with his brother Howard, *Fundamentals of Ecology*, published in 1953.

As a result of the contributions of Odum, Carson, and many others, countless studies have since been undertaken throughout the world that are concerned with the adverse effects people and their lifestyles, behaviour, and ways of life have on the natural environment. These studies fuelled a growing realization that things could not go on as they had in the past. It was rapidly becoming apparent that a basic paradigm shift was needed in the world from *unsustainable* to *sustainable* development. Like the idea of an ecological civilization, the idea of sustainable development was based on the belief that the natural environment and the needs of future generations—and not just the present generation and its needs—must be taken into account in all present and future developments, plans, policies, and decision-making processes. In order to do this, it was mandatory to undertake environmental assessments of all major development and construction projects, as well as to realize an effective balance and harmony between human beings and the natural environment—a balance and harmony that had been badly needed but lacking in the world for a long time. For that matter, it is still lacking today.

Action on these concerns by governments and international organizations can be traced back to the creation of the United Nations Environmental Programme in 1972, the United Nations World Commission on Environment and Development (also known as the Brundtland Commission) from 1983 to 1987—where the idea of sustainable development was introduced for the first time—and the United Nations Conference on Environment and Development in Rio de Janeiro in 1992. These initiatives helped to open the doors to the acceptance of such ideas as an ecological culture and an ecological civilization.

It was about this same time that the idea of the *ecological footprint* made its appearance on the world scene. This concept was designed to illustrate the fact that human beings were making colossal and rapidly escalating demands on the natural environment in countless ways. The importance, implications, and consequences of this were seen several decades ago by two highly creative scholars from the University of British Columbia—William Rees and Mathis Wackernagel—who first developed the idea. This concept, since adopted, adapted, and refined by many scholars, environmental and ecological organizations, governmental departments, and international agencies, is designed to show in concrete, measurable, and practical terms how much of the natural environment and world's scarce resources are required to support human beings and their material habits, needs, lifestyles, behaviours, and ways of life.

In individual terms, every person makes demands on the natural environment and nature's scarce resources due to their need for food, clothing, shelter, transportation, and the fulfillment of many other wants and needs. In addition, every person returns large amounts of garbage and waste to the natural environment. And what is true in individual terms is also true in collective terms. All people and countries in the world impose their ecological footprint on the natural environment by consuming natural resources on the one hand and emitting pollutants on the other.

It was but a short step from this to the creation and development of forms of measurement that could determine with great scientific accuracy and statistical precision the actual ecological footprint of individuals, towns, cities, regions, and countries. The footprint of individuals, for instance, is determined by calculating the land mass that is needed in a number of different categories to support people's level of consumption with existing technologies. This varies substantially from individual to individual, country to country, and one part of the world to another depending on a variety of factors, such as people's standard of living and quality of life, the demands and severity of the different seasons of the year, energy requirements to meet such needs as heating, lighting, air conditioning, transportation, and communications, and so on. It was estimated some time ago that the planet would have to be many times larger than it actually is were the entire population of the world to have the same ecological footprint as the wealthiest nations.

It was not long after this that scientists began to develop more sophisticated and specific types of footprints—such as "carbon footprints"—that are designed to ascertain the impact that human beings are having on specific aspects of the environment, such as climate change. In recent years, this has led to numerous studies that document in considerable detail the rapid deterioration of the natural environment. Research indicates that humanity is so far losing the battle against global warming. And this is not the only dimension of the environmental crisis. Resources and basic foodstuffs are being consumed at a phenomenal rate, other species are disappearing at a rate that is a thousand times greater than the natural rate of extinction, and the increase in average global temperature threatens to exceed the 1.5 degree Celsius limit that was agreed to by participants in the 2015 Paris Agreement. This is now an acute, urgent, and life-threatening problem, one which will only get much worse if more is not done.

Most scientists and ecologists agree that humanity is rapidly running out of time to make the changes that are imperative. With the world's population reaching eight billion and still growing, there are in the future bound to be many more shortages of natural resources, basic foodstuffs, and other necessities of life.

A completely different type of relationship is required between human beings and the natural environment if this looming catastrophe is to be avoided. This relationship must be based on creating a great deal more consciousness and comprehension of the importance of the natural environment. This relationship must be based on the fact that we simply can't live without the natural environment.

Creating such a relationship will not be easy. In fact, it will probably be the most difficult task humanity has ever faced. Compounding the difficulty is the fact that people are rapidly losing contact with nature as a result of urbanization as well as advances in technology. With about 56 percent of the world's population now living in urban areas, it is going to take a quantum leap in the right direction for people to be conscious of the crucial importance of the natural environment.

There are many ways in which expanding and enhancing human consciousness of the natural environment can be realized. This requires making concerted attempts at every conceivable opportunity to connect with nature, whether by taking long walks on nature trails and in forests as well as in parks, conservation centres, and wilderness areas, driving or cycling through the countryside on a regular basis, taking eco-holidays of one type or another if possible, and keeping informed about developments with respect to the environmental crisis. It also means being sensitive to the state of natural habitats and cherished ecosystems, enjoying plants, flowers, trees, and shrubs, digging in the earth and savouring the feel of the soil, creating vegetable gardens, planting and pruning trees, adopting and looking after animals and pets, landscaping, beautifying homes, towns, cities, and rural areas, and a great deal else.

Since many people may be doing some or most of these things already, what is most essential is increasing the frequency of these things and intensifying involvement in them. While this is not a sufficient solution to this problem, it is a necessary step in the right direction because it increases our interaction with the natural environment and other species in positive rather than negative ways and does so on a sustained basis.

To progress further in this area, it is helpful to turn our attention to the arts, artists, and arts organizations. This is because, as Gregory Bateson observed, "When we find meaning in art, our thinking is most in sync with nature."[3] This explains why so many artistic works are concerned with nature, as well as how understanding and awareness of nature can be enhanced by the arts. As Marc Chagall put it, "Great art picks up where nature ends."

Music is undoubtedly one of the most effective ways of connecting with and appreciating nature and providing profound insights into nature's diverse elements and manifestations in one form or another. In the western musical tradition alone, think, for instance, of Richard Strauss's *Sunrise Prelude* from *Also Sprach Zarathustra*, Dvořák's *Song to the Moon*, Debussy's *Clair de Lune*, Hildegard of Bingen's *Symphonia armonie celestium Revelationum* (*Symphony of the Harmony of Heavenly Revelations* or *Celestial Harmonies*), Britten's *Four Sea Interludes*, Wagner's *Forest Murmurs*, Hovhaness' *Mysterious Mountain* symphony (*Symphony No. 2*), and countless others. Not only are these works exceedingly beautiful, but also they convey a great deal about the natural environment in a multitude of different ways.

The seasons figure prominently in this. Many composers have written music about spring, summer, fall, and winter, such as Haydn, Glazunov, and most notably Vivaldi and his remarkable work *The Four Seasons*. This piece conveys the sense of excitement, renewal, and revitalization that is experienced at the first signs of spring, the scorching and torrid heat of the summer, the beauty, elegance, and nostalgia of fall with its exquisite colours, falling leaves, and pungent aromas, and the harshness and cruelty of winter with its ice, snow, and bone-chilling cold.

Like the seasons, rivers have also been a favourite subject of composers for centuries. This is because rivers involve water, flow, and movement, which are all crucial elements in nature and the life process. Some of the most obvious examples are Handel's *Water Music* and Telemann's *Wassermusik*, Smetana's *The Moldau*, Johann Strauss II's *The Blue Danube*, Peter Boyer's *Rolling River*—a series of sketches dealing with the beloved Shenandoah River in the United States—as well as Henry Mancini and Johnny Mercer's *Moon River*, Yin Chengzong and Chu Wanghua's *Yellow River Piano Concerto* based on Xian Xinghai's *Yellow River Cantata*, and Robert Burns and Jonathan Spilman's *Flow Gently, Sweet Afton* with its captivating melody and enticing lyrics.

What is true for composers and music is also true for visual artists and painting. The Impressionist painters in France play a dominant role in this. Not only were they interested in painting nature outdoors in all its different moods, manifestations, and transformations, but they portrayed nature in a way that helped people gain a clearer and more profound sense of gratitude, respect, and appreciation for nature and all its multifarious elements. This is true regardless of whether we are thinking of the works of Édouard Manet, Pierre-Auguste Renoir, Alfred Sisley, Paul Cézanne, Camille Pissarro, or many others.

Claude Monet and Vincent van Gogh were undoubtedly the masters at this. Beginning with *Impression, Sunrise* (1872), Monet showed a remarkable penchant for depicting the natural world. His favourite subject was water lilies. He painted them countless times, especially those in his garden in Giverny, France. Particularly important in this regard are his huge murals of water lilies that grace the walls of the Musée de l'Orangerie in the Tuileries Gardens in Paris. Like Monet, van Gogh also painted numerous nature scenes, many of them outdoors in the south of France. Included among his many "nature paintings" are *Wheat Field with a Lark*; *Orchard in Blossom; The Pink Peach Tree*; *Almond Blossoms*; *Irises*; and *Starry Night over the Rhone*. Nature figures prominently in most of van Gogh's artistic masterpieces and tends to take precedence over everything else.

Of course, interest in nature and the natural environment is by no means limited to western artists, the western world, or the western artistic tradition. Brush painters in China, Japan, and many other parts of Asia and elsewhere in the world have also been captivated by nature for centuries. Indeed, brush painting has been practised in China for more than a thousand years. Is it any wonder that the Chinese have a special affinity for birds, horses, fish, flowers, mountains, lakes, rivers, trees, and plants such as the lotus and the bamboo, since these things are depicted prominently in Chinese brush painting as well as in other areas of Chinese cultural life? W. Scott Morton emphasized this point when talking about the keen interest Chinese brush painters have always had in nature and its diverse elements in his book *China: Its History and Culture:*

> Nature in her various moods of sunshine and mist, in the changing seasons, in the balance of high mountains and low water-courses, not only solaced and uplifted the spirit of the artist but appealed to his mind as a clue to the harmonious

> working of the universe, its *dao* or Way.... Landscape painting was thus the grandest and most satisfying way to represent Nature as a whole, to feel a sense of communion with Nature and know oneself to be part of an orderly cosmos.[4]

Countless poets have also been interested in nature for centuries. Poets in England and the United States were writing poems about nature at about the same time that the Impressionist painters were producing nature paintings that stood head and shoulders above the rest. This is especially true in England, where poets such as Blake, Coleridge, Keats, Wordsworth, Byron, and Shelley were reacting strongly to the Enlightenment and especially the Industrial Revolution by emphasizing intuition over reason and the pastoral and rural over the technological and urban. They were interested in nature because it was "spontaneous," "real," and "authentic" whereas human creations were "planned, "deliberate," and "devised." As a result, nature figures prominently in many of their poems, such as Shelley's *Ode to the West Wind*, Keats' *Ode to a Nightingale*, Blake's *The Lily*, and Coleridge's *On Nature*.

Leading the way in the United States in writing about nature were Ralph Waldo Emerson, Henry David Thoreau, Walt Whitman, James Fennimore Cooper, and especially Emily Dickinson, who was better known as a gardener than a poet during her life. Dickinson wrote numerous "nature poems" about her gardens and gardening, such as *My Garden, Like the Beach*; *May-Flower*; *The Bee Is Not Afraid*; *The Grass*; *The Sea of Sunset*; and *Purple Clover*.

Interestingly, poets have had a fascination with trees in much the same way that composers have had a fascination with rivers. This is especially true for poets such as Robert Frost and William Butler Yeats, as Frost's *The Sound of Trees*, *Birches*, *Tree at my Window*, and *On a Tree Fallen across the Road,* as well as Yeats' *The Two Trees* reveal. But the most famous poem ever written about trees is undoubtedly the one written by Alfred Joyce Kilmer and simply called *Trees*. It was written in 1913 and published in a collection titled *Trees and Other Poems* in 1914. In it, Kilmer reveals his strong commitment to the beauty of nature in general and trees in particular. His deep religious faith and convictions are revealed in this venerated and oft-quoted poem:

I think that I shall never see
A poem as lovely as a tree.

A tree whose hungry mouth is prest
Against the earth's sweet flowing breast;

A tree that looks at God all day,
And lifts her leafy arms to pray;

A tree that may in Summer wear
A nest of robins in her hair;

Upon whose bosom snow has lain;
Who intimately lives with rain.

Poems are made by fools like me,
But only God can make a tree.

This poem was so popular that Oscar Rasbach set it to music in 1922, and a number of other composers followed suit shortly thereafter. Its popularity grew rapidly after this, especially when it was sung by such world-famous singers as Nelson Eddy, Robert Merrill, and Paul Robeson in the 1940s and 1950s. What makes this poem so noteworthy today is the fact that trees play an essential role in taking toxins out of the air; small wonder many organizations and countries in the world have been planting millions of trees in recent years.

Animals and their behaviour are another favourite subject for artists. The best-known example of this in a musical sense is obviously the *Carnival of the Animals* composed by Camille Saint-Saëns. This piece was written in 1886 but not performed in public until after Saint-Saëns' death in 1922 because he didn't want it to spoil his reputation as a serious composer.

Despite this, it is a legendary composition that includes a parade of animals not unlike that which entered Noah's Ark. It commences with lions, hens, roosters, wild asses, tortoises, kangaroos, and an elephant, and concludes with fish, donkeys, a cuckoo, other birds, fossils, a swan, and a grand finale when all the different animals "strut their stuff." What is particularly clever about this masterpiece is the way all the different animals are depicted in musical terms as well as how specific characteristics and personality traits are accorded to them, many of which are extremely funny in addition to being exceptionally beautiful. Saint-Saëns played these characteristics and personality traits up to the hilt, such as the slow and cumbersome gait of the elephant and the smooth and graceful glide of the swan; the latter is without doubt one of the most beautiful pieces of music ever written in general and about animals in particular

Other musical works in the western tradition concerned with animals include Ralph Vaughan Williams' *The Lark Ascending*, Stravinsky's *Firebird Suite*, Bach's *Sheep May Safely Graze*, Schubert's *Trout Quintet*, Prokofiev's *Peter and the Wolf*, Ravel's *Mother Goose* suite, Rimsky-Korsakov's *The Flight of the Bumblebee*, and many others. Numerous composers have also been fascinated with birds and bird calls, which figure prominently in works such as Janequin's *Le Chant des Oiseaux* (*Song of the Birds*), Handel's *The Cuckoo and the Nightingale*, Messiaen's *Oiseaux Exotiques* (*Exotic Birds*), Tailleferre's *Le Marchand d'oiseaux* (Bird Trader), Vivaldi's *Il Gardellino*, and Mozart's tribute to his pet starling. If you listen to the way starlings mimic sounds—often slightly off key and usually in a rather repetitious manner—it is understandable why Mozart had his pet starling in mind when he wrote this tribute, since it is frequently off key and Mozart often whistled, sang, and hummed while he wrote music.

Interestingly, compositions with songbirds in them are the norm rather than the exception in traditional Afghan music. Moreover, the singing of birds is considered a "musical culture" in Sufism and mystical Islam because every tweet and twitter sounds like one of Allah's sacred names. Italy's Ottorino Respighi and Enrico Toselli were also fascinated with birds: Respighi wrote a popular piece called *The Birds* (*Gli Uccelli*); and Toselli wrote an equally popular composition called *Nightingale Serenade*, made popular by André Rieu.

Artistic depiction of animals is not confined to music. Far from it. It is also evident of this in the visual arts. The most obvious examples are likely Salvador Dali's *The Elephants*, Albrecht Dürer's *Young Hare*, Henri Rousseau's *Surprised! (Tiger in a Tropical Storm)*, Andy Warhol's *Cow*, Ai Weiwei's *Circle of Animals/Zodiac Heads*, and many others.

Flowers are also popular subjects for both composers and painters. Think, for instance, of Johann Strauss II's *Roses from the South Waltz*, Rodgers and Hammerstein's *Edelweiss*, Edward Macdowell's *To a Wild Rose*, Bizet's *Flower Song* from *Carmen*, Fauré's *Les Roses d'Ispahan*, and Delibes' *Flower Duet* from *Lakmé*. Famous paintings in this vein include van Gogh's Sunflower series, Hiroshige's *Hibiscus*, Mondrian's *Amaryllis*, and Georgia O'Keeffe's more than two hundred large-sized paintings of flowers.

While the remarkable role the arts and artists play in expanding our knowledge, understanding, appreciation, and consciousness of nature and its many diverse elements is exceedingly important, they perform many other roles as well. For instance, the arts provide an ideal model for resource and environmental conservation. Unlike many other activities, the arts do not make excessive demands on nature and its resources. Artistic work is largely labour-intensive rather than capital- or material-intensive. Apart from the need for basic supplies—paints, brushes, easels, and paper for painters, stone, wood, metal, and other materials for carvers and sculptors, clay and kilns for potters, musical instruments and score paper for musicians and composers, and sets and props for actors, actresses, singers, and dancers—artists and arts organizations do not make unreasonable demands on nature's precious resource legacy. Even opera, which is the most expensive and elaborate art form of all as far as the need for resources is concerned, requires far fewer resources than industrial, manufacturing, technological, and commercial activities.

This fact has powerful implications. The more we engage in the arts and artistic activities, the less damage we do to the natural environment. This is why Tibor Scitovsky, a well-known economist, wrote *The Joyless Economy*, and B. F. Skinner, a celebrated psychologist, wrote *Walden II*. Both authors viewed involvement in the arts as a way to conserve rather than consume resources, as well as produce much more fulfillment, happiness, and contentment in life. Perhaps this is why John Muir, generally regarded as the principal founder of the national park movement in the United States, said, "It's into the forest I go, to lose my mind and find my soul."

In recent years, artists have become much more interested in nature, presumably because of the environmental crisis. This has given rise to what are increasingly being called *environmental art* and *environmental artists*—art and artists deriving inspiration, motivation, and satisfaction from nature, with many works produced outdoors in natural settings. Open-air concerts and festivals, outdoor painting and sketching, murals on the sides of buildings, sculptural pieces in parks, and performances on lakes or beside rivers as well as in mountainous areas and forests embellish and consecrate the communion and connection that exist among nature, people, and the arts. When works of art are brought together with the best nature provides, the results can be and often are sublime.

A good example of this are the artistic compositions of R. Murray Schafer, a Canadian composer deemed by many an environmental artist first and foremost. While he wrote many pieces that are performed indoors in concert halls and other venues, he has also written many pieces for presentation outdoors, especially in his *Patria* series of music theatre works. His *Music for Wilderness Lake*, for instance, takes place with musicians strategically situated around a lake and is usually performed very early in the morning; his *Enchanted Forest* takes place in many different locations in dense forests and deep woods at night; and his *Princess of the Stars* is performed on a lake when the sun is just rising with actors, actresses, and musicians standing or sitting in canoes and other boats on the lake and the audience seated along the shoreline.

Although appreciation of the natural environment is exceedingly important, the greatest requirement of all is to revere nature as a sacred and spiritual entity. We will never solve the environment crisis until we develop a different approach and attitude towards the natural environment, one grounded in reverence for nature.

Interacting with nature and nature's elements is obviously one of the best ways to create such reverence. No city in the world has been more successful at this—or provides a better example of it—than Singapore, which is known internationally as "the garden city." This understanding of what a city could and should be like was initiated by the prime minister of Singapore, Lee Kuan Yew, who in 1967 set out to transform Singapore into a city with abundant and lush greenery and a clean environment that would make it possible for people to live more pleasant, satisfying, and fulfilling lives.

In order to incorporate nature into all sectors, segments, and districts of Singapore with its huge condominiums and colossal office towers, regulations were passed in 2008 that made it mandatory to include or depict plant life in the form of vegetation, green roofs, cascading vertical gardens, verdant walls, and especially green buildings. Here again, Marc Chagall had something precious and meaningful to say when he observed that "Green is the prime colour of the world and that from where its loveliness arises."

These seminal developments in Singapore, and others, were carried further by Cheong Koon as the director and first woman to lead the Singapore Urban Development Agency. They included such initiatives as a total reshaping of the skyline through a variety of landmark projects that have made Singapore the largest freshwater city in the world as well as the development of Marina Bay, which is set on 250 acres of prime land in the residential, waterfront, and entertainment area of Singapore and includes many gardens on the roof tops of huge buildings, and the Jurong lake district that links Singapore to neighbouring Malaysia. This area is interspersed with countless parks, rivers, ponds, and bridges between high-rise buildings as well as lush plants that provide Singaporeans with several hundred kilometres of cycling and walking trails in addition to three million trees that cover the city. As well, a vast virgin rainforest with rich biodiversity exists right in the centre of this urban metropolis.

Developments like these, and many others, have done a great deal to accelerate attempts in many parts of the world to come to grips with the environmental crisis in more concrete ways. This includes creating greener, cleaner, low-carbon, creative, sharing, and humane economies, introducing and implementing carbon taxes, carbon pricing agreements, and "cap-in-trade" policies, making the transition from gas-guzzlers to electric cars, trucks, and planes, and shifting from "quantity first" to "quality first" in diets, lifestyles, and ways of life. This also includes creating carbon-neutral towns, cities, regions, and countries by balancing carbon dioxide emissions with offsetting amounts of renewable energy, the planting of millions of trees to absorb carbon dioxide from the air, evolving and utilizing alternative energy sources such as wind and solar power, creating a "Green Deal" in the United States similar to the "New Deal" of the 1930s, and many others.

These developments have been accompanied in recent years by legal and political attempts to protect other species through such vehicles as the One World, One Health initiative, recognition of animal rights and the enforcement of these rights in courts of law, the creation and declaration of the Earth Charter, the creation of a very timely and badly needed book on Earth Law, and others.

The One World, One Health initiative is predicated on the conviction that the world is in urgent need of a single integrated health care system that includes all species in a holistic, collective, and integrated fashion. This need is due to the rapidly escalating and multitudinous interactions and interrelationships that are constantly going on between humans and other animals. Infectious diseases such as COVID-19 originated in wild animals and were then transmitted to human beings. This problem is being compounded considerably as animals are forced out of their natural habitats by vast construction projects and the destruction of forests.

In recent years there have also been attempts to create legislation that recognizes animal rights and develop the laws that are required to protect and enforce these rights. Concerns over the way animals are treated can be traced back to ancient Greece and especially Aristotle, if not further back. Since that time, there has been a long list of advocates for better treatment of animals, such as Thomas Aquinas, Saint Francis of Assisi, Descartes, Kant, Shelley, Isabella Beeton, John Stuart Mill, and Charles Darwin in earlier times, and Jane Goodall, Diane Fossey, Bryan Adams, Brigitte Bardot, Maneka Gandhi, and many others in the contemporary world. This concern is also evident in many religions such as Jainism, Taoism, Hinduism, Buddhism, and Shintoism, as well as in the work of organizations such as the Society for the Prevention of Cruelty to Animals (SPCA), People for the Ethical Treatment of Animals (PETA), the World Wildlife Federation, and many others.

Until recently, it was generally held that animals do not have responsibilities and therefore cannot be accorded rights since rights and responsibilities must always go together in the legal sense. This is clearly impossible in the case of animals, however, because animals cannot hire their own lawyers or compensate legal experts for the costs involved in creating laws and rights to protect them. This same problem confronted lawyers and law firms half a century age ago when they manifested a strong desire and keen commitment to getting involved in environmental issues. This problem was eventually solved to a significant extent by creating environmental defence funds that could be used specifically for this purpose.

Fortunately, lawyers and legal experts in the animal rights movement have plunged in and ploughed forward in recent years in this area by creating animal rights funds. Animal rights issues are proving attractive to many young lawyers and while this field is still in its infancy, the prospect for the creation of animal rights legislation is much brighter than it was a decade ago. This augurs well for the compassionate treatment of animals in the years and decades ahead.

Another initiative that also holds great promise for the future is the creation of the *Earth Charter*. This is an international declaration of fundamental values and principles concerning the sanctity of the Earth deemed to be imperative in building a just, sustainable, and peaceful global society and greater reverence for nature and the natural environment in the twenty-first century. The creation of this charter commenced in 1987 when Maurice Strong, a Canadian environmentalist, businessman, activist, and diplomat, and Mikhail Gorbachev, the former president of the Soviet Union, launched the idea. The United Nations requested a document on this matter in 1992; a six-year consultative process was commenced and undertaken between 1994 to 2000 that was aimed at drafting the text for an Earth Charter, and was overseen by an independent Earth Charter Commission. The final text of this charter was approved at UNESCO headquarters in Paris in March 2000.

The Earth Charter is erected on four fundamental pillars and sixteen basic principles. The four pillars are: *Respect and Care for the Community of Life*; *Ecological Integrity*; *Social and Economic Justice*; and *Democracy, Nonviolence, and Peace*. The sixteen basic principles range all the way from respecting earth and its life forms in all their diversity and caring for the community of life with understanding, compassion and love to upholding the rights of all without discrimination to a natural and social environment supportive of human dignity, bodily health, and spiritual well-being with special attention to the rights of Indigenous peoples and minorities, as well as promotion of a culture of tolerance, nonviolence, and peace.[5]

While it will take time for the Earth Charter to be accepted and implemented in the world—much as has been the case for other documents of this type such as the UN Declaration of Human Rights—there is no doubt that this charter will slowly but surely work its way into the legal and judicial systems of all countries and the world as a whole. One of the most interesting things about this particular charter is that it concludes by stating the need to create a culture of tolerance, nonviolence, and peace, thereby asserting and confirming the fact that culture in general—and tolerance, nonviolence, and peace in particular—have an indispensable role to play in the world in environmental and ecological terms in the years, decades, and centuries ahead.

Complementing and reinforcing the creation of the Earth Charter is the publication in 2021 of a very valuable and timely book on *Earth Law: Emerging Ecocentric Law—A Guide for Practitioners*, co-edited by Anthony R. Zelle, Grant Wilson, Rachelle Adam, and Herman Greene.[6] As stated by the co-editors in the introduction to this book:

> *Earth Law: Emerging Ecocentric Law—A Guide for Practitioners* is a book for students and practicing lawyers who seek to preserve a habitable planet and question whether current environmental law is sufficient for the task. Earth law is the emerging body of ecocentric law for protecting, restoring, and stabilizing the functional interdependency of Earth's life and life-support systems. Earth law may be expressed in constitutional, statutory, common law, and customary law, as well as in treaties and other agreements both public and private. It is a rapidly developing field in many nations, municipalities, Indigenous communities, and international institutions. This

> course of study is for students and lawyers who know that nature and human environmental rights need to have seats at the table of law—in courts, legislatures, administrative bodies, enforcement agencies, and civil society.[7]

In some ways, publication of this book is an outgrowth of the Earth Charter because it is concerned with the creation and development of an "ecological social contract" for orderly and community living, moral development, and the flourishing of all species and the earth as a whole and not just the human species. As with the concern for the rights of animals, major contributions to the creation of an Earth Law came in earlier centuries from such scholars as Thomas Hobbes, John Locke, and especially Jean Jacques Rousseau, who was largely responsible for creating the idea of the *social contract*, something initially restricted to human beings. This concept is being enlarged in the twenty-first century with the emergence of an *ecological social contract* that includes other species and the Earth as a whole and not just humans. Two of the most important contributors to this area in recent years have been Bruno Latour and especially Bruce Jennings and the publication of his book *Ecological Governance: Toward a New Social Contract with the Earth* in 2016.

According to Jennings, the concept of the "general will" is a precious "achievement in human history ... and the highest expression of our communal humanity which emanates from *the development of humanity out of nature through culture*."[8] Jennings developed this idea in his own book, as well as for inclusion in the aforementioned book on *Earth Law*, by quoting Pope Francis's *Laudato Si': On Care for Our Common Home*, as illustrated in the following passage:

> Ecological culture cannot be reduced to a series of urgent and partial responses to the immediate problems of pollution, environmental decay and the depletion of natural resources. There needs to be a distinctive way of looking at things, a way of thinking, policies, an educational programme, a lifestyle and a spirituality which together generate resistance to the assault of the technocratic paradigm.... To seek only a technical remedy to each environmental problem which comes up is to

> separate what is in reality interconnected and to mask the true and deepest problems of the global system.[9]

While all these initiatives, and many others, illustrate the practical activities and concrete actions that are and must be taken to protect nature and other species, they fall short of what is needed to create the new lifestyles and overall ways of life that are necessary to come to grips with the environment crisis and create a new environment reality. In order to do this, it is essential to treat nature and the natural environment as *spiritual entities* to be revered and respected rather than as economic assets to be exploited, as well as to assign legal rights to rivers, lakes, forests, mountains, and so forth that are recognized in courts of law in the same way that legal rights are accorded to animals and human beings today. Fortunately, this is beginning to occur in such countries as Bolivia, Mexico, Colombia, New Zealand, Australia, Bangladesh, the United States, and Canada.

The ways of life of the Indigenous peoples could prove helpful and timely here. Throughout their history and despite all the myriad injustices, setbacks, and prejudices they have been compelled to endure in many different parts of the world, the Indigenous peoples have survived and sustained their commitment to treating nature and the natural environment as well as their interactions with them in a deeply spiritual sense. This is manifested in their sacred songs and dances, languages, rituals, and celebrations. In so doing, they have provided excellent models of behaviour with respect to how to love the earth and "the land" in a variety of ways that most people in the world still know very little about and do not fully comprehend. There are valuable lessons to be learned from the Indigenous peoples that need to be heeded by all societies. Without doubt, the Indigenous peoples have created a "permaculture" over the centuries that shines a light brightly on human activities that work with nature rather than against it.

It is clear from developments such as these, and many others, that the ecological manifestation of culture is not only much more all-encompassing in the holistic sense than the manifestations dealt with earlier, but also possesses the ability to include all living organisms and non-living elements in a perception and understanding of culture, cultures, and "the whole" that is capable of playing a vital role in the world. This is a perspective and a manifestation of culture whose time has come.

Chapter Eleven

Mythology, Worldview, and Cosmology

> Every culture, every people, every society must rediscover its own interior cosmology, must arrive at a coherent account of its being in the world, must be able to locate itself in a recognizable world and find for itself the organizing principle of its world.
>
> —Pierre Pascallon[1]

Just as culture as cultivation of the soul, the arts, humanities, and heritage of history can be traced back at ancient times, so can culture as mythology, worldview, and cosmology. This manifestation of culture—one of the most neglected but necessary manifestations of culture of all—is required more than ever since it is concerned with what constitutes the foundations and context of everything that exists in the universe: how things came into existence originally, how they function today, and the nature and meaning of culture and the whole in the broadest and most all-encompassing sense possible. Everything in the universe is included in this manifestation of culture in one form or another.

Whether culture is seen in this way, or any other all-encompassing way, it can be visualized as a gigantic tree with roots, trunks, branches, leaves, flowers, and fruit. Metaphorically speaking, mythology, worldview, and cosmology constitute the roots; agricultural processes, industrial activities, economic and scientific systems, technological devices, political ideologies, social structures, behavioural practices, environmental elements, and so forth the trunk and branches; and values, value systems, ethical beliefs, intellectual, aesthetic, and humanistic endeavours, and religious, philosophical, and spiritual endeavours and ideals the leaves, flowers, and fruit.

In his book *The Paths of Culture: A General Ethnology*, Kaj Birket-Smith carries this tree metaphor concerning culture a step further when he states:

> Culture is like a tree, a fabulous tree in which each branch is formed differently from its neighbour, each flower has its own color and fragrance, each fruit its special sweetness. This wealth and abundance has developed naturally. Each culture and each people bears its individual stamp; but the branches are all shoots of the same trunk and are fed by the same sap. If the branches are cut and detached from the trunk, the flowers wither. We are all members of the great society of mankind [humankind]; our national cultures are part of the culture of the whole world, which we must continue to build up.[2]

This metaphor of culture as a tree provides an effective way of thinking about and visualizing culture and cultures in general and the whole and wholes in particular. Not only does it deal with culture and cultures in holistic rather than partial or specialized terms—thereby focusing attention on culture and cultures' all-embracing character and integrative and all-inclusive potential—but it highlights the fundamental relationships, connections, and interdependencies that exist between and among the component parts of culture and cultures. It also depicts culture and cultures as dynamic and living entities as well as organic systems—much like trees—that are constantly changing, evolving, mutating, and adapting over time, much as all living things do.

Having spent the first ten chapters of this book dealing with the trunks, branches, leaves, flowers, and fruit of culture and cultures, it is time to deal with the most essential component of culture and cultures, namely the roots. While the roots cannot be seen because they are buried under the ground and therefore hidden from view, there is no doubt that they play the most important role of all in the nurturing, functioning, development, and flourishing of culture and cultures, much as they do for trees. As the old saying goes, "Look after the roots properly and everything else will take care of itself."

Take mythology, myth, and myths as one of the best illustrations of this. The ancient peoples were very conscious of the mythological dimensions of culture and cultures because they played the principal role in the growth and development of their lives and societies as complex, dynamic, and organic wholes. As a result, they created many sophisticated *cultural myths* to explain how the world and the universe came into existence in the first place, how things occurred in the world that they couldn't explain, how they became a group, tribe, community, society, or nation, what was most important to them, how they should live their lives and deal with the many challenges and problems that confronted them, how their burial services should be conducted, whether or not there was an afterlife, and what their ultimate purpose and destiny was. As Joseph Campbell, the well-known cultural scholar and expert on mythology, myth, and myths, put it, "the first function of a mythology—myths and mythic rituals, sacred songs and ceremonial dances—is to waken in the individual a sense of awe, wonder, and participation in the inscrutable mystery of being."[3] And what is true for individuals is also true for groups, communities, tribes, societies, nations, and all other human collectives. For Campbell, mythology is "the song of the universe" and "the music of the spheres."

A whole series of cultural myths were created by the ancient peoples to explain the diverse experiences, mysteries, and phenomena they encountered. There were *supernatural creation myths* that explained how something could be created from nothing, especially through words, deeds, dreams, and even bodily secretions from some divine source or supernatural power, as well as *earth-driven creation myths* in which some sacred authority, such as a bird or an amphibian, cut through a primordial ocean and brought some substance up from the ocean floor such as sand, mud, or cinders that eventually became the foundation of life and the terrestrial world. There were also *emergence creation myths* in which progenitors passed through a series of different steps, stages, worlds, and metamorphoses until the present world was reached, including primordial beings who were dismembered to form creation, the splitting up and ordering of various entities such as the cracking of "cosmic eggs" that was required to create order out of chaos, and many others.

For centuries, most of these myths were based on superstitions of one type or another.

As ancient peoples in all parts of the world began to study the sky more systematically and carefully, earlier myths grounded in superstition began to give way to either myths based on astronomical observation on the one hand, or religions incorporating one or many gods on the other. Even in religions with many gods, one god generally was recognized as superior to the others, such as Zeus in Greek mythology. Gods usually had abilities far transcending those of human beings, such as the ability to create floods or hurl lightning bolts. But they also displayed many human characteristics as well, such as love, lust, hate, anger, and so on. It was often necessary to make sacrifices to the gods, including offering up animals or sometimes even humans, to gain the gods' favour.

Take early Greek mythology as an example. Not only did the Greek gods act like humans (albeit humans with superpowers), but they involved themselves in mortals' lives in ways that involved rewards and punishments, retributions and rituals, realities and divinations, and much more.

The Greeks created numerous myths to try to understand the way the world worked. Over time these myths grew more and more complex. Joseph Campbell, mentioned earlier, made us aware of the incredible power of myths and their role in making and shaping all the various cultures in the world in his popular book *The Power of Myth*.[4] Ronald Wright elaborated on this when he said:

> Most history, when it has been digested by a people, becomes myth.
>
> Myth is an arrangement of the past, whether real or imagined, in patterns that resonate with a culture's deepest values and aspirations. Myths create and reinforce archetypes so taken for granted, so seemingly axiomatic, that they go unchallenged. Myths are so fraught with meaning that we live and die by them. They are the maps by which cultures navigate through time.[5]

Over time, other worldviews and cosmologies came into existence, ones that relied on natural processes as explanations of how the world worked, rather than the doings of gods. For instance, Plato concluded that the earth was at the centre of the universe, with the sun, moon, planets, and stars circling around it.

Although a few ancient philosophers like Aristarchus of Samos argued that the earth revolved around the sun, not vice versa, such views made little headway in ancient times as they seemed to defy common sense and everyday observation. The earth-centred or *geocentric* view of the universe reached its pinnacle with the work in the second century A.D. of Claudius Ptolemy, who lived in Alexandria, Egypt. Ptolemy drew on centuries of research and observations by the ancient Greeks and Babylonians to put together a description of the universe with the earth at its centre that remained the dominant cosmology for more than 1400 years. The Ptolemaic system also asserted there were clear links between the nature of the external universe and human nature:

> With regard to virtuous conduct in practical actions and character, this science [astronomy], above all things, could make men [women] see clearly; from the constancy, order, symmetry and calm which are associated with the divine, it makes its followers lovers of this divine beauty, accustoming them and reforming their natures, as it were, to a similar spiritual state.[6]

Though it held sway for nearly a millennium and a half, the Ptolemaic worldview eventually proved unable to accommodate increasingly precise and sophisticated observations of the motions of the heavenly bodies and in trying to do so became overly complex and implausible. In 1543, Nicolaus Copernicus, a Polish mathematician and astronomer, published a book asserting that the sun, not the earth, lay at the centre of the universe. The fact the earth makes one complete turn on its axis each day makes it look as though the sun revolves around the earth—but that is an illusion.

In the years after Copernicus advanced his notion of the *heliocentric* (sun-centred) universe, interest in astronomy intensified dramatically. Johannes Kepler, a seventeenth-century German scientist, arrived at laws governing planetary motion that still undergird our understanding of the workings of the solar system today.

The Italian astronomer Galileo was the first to systematically study the night sky with a telescope, in the process discovering mountains on the face of the moon, the four large satellites of Jupiter (they are still called the "Galilean satellites" today), and the phases of Venus, which served as convincing proof that the planets revolved around the sun and not the earth. Following in these scholars' footsteps, Isaac Newton, an English mathematician, developed the theory of universal gravitation and the three basic laws of motion that form the foundations of the science of physics. Although early in the twentieth century Albert Einstein's theory of relativity resulted in modifications in Newton's theories, the differences between the physics of Newton and of Einstein only become apparent in what, by earthly standards, are unusual conditions involving extremely high velocities and masses. In everyday life, including the sending of spacecraft to the moon or other planets, Newton's laws are entirely sufficient.

Just as the new ideas of Copernicus, Galileo, and Newton supplanted earlier scientific views of the universe, so have many of the religious myths, theories, and beliefs concerning the existence of one God or many gods as well as their creation of the universe been challenged as well. Modern views of the origin of the universe date from the 1920s, when it first became clear that many large collections of stars ("galaxies") existed beyond the boundaries of our home galaxy, the Milky Way, and that almost all of these distant galaxies were moving away from us into deep space. To try to explain this puzzling observation, the Belgian cosmologist and Catholic priest, Georges Lemaître, suggested that all the matter and energy of the universe was originally packed into a single dense particle—a "cosmic egg" or "primeval atom"—that for some reason suddenly exploded, giving rise to the expanding universe that we observe today.

In the century since Lemaître's time, the so-called "Big Bang" theory of the creation of the universe has been refined and elaborated upon by generations of astronomers, cosmologists, and physicists, to the extent that its current iteration bears about as much resemblance to Lemaître's original theory as does a late-model Tesla electric car to Henry Ford's Model T. Although many challenges to the Big Bang theory have emerged over the decades, today it remains the most widely accepted scientific theory of the origins of the universe.

One might think that Lemaître would have found it difficult to carry out his scientific work given that he was a Catholic priest. However, he kept his scientific work quite separate from his religious beliefs, writing:

> As far as I can see, such a theory remains entirely outside any metaphysical or religious question. It leaves the materialist free to deny any transcendental Being.... For the believer, it removes any attempt at familiarity with God.... It is consonant with Isaiah speaking of the hidden God, hidden even in the beginning of the universe.[7]

While separating the scientific and religious worldviews was not a problem for Lemaître, it has proved a problem—and a huge problem indeed—for many religions and religious institutions and leaders since that time. The pendulum has swung to the point that while the Big Bang theory is now taught in countless educational institutions throughout the world, religious ideas about the origins of the universe receive far less attention. This reflects an overall trend in western society in which science has taken on increased importance while religion is viewed as less important.

This is largely where matters stand at present, although an enormous amount of research continues in the fields of cosmology and astronomy today. The importance of this subject should not be ignored or dismissed. This is especially true with respect to worldview in general and worldviews in particular. Here is what Albert Schweitzer had to say about this subject:

> Even as a student, I used to be struck by the fact that the history of thought was always presented as the history of philosophical systems, not as that of a struggle for a world-view....
>
> Western thought has failed to realize the unsatisfactory nature of the results of its search for a securely based world-view of real value. [Philosophy] has become more and more involved in the discussion of secondary issues. It has lost touch with the elemental questions regarding life and the

> world which it is man's [humanity's] task to pose and to solve, and has found satisfaction more and more in discussing problems of a purely academic nature and in a mere virtuosity of philosophical technique. It has become increasingly absorbed in side issues. Instead of genuine classical music it has frequently produced only chamber music, often excellent in its way, but not the real thing. And so this philosophy, which was occupied only in elucidating itself, instead of struggling to achieve a world-view grounded in thought and essential for life, has led us to a position where we are devoid of any world-view at all, and, as an inevitable consequence of this, any real civilization....
>
> Our only possibility of progress lies in thorough comprehension of and immersion in the problem of world-view.[8]

Searching for an acceptable and authentic worldview should be given an extremely high priority going forward into the future, since it is of the utmost importance. At the individual level, every person is compelled to develop a personal worldview that includes thoughts about how the universe came into existence, how individuals function and position themselves in the world, how they should live their lives, and what life and living are really all about. As Anthony Wallace observed:

> "World view" attends especially to the way a man [woman], in a particular society, sees himself [herself] in relation to all else. It is the properties of existence as distinguished from, and related to, the self. It is, in short, a man's [woman's] idea of the universe. It is that organization of ideas which answers to a man [woman] the questions: Where am I? Among what do I move? What are my relations to these things?[9]

Just as individuals are compelled to develop personal worldviews, so groups, societies, countries, cultures, and civilizations are also compelled to develop collective worldviews. This is particularly important in terms of people's cultures:

> The culture of a people is, then, its total equipment of ideas and institutions and conventionalized activities.... The "world view" of a people ... is the way a people characteristically look outward upon the universe ... "world view" suggests how everything looks to a people, "*the designation of the existent as a whole*" ... "World view" may be used to include the forms of thought and the most comprehensive attitudes towards life.[10]

It is the all-encompassing potential and character of culture in this holistic sense that makes it very different from disciplines such as economics or political science, to name only two examples. Whereas most academic disciplines are specialized efforts to enhance human knowledge and understanding of the intimate nature and intricate workings of particular parts of the whole, culture is an all-encompassing, unifying discipline, one designed to enhance knowledge, understanding, and awareness of the structure and functioning *of the whole*, regardless of whether that whole is defined as all human beings, all living species, all interactions in the natural environment, or the entire universe.

This explains why culture and cultures are not just the roots, trunks, branches, leaves, flowers, and fruit of the tree, but, also, organic and dynamic wholes composed of countless interrelated parts or elements taken collectively and in totality. The ultimate purpose is to see and understand culture and cultures as holistic entities, and therefore, among many other things, the "contexts" within which all the diverse component parts of culture and cultures as wholes are situated and can be analyzed, understood, explained, and discussed. In other words, culture and cultures are the multidisciplinary, theoretical, and practical containers that are required to house many different disciplines and fields, and therefore act as the unifying forces necessary to see, understand, and order reality.

The crucial importance of this point is amplified by the Canadian philosopher and cultural scholar Jerzy A. Wojciechowski:

> Central to each culture are convictions about the universe and about man [people], about his [their] nature, his [their]

> relation to the external world, his (their) place in the universe, the meaning of human life, the supreme values, and the distinction between right and wrong, good and evil.... The sum of these convictions forms in each case a unique and distinctive system, differing from culture to culture, even though some of its elements are similar in different cultures.[11]

If this problem of creating and developing a personal and collective worldview through culture in general and cultures in particular is not taken seriously and fully into account, people will be compelled to accept or adopt other worldviews and cultures or have them thrust on them by other individuals, groups, institutions, governments, or cultures. The trouble with this is that "adopted," "imposed," "imported," or "imitative" worldviews and cultures may be at odds with people's own individual and collective worldview, perceptions, convictions, beliefs, aspirations, and needs, compelling them to accept things in life that they may not agree with or believe. Cleary it is in the best interests of all people, groups, cultures, and countries to examine their own individual and collective worldviews in detail and in depth, as well as to develop worldviews that are consistent with their own cultural needs, wants, circumstances, and requirements.

To progress further in this area, it is necessary to enter the highly complex but very evocative domain of cosmology. While mythologies, worldviews and cosmologies share certain aspects in common, they are not identical. Speaking generally, mythology, myths, worldview, and worldviews tend to be more concerned with describing and explaining specific situations, including peoples' beliefs about the original creation and basic functioning of the world, their views on major problems, challenges, needs, and opportunities with respect to these matters, as well as their specific roles, responsibilities, and relationships in the world and the universe.

In contrast, cosmology and cosmologies tend to be more concerned with the substantially larger and vastly more complicated problem of trying to ascertain, understand, and explain the structure and evolution of the universe. This includes how the universe came into existence in the first place; evolved historically; functions today;

and how these matters are most effectively visualized, interpreted, understood, and explained. Some thinkers take an even broader view of cosmology to include such matters as the place of human beings in the universe, how groups, communities, and cultures should be structured, how geographical space is and should be occupied, and how relations should be conducted within and between countries, cultures, species, and the world and the universe at large.[12]

Interestingly, cosmology is derived from two Greek words: *kosmos* (meaning an ordered and harmonious whole) and *logos* (meaning the study of or discussion or discourse about a subject). *Cosmology*, then, concerns itself with discussion or discourse about the universe as a whole, including the logical principles underlying the workings of the universe as an ordered whole or, as the *Cambridge English Dictionary* puts it, "the universe considered as a system with an order and a pattern." (As a side note, the word "cosmos" is also the name of a beautiful flower that grows in hot climates such as Greece and Mexico. It is a perfect circle in most cases with beautiful petals that are usually pink, red, or multi-coloured.)

And this is not all. Over the centuries, some scholars manifested a belief in what they called "the harmony of the spheres." This belief was based on the conviction that the universe is governed by numerical proportions as well as the harmonious movement of the heavenly bodies, the sounds of which formed music when blended together. This idea was first put forward by the Greek philosopher Pythagoras in the sixth century B.C. It was also espoused by the early modern astronomer Johannes Kepler (1571–1630), who was convinced that the orbits of the planets followed a particular mathematical pattern and that each planet emitted a unique sound that, taken together, resulted in the "music of the spheres." Although such ideas are no longer held by modern astronomers, it is undeniably true that precise yet complicated mathematical principles underlie the structure of the universe, including such constants as the speed of light in a vacuum and the fine-structure constant, which determines the strength of electromagnetic interactions. As well, a major breakthrough in modern cosmology came with the detection of the *cosmic background radiation*, a faint microwave signal which many astronomers believe to be the fading echo of the Big Bang itself. All in all, the more we study the cosmos, the more we realize it is a harmonious, ordered, and regenerative whole.

Cosmology, then, is a discipline of crucial importance to people, groups, communities, countries, cultures, and civilizations in all parts of the world, as well as being connected to culture and cultures in a whole series of quintessential and dynamic ways. As Milton Munitz put it:

> One of the characteristic, persistent, and irrepressible needs of the human mind is to have a cosmology. It consists in the interest in being able to describe and understand the large-scale global structure of the universe in which we live. An interest in cosmology ... is to be found in virtually every period and culture of recorded history.[13]

Unfortunately, cosmology is often confused with astronomy, with which it shares certain similarities. However, whereas astronomy is concerned with the nature and evolution of individual stars, planets, and galaxies in the universe, cosmology is concerned with the nature and evolution of the universe *as an ordered or structured whole*:

> Cosmology is thus the all-embracing science, for it deals with the structure and evolution of the entire universe—everything that we now observe and that we can ever hope to observe in the future. Astronomy, by contrast, deals with the properties of individual objects, such as stars and galaxies.[14]

This concern with the organization, nature, functioning, and evolution of the universe as an ordered and structured whole makes cosmology, like culture, a holistic and integrative discipline or field of study rather than a partial and specialized one:

> Cosmology is a joint enterprise by science, philosophy, religion, and the arts that seeks to gain understanding of what is unified and is fundamental. As a science, it is the study of the large-scale structure of the universe....
>
> Cosmology is the one science in which specialization is

> rather difficult. Its main aim is to assemble the cosmic jigsaw puzzle, not to study in detail any particular jigsaw piece. While all other scientists are pulling the universe apart into more detailed bits and pieces, the cosmologists endeavour to put the pieces together in order to see the picture on the jigsaw puzzle.... The cosmologists, unlike other scientists, take the broad view. *They are like the impressionistic painters who stand well back from their canvas in order not to see too much distracting detail ...*
>
> We cannot study cosmology in the broadest terms unless we pay heed to the pageantry of world pictures that have shaped the history of the human race.[15]

It is the all-encompassing nature of cosmology and its intimate connection with culture in the holistic sense that makes it possible to talk about culture being the centrepiece of the world in the next age of human history. Not only are cosmology and culture concerned with seeing the world and the universe from an all-inclusive rather than partial or specialized perspective, but they make it possible to create theoretical and practical frameworks as well as evaluative and assessment mechanisms that are capable of comprehending, confronting, and coming to grips with present and future challenges, problems, and possibilities in the most all-encompassing sense, as well as developing effective, systematic, and impartial methods, techniques, approaches, and systems for dealing with such matters.

Several decades ago, the well-known environmentalist Barbara Ward said, "The chief environmental insight is that all things are linked; but if all things are linked, where is the thread which will lead us through the maze?" It is now clear that culture is this thread, particularly when it is seen and dealt with in the all-embracing, cosmological sense. Surely this explains why Wole Soyinka, the Nigerian Nobel laureate for literature, advocated seeing, understanding, and treating culture as *source*—the source from which all things in the world and the universe flow and to which all things return. It is only by travelling back to the source in this profound and all-encompassing cosmological and cultural sense that it will be possible to comprehend and deal with the most debilitating ecological, economic, social, political, ethical, environmental, spiritual, and other problems that exist in the world today.

One of the most prominent contributors to the development of cosmology and culture in this profound, powerful, and all-encompassing sense was Thomas Berry. Not only was Berry well educated, experienced, and deeply involved in culture, cultures, cultural history, "cultural coding," and other matters as an internationally renowned and celebrated cultural scholar and historian, but he was a world-famous theologian, Catholic priest, and what he himself called a "geologian," or a person who is well versed in and very knowledgeable about the arts, sciences, religion, ecology, geology, and cosmology. Berry took a long-term and very expansive cultural and cosmological approach to the vast array of crucial problems related to human life on earth, as well as to community, solidarity, environmental and ecological sustainability, and the well-being of people, the planet, and the universe.

During the course of his life, Berry wrote numerous articles and many books on these matters, such as *The Dream of the Earth*, *The Great Work: Our Way into the Future,* and *The Sacred Universe: Earth, Spirituality, and Religion in the Twenty-First Century.* These books, and others, were predicated on Berry's belief that the "traditional story" of the earth and the universe is outmoded and ineffective, largely because cosmology over the last few centuries has been grounded in the physical sciences, rather than in a much broader range of disciplines and such key matters as truth, beauty, adventure, art, and peace, as advocated by Alfred North Whitehead in books such as *Adventures of Ideas, Process and Reality*, and others.

This problem was addressed at length by Rémi Brague, author of *The Wisdom of the World: The Human Experience of the Universe in Western Thought*:

> The image of the world that emerged from physics after Copernicus, Galileo, and Newton is of a confluence of blind forces, where there is no place for consideration of the Good....
>
> The world was no longer a whole, but a result of disparate forces. Cosmology gave way to cosmography—the stars, for example, no longer reflected the order of heaven, an ethical

> model which one was to adapt oneself, but lacked any significance until some new theory might account for the facticity of their existence.[16]

As a result of such problems, Berry believed that it was time to create a new story of the universe based on understanding the profound role that culture, religion, ecology, the arts, and cosmology play in the creation, telling, and diffusion of that story. The key to this in Berry's opinion was to understand that "the universe is not a collection of objects, but rather a communion of subjects." This was of vital importance in coming to grips with the present and prospective problems confronting humanity, the world, and the universe, as well as making it possible for all species and not just the human species to flourish in the future. Many of Berry's thoughts on matters like this were stated in a book he co-authored with Brian Swimme entitled *The Universe Story: From the Primordial Flaring Forth to the Ecozoic Age—A Celebration of the Unfolding of the Cosmos.*

Unlike many contemporary cosmologists who have tended to emphasize scientific views of the universe, Berry was a great believer that the arts had a crucial role to play in the development of this new story of the universe, working with science rather than separate from it. As David Schenck pointed out in his article, "Cosmology and Wisdom: The Great Teaching Work of Thomas Berry":

> For Berry cosmology is at once science and poetry, and most fundamentally, a matter of vision and myth and epic. A geologian might then fairly be considered a visionary for the earth.
>
> Thomas Berry, in addition to being our contemporary, is both behind us and ahead—a historian preserving the living core of wisdom traditions of human cultivation—and a visionary listening towards the future cultivation of human presence on and to the earth.
>
> We need new means of cultivating ourselves if we are to live differently on the earth. Developing and telling the new story is one component of establishing such cultivation. But the grand sweep of the longed-for cultivation is found only

> in Cosmology envisioned as the comprehensive presentation of the mystery of presence of the universe in myth, ritual and dream; in liturgy, poetry and music; in wisdom literature and renewed philosophies and theologies; and in the plastic arts of all kinds—painting, sculpture, architecture.[17]

In the development of his thoughts and ideas on these fundamental matters, Berry often teamed up with the evolutionary cosmologist Brian Swimme. Both scholars were strongly influenced in these matters by the thoughts and beliefs of Pierre Teilhard de Chardin, who believed that everything in the universe has a spiritual as well as a physical aspect. In consequence, all three scholars would probably have answered "yes" to the fundamental cosmological question raised for both science and religion by John F. Haught—author of *The Cosmic Adventure: Science, Religion, and the Quest for Purpose*—when he asked if "the evolutionary processes of nature have any purpose or meaning." In a similar vein, Albert Einstein was once asked, "What is the most important question you can ask in life?" Einstein's response was another question: "Is the universe a friendly place or not?" Without doubt, Berry, Swimme, de Chardin, and many others in the cosmological, cultural, and religious realms would likely assert that the universe is a "friendly place," especially if humanity can make it not only an ordered and regenerative whole but also a harmonious whole in the future.

According to Angela T. Lydon, author of *Cosmology and Curriculum: A Vision for an Ecozoic Age*, "the very survival of the human community requires the creative articulation of a new mode of human presence within universal processes." She went on to explain this in more detail by affirming her and Berry's belief that it is not just the physical and material aspects of universal processes that must be considered, but also the metaphysical, philosophical, artistic, and aesthetic aspects:

> What is needed is a meaning-filled story that sees humankind as part of cosmic processes. Such stories as narrated in ancient cultures, overflow in eventment and in celebration.... Dance, song, art, drama, and spoken narratives can make

> explicit the bondedness and interdependence of all species.... The very survival of the human community requires the creative articulation of a new mode of human presence within universal processes.[18]

Since cosmological questions, like cultural questions, originate in the human mind and imagination, a related set of questions exists with which cosmology and culture are and must be concerned. These questions have to do with how human beings see and relate to the world. Milton Munitz confirmed the fundamental importance of cosmology and culture in this sense when he wrote:

> We wish to know our "place," where we fit in among all the other entities that make up the universe. What forces, powers, and causes brought us into existence and sustain us? What should be our goals, purposes, and values? Is there some cosmic design of which our lives are a part? Being able to answer these kinds of questions is one way of responding to what is frequently referred to as a search for the meaning of life?[19]

We would probably be wise to leave the last word on cosmology and the cosmic whole to ancient and contemporary scholars from India such as Thanu Padmanbhan, Swami Vivekananda, Rana P. B. Singh, and many others who have delved deeply into this matter. As Fritjof Capra points out in his book *The Tao of Physics*, at its most elementary level, traditional Indian philosophy is predicated on "an awareness of the unity and mutual interrelation of all things and events, the experience of all phenomena in the world as manifestations of a basic oneness. All things are seen as interdependent and inseparable parts of this cosmic whole, as different manifestations of the same ultimate reality."[20]

Here we have it then as far as the most all-encompassing manifestation of culture is concerned. Not only is it concerned with the universe as a whole in the broadest sense possible, but it is also concerned with the universe as a structured, ordered, and eventually harmonious whole. A new course must be charted—one that is set in a long-term time frame and viewed from a cultural perspective. This is where culture in the cosmological sense comes to the fore. Without it we will be unable to come to grips with the many problems that threaten our world.[21] Bringing the world as culture into existence and enabling it to flourish is a categorical imperative. It is to this matter that our attention is directed in the final chapter of this book.

Chapter Twelve

Making the World as Culture a Reality

> In the great movement of time which we call human history, we must ask ourselves the question, "Where are we, and where is our road leading to?" in the hope that through an understanding of the growths and declines, of the successes and the failures of cultures, we will acquire some clues that will lead us to the right decisions in our time.
>
> —S. Takdir Alisjahbana[1]

We have reached the end of a long and fascinating journey together to determine how culture as an idea and a reality has evolved and manifested itself in the world over the course of human history and what countless cultural scholars, historians, and practitioners have had to say about this.

In the process of doing so, we have seen that the vast and unwieldy array of perceptions and definitions of culture that have been advanced over the last two thousand years and more can be reduced to a much smaller and more manageable number of manifestations of culture as most of these perceptions and definitions are variations on the same theme or a similar theme. This made it possible to identify the main manifestations of culture that have been created over more than twenty centuries, from culture as cultivation of the soul—espoused by Marcus Cicero in Roman times—to culture as mythology, worldview, and cosmology, as advocated by Joseph Campbell, Thomas Berry, and others very recently. These main manifestations all exist and are legitimate. They expose the true nature, meaning, potential, and capabilities of culture when they are considered collectively, and are being used by many different people, groups, scholars, practitioners, and institutions in the world on an ongoing basis.

If, as John McHale, the well-known futurist, claimed, "people survive, uniquely, by their capacity to act in the present on the basis of past experience considered in terms of future consequences,"[2] then it makes a great deal of sense to examine what can be learned from past experiences with culture as an idea and a reality that can be used, refined, built on, and carried forward into the future. This is required to put ourselves in the strongest possible position to come to grips with the complex and debilitating problems that exist throughout the world today, as well as to take advantage of the limitless opportunities that are available in the years and decades ahead.

What is most obvious when we look back over the course of history is the fact that we can simplify the process of determining the true nature, meaning, potential, and capabilities of culture even more if we subdivide culture's main manifestations into two distinct and interrelated groups based on what they are most concerned with and have in common. When this is done, it is evident that some of these manifestations have to do with culture as *parts of something larger*, such as cultivation of the soul, the arts, humanities, and heritage of history, whereas others have to do with culture as *the whole,* regardless of whether this whole is seen in terms of the whole person, the complex whole or total way of life of people, societies and social systems, the ways of life of other species, all the interactions that take place in the natural environment, or mythology, worldview, and cosmology.

Taken together, these two groups of ideas possess the potential to play a powerful role in bringing the world as culture into existence and enabling it to flourish. Not only do they confirm how culture and cultures should be perceived, understood, and dealt with in the world in the future, but they also contribute a great deal to establishing the theoretical and practical foundations that are necessary to make the world as culture a reality. This makes it possible to confront the present and the future with optimism and enthusiasm rather than pessimism and apprehension.

With the exception of culture as cultivation of the soul, the remaining manifestations of culture in the first group—the arts, the humanities, and the heritage of history—constitute the way most people and organizations in the world see, understand, and deal with culture today. This is especially true when the cultural industries as well as such activities as sports and recreation are added to this list. This is also how most governments, corporations, foundations, and private benefactors see and deal with culture for funding purposes, as well as how public authorities and ministries of culture formulate and implement their cultural plans and policies. It is important to emphasize at this point that many of humanity's greatest goals and objectives as well as its highest ideals and beliefs are included in this group. If these manifestations of culture are not attended to properly, or are downplayed and ignored, we run the risk of losing a great deal that is of quintessential importance.

At the same time, interest in the second group of manifestations of culture is escalating rapidly throughout the world at the present time. This is because they are concerned with one of the greatest needs in the world today and going forward into the future—namely, the need to see, understand, and deal with the big picture in holistic rather than partial or specialized terms. This is what is most lacking in the world today. We need to see, understand, and deal with the big picture in this sense if we are to be successful in dealing with the numerous problems that exist in the world today, as well as cross over the threshold to a very different kind of world in the future.

While there are many benefits to be derived from breaking the whole up into parts and studying those parts in detail, it is now essential to bring things together rather than split them apart—to *unite* rather than *divide*—since this makes it possible to take advantage of one of culture's most powerful assets, namely the capacity for holism. This is true regardless of whether we are considering the earlier psychological, anthropological, and sociological manifestations of culture or the more recent biological, ecological, or cosmological ones. It is the all-inclusive capacity culture possesses as "the whole" that will make it possible to achieve more unity, cooperation, solidarity, and harmony—as well as less disunity, division, competition, polarization, and discord—in the world. *Consequently, what specialization and reductionism have been to the world of the past, holism and the holistic perspective must be to the world of the present and the future.*

Looking back over the past, we also see that culture as an idea and a reality has been dynamic, organic, and fluid rather than static, inorganic, and fixed. It has also broadened, deepened, and intensified substantially over time in order to stay in tune with the most important developments and changes that have occurred in the world. Not only has culture demonstrated a remarkable capacity for moving across a vast panorama of disciplines and fields over the centuries, as we have seen, but there is also very little in the world that is not concerned with culture in general and cultures in particular in one form or another. Culture and cultures constitute the real foundations and fundamental essence of human existence and the existence of all other forms of life.

It follows from this that few if any other disciplines or activities possess the breadth of vision, depth of understanding, and theoretical and practical potential that culture does, especially when it is visualized and dealt with in all-encompassing terms. Whereas most disciplines and activities derive their power, potential, and utility from being perceived, defined, and dealt in one particular way—economics, for instance, is perceived and defined as production, distribution, and consumption of goods and services and creation of material and monetary wealth, while science is perceived and defined as exploration, discovery, articulation, and application of the laws of nature—culture derives its power, potential, and utility from being perceived and defined in many different ways rather than just one way. The longer we fail to realize this and capitalize on it, the more devastating the consequences will be.

This is what makes the relentless trend over the course of history toward ever more holistic and all-inclusive manifestations of culture so relevant and timely. While this trend began in the nineteenth century when the anthropological, sociological, and psychological manifestations of culture were created, it has been strengthened and expanded considerably in the twentieth and twenty-first centuries with the addition of the biological, ecological, and cosmological manifestations of culture.

This is because these much more far-reaching and all-inclusive manifestations of culture are no longer confined to the human species but include other species, the natural environment, and indeed the entire universe. This is most obvious in the case of the cosmological manifestation of culture because it is based on the conviction that the universe is not only an ordered and structured whole, but also a self-regulating system or organism. We are beginning to understand the crucial importance of this as we expand our knowledge, understanding, and activities beyond the earth. We are also learning that the universe possesses certain capabilities that human beings do not—such as the capacity for sustainability and regeneration—but which we must learn in the future if human survival and well-being as well as the survival and well-being of other species and planet earth are to be assured.

This is what makes the paradigm shift that is going on in the world today from seeing culture as part of something larger to seeing culture in holistic terms as the whole or total way of life so timely, valuable, and indispensable. This is what is most needed in the world to come to grips with climate change, global warming, and the environmental crisis, colossal disparities and inequities in income and wealth, escalating tensions and open conflicts between different races, tribes, ethnic groups, countries, cultures, and civilizations, and the intermingling and interaction of people with very different customs, traditions, and beliefs as well as worldviews and value systems.

Nothing confirms the power, potential, and potency of the holistic perception of culture better than the realization that culture and cultures are the change agents that are urgently needed during this difficult period in human history. How often have we heard people and organizations say in recent years that it is necessary to "change the culture"?

Why is this? Surely it is because what is most needed in the world is not piecemeal change or tinkering with a few individual parts, but rather wholesale change that is fundamental, foundational, systematic, and systemic. This is imperative if the aforementioned problems, and others, are to be dealt with effectively. This makes culture and cultures the change agents that are required in the world. They go right to the core and substance of problems, thereby making it possible to change people's, organizations', and humanity's worldviews, value systems, lifestyles, habits, consumer practices, and overall ways of life.

There is something else of crucial importance that is occurring in the world today that is intimately connected to this fundamental paradigm shift. It is the fact that the first group of manifestations of culture is being seen, understood, and treated more and more as the "gateways" or "keys" that are necessary to open the doors to the second group. This is because cultivation of the soul and artistic, humanistic, and heritage activities are not only ends in themselves, but also have incredible symbolic potential and significance when it comes to broadening and deepening knowledge and understanding of culture and cultures in the holistic sense as well as their development, functioning, and cultivation in the world. Rich rewards are standing in the wings and waiting to be realized as a result of this.

Take the arts as one of the most obvious examples of the incredible symbolic potential and significance of certain parts of culture to shed light on culture and cultures as wholes and total ways of life. Many people in Finland believe that Jean Sibelius' evocative composition *Finlandia* should be their national anthem—it isn't today—because it says so much about Finnish culture as a whole and the total way of life of Finnish people. This also explains why the European Union made Beethoven's monumental *Ninth Symphony* and especially its *Ode to Joy* its anthem: it symbolizes European culture as a whole and not just specific cultures or countries in Europe. Moreover, think about how brilliant Mahatma Gandhi was when he selected "homespun"—which has always had great symbolic significance as a material art in India and Indian culture as a whole—to bring an end to British rule in India. And what is true for the arts in this symbolic sense is also true for the humanities, the heritage of history, the cultural industries, and many other parts of the whole such as languages, architecture, cuisine, sports, science, recreation, traditions, and so forth.

There is another aspect to this matter that is also revealed by looking back over the past and which has great importance for the world of the present and the future. It is the fact that, like all disciplines and activities, culture has negative as well as positive consequences and effects. These have been demonstrated throughout history and documented in some detail in this book. This means that culture must be able to act as a real "beacon" going forward into the future if it is to function effectively. In order to do so, it must possess a dual capability like all successful beacons. One the one hand, it must be capable of illuminating a vital, viable, safe, and sustainable path into the future, ensuring that humanity and the world are headed in the right direction. On the other hand, it must be capable of warning of impending danger and ensure that all the requisite safeguards, precautions, checks, and balances are put in place to prevent atrocities.

The well-known cultural scholar and pioneer in the creation of the cultural interpretation of history, Jacob Burckhardt, proposed an excellent way of realizing this dual capacity of culture as a beacon of the future when he visualized humanity's journey over the centuries as a *cultural continuum* where with "undulled senses" it is essential to pursue "the great" amidst "the perishable" and "the barbaric." He went on to say, "There exists a marvellous, universal, silent promise to bring an objective interest to everything, to transform the entire past and present world into a spiritual possession."[3] Many other cultural scholars such as Kenneth Clark, Jacob Bronowski, and Thomas Berry have advocated something similar to this, as well as the need to focus on the ascent and accomplishments of humanity.

This is what makes it so necessary to preserve, protect, build upon, and share the cultural and natural heritages of all the different countries and cultures of the world as well as come to grips with the world's diversity and complexity. It would be foolhardy to embrace any discipline or activity that doesn't take all these factors as well as the fate of other species and the natural environment fully and forcefully into account in the creation and development of plans, programs, policies, and decision-making processes.

When culture is perceived and understood in both the partial and holistic sense as it is here, it is a seamless web that should be made the centrepiece of the world as culture in general and the world system in particular. While we have become accustomed to treating economics and economies in this way—largely because we are living in the world as economics at present and have been for more than two centuries—it is really culture and cultures that deserve this position in the future as the real foundations of municipal, regional, national, and international development as well as human affairs. Rajni Kothari, the Indian cultural scholar, captured this best when he said, "Development is not merely an economic and political concept; it is more fundamentally a process of culture and civilization."[4]

Capitalizing fully on culture as a seamless web in the partial and holistic sense does not mean rejecting the crucial importance of economics, economies, and all other activities in the overall scheme of things. Rather, it means incorporating economics, economies, and all other activities in a substantially broader, deeper, and more fundamental and all-encompassing way of looking at and dealing with the human condition and world situation. Not only is it necessary to accept this as a fundamental necessity, but also it is necessary to ensure that the development of economics, economies, and all other activities is informed by environmental, cultural, and human values and ideals and not just industrial, commercial, and technological interests and concerns.

This is equally true of the need to develop culture and all the diverse cultures in the world in breadth and depth, as well as situate them effectively in the natural, historical, and global environment. This is especially important with respect to achieving and maintaining balance and harmony between all the different activities and relationships that constitute culture and cultures. While this is of utmost importance in terms of the relationship between human beings, other species, and the natural environment as well as the qualitative and quantitative dimensions of development, it is also essential in terms of the relationship between all the diverse peoples, races, ethnic groups, cultures, and civilizations of the world, rich and poor countries and rich and poor people, the public sector and the private sector, the arts and the sciences, technology and society, and human rights and responsibilities. Imbalances and disharmonies exist in all these areas, and others, that are inimical rather than conductive to balanced and harmonious development in the future.

There is one final matter that stands out and needs to be addressed when we cast our eyes back over the past. It is the need to take full advantage of the rich legacy of thoughts, ideas, ideals, insights, and writings of cultural scholars, historians, and practitioners over the centuries. Unfortunately, this legacy has been largely ignored over the last two hundred and fifty years because the world has been preoccupied with economics and the theories and publications of economists.

For those who believe that the thoughts, ideas, ideals, and insights of cultural scholars, historians, and practitioners who lived in the past have little or no relevance for the world of the present and the future, it is necessary to recall that this would not be the first time in the history of the world that major contributions have been made in the past that have been ignored for very long periods of time, only to be to revived much later due to their relevance. The Renaissance is probably the best example of this. It was based on thoughts, ideas, ideals, and insights created in Roman times that remained dormant and ignored for the better part of a thousand years before they were revived because they were so relevant, first in Italy, then in Europe, and ultimately throughout the world. On a smaller scale, this also holds true for the musical achievements of Johann Sebastian Bach, who most musicologists now believe was the greatest composer who ever lived. His phenomenal talents, vast repertoire, and countless musical accomplishments were ignored for a long time before Felix Mendelssohn came across some of his manuscripts in a library in Leipzig one day, revived them, and set Bach on the path to being enjoyed and cherished by millions of people throughout the world today. Or, to cite a final example among countless others, what about Johann Pachelbel's famous *Canon*? This musical masterpiece was written in the late seventeenth century and ignored for centuries before it became a "smash hit" in the latter part of the twentieth century.

Something similar must now be true for the cornucopia of research and writing provided by generations and indeed centuries of cultural scholars, historians, and practitioners. The time has come to examine their works in considerable detail and utilize them fully. They contain an incredible amount of knowledge, wisdom, and understanding, and have a great deal to say that is relevant to the world today and going forward into the future.

When all these diverse factors and developments are combined together and considered collectively, it is important to emphasize that the world as culture is not the be-all-and-end-all or final stage in human history or global development. Unlike the world as economics, which is based on the economic interpretation of history and Marx's conviction that humanity is destined to live in such a world forever, the world as culture is based on the belief that history is always an open book to be charted in accordance with humanity's and the world's most basic needs and fundamental requirements at each and every stage of development.

Visualized and dealt with in this way, humanity possesses the freedom and independence that are needed to create and enter any age, stage, period in history, or type of world, and therefore is not forever locked in a deterministic straitjacket. Whereas economics and the economy may dominate one age, stage, period of history, or type of world, culture, ecology, cosmology, spirituality, or some other activity may dominate another age, stage, period, or type of world. It happens to be culture that is most needed at this specific time in the history of humanity and the world.

This confirms the conviction stated earlier that it is essential to bring the world as culture into existence and enable it to flourish as the next great epoch in human history. As Valerie Lynch Lee, editor of *Faces of Culture*, put it:

> The future of humanity is one and the same with the future of culture, for culture is the chief means by which we adapt to our environment. Cultural adaptations have allowed us to build large cities, increase food production, and travel quickly to all parts of the world. In fact, human inventiveness has so changed the world that our old ways of living may no longer be suitable. We have changed the world to such an extent that it may now be necessary to change ourselves if we are to survive in it.[5]

This quotation brings us, via a rather circuitous route, to what is undoubtedly the most important requirement of all at present and going forward into the future. It is the need to cultivate the capacity to see the world from a cultural perspective and develop a much high level of *cultural consciousness*. This means changing the way we see the world, organize ourselves, conduct our affairs, interact with other people and other species, enhance and embellish our lives, position ourselves in the world, and, most importantly of all, create a new environmental reality. Jean d'Ormesson, the French novelist, former director of *Le Figaro,* and dean of the Académie française, stated this most effectively when he said, "Culture used to look backwards in order to try to understand the world; now, all of a sudden, it is looking forward in order to change it."

It is one thing to talk about creating the world as culture in theoretical, idealistic, and conceptual terms. It is quite another to talk about creating this world in practical, concrete, and operational terms. Having dealt with the first requirement, it is now time to deal with the second.

This requirement will not be realized without powerful and proactive contributions coming from three specific groups: people and organizations in the cultural field; people and institutions in government, politics, and international affairs; and the general public. Let us examine the most essential roles and responsibilities of these three groups because this is of quintessential importance in making the world as culture a reality.

Of the three groups, people and organizations working in the cultural field have the most important role to play in ushering in the world as culture and making it a reality. Not only is this group the most committed to the centrality of culture, the development of culture and cultures in breadth and depth, and advancing the cultural cause, but it also has to provide the leadership, impetus, and inspiration that are required to make the world as culture a concrete entity and demonstrable fact.

Unfortunately, this group is at present spread across many different disciplines, activities, and areas. This includes all the different art forms, the cultural industries, the humanities, cultural studies, psychology, sociology, anthropology, ecology, biology, mythology, cosmology, philosophy, cultural history, and others. This problem is compounded by the fact that there is very little communication taking place between people and organizations in these different areas. While this is consistent with the way culture has evolved as an idea, reality, discipline, and activity over more than two thousand years, it is a very serious problem today because there is not a great deal of interaction and discussion going on between people, organizations, and disciplines working in all these different fields. This makes bringing these people, organizations, disciplines, and activities together and enabling them to share thoughts, ideas, and insights about the role of culture and cultures in the world a categorical imperative. It also makes coalescing them into a powerful, persuasive, cohesive, and united cultural community the most important priority in the cultural domain today.

A similar challenge faced people and organizations in the environmental field more than half a century ago. They were also spread across many different disciplines and activities and had to be brought together to coalesce into the powerful environmental community they are today. They did this largely through the commitment of many dedicated environmental activists, practitioners, and policy makers, as well as organizations such as Greenpeace International and myriad others. A similar development is urgently needed in the cultural field today. A strong, vocal, and cohesive cultural community needs to be created that is capable of making culture and cultures the centrepiece of the world system and the principal preoccupation of municipal, regional, national, and international affairs.

There are many ways the cultural community can fulfill its mandate and responsibilities in this area. People working in the arts, humanities, cultural studies, anthropology, psychology, sociology, ecology, biology, and cosmology, for instance, can create the educational resources and academic programs and courses that are required to broaden, deepen, and intensify knowledge and understanding of the intricacies and complexities of culture in general and cultures in particular, in both theory and practice. They can also improve awareness of the similarities and differences between all the diverse human cultures and civilizations in the world, as well as the cultures of other species.

And this is not all. They can also enhance people's appreciation of the natural and cultural heritage of humankind as well as facilitate the development of the algorithms, artificial intelligence capabilities, and digital technologies and devices that are required to celebrate the best in human nature, conduct, and character, as well as reduce violence, conflict, racism, terrorism, and genocide in the world through more effective interpersonal, interorganizational, and intergenerational relations. While some of these needs and resources already exist, what is needed more than anything else at this time is a much more systematic, sustained, and comprehensive approach to these requirements, as well as expansion of them far beyond esoteric and specialized groups to make them far more accessible to other groups and the public at large.

They can also create many more exchanges between the different peoples, countries, cultures, and civilizations of the world. This is especially important in terms of countries, cultures, and civilizations that are experiencing conflicts, tensions, and hostilities. Activities and initiatives like this are essential in opening the doors to fruitful and productive developments in more quintessential, human, and humane terms, thereby promoting greater understanding of and sensitivity to the similarities and differences between all the diverse peoples, countries, cultures, and civilizations of the world.

Most importantly, people and organizations working in the cultural field need to spread the word throughout the world that it is time to enter the world as culture, explain why this is so essential at this point in human history, and what the world as culture can and should be like, using their own activities and commitments as the principal illustrations of this. In order to do this, it will be necessary to move culture and cultures in general—and cultural development and policy in particular—out of the margins and into the mainstream of public and private life in all parts of the world. Margaret Mead stated the need for this most admirably and effectively when she said:

> For even the small children were collaborators in an undertaking that transcended both me and them—the attempt to understand enough about culture so that all of us, equally members of humankind, can understand ourselves and take our future and the future of our descendants safely in our hands.[6]

Next to people and organizations directly working in the cultural field, people and institutions in government, politics, and international affairs have the most important role to play in creating and developing the world as culture in practical terms. They also must play a powerful, proactive, and leadership role, but in a very different way.

In order to fulfill this role, governments, politicians, and people in international affairs will have to achieve two major cultural breakthroughs. The first involves seeing the world and political and governmental affairs from a cultural rather than economic perspective. The second involves creating the administrative structures, policies, procedures, and practices that are required in operational terms to achieve this.

Taken together, these two cultural breakthroughs will make it possible for political, governmental, and international authorities, institutions, and agencies to concern themselves with the total picture and not just selected or privileged parts of it, thereby taking maximum advantage of culture's holistic potential and integrative capacity. This is essential, since politics, politicians, governments, international authorities, and culture share one of humanity's greatest, wisest, and most important ideals in principle if not often in practice, namely commitment to "the whole" and not just privileged parts of the whole or special interest groups. This requires acting in the best interests of all people, activities, countries, and species and not only some people, activities, countries, and species, which remains the case today in virtually all parts of the world.

If this holistic requirement and all-inclusive principle is not embraced, employed, and realized by political and governmental authorities and institutions, as well as by such international agencies as the United Nations, the World Bank, the International Monetary Fund, the World Trade Organization, the Organization for Economic Cooperation and Development, the World Economic Forum, and others, *it will not be embraced, employed, or realized at all.* This is because all other individuals, institutions, groups, people, agencies, and sectors of society—be they in business, agriculture, industry, education, social affairs, science, sports, religion, recreation, the arts, the humanities, or any other area—are involved in and committed to developments in their own specific areas of employment, expertise, interest, and activity, and therefore not those of culture and cultures as wholes or total ways of life. This is why politicians, governments, and people and institutions working in international affairs must accept responsibility for developing culture and cultures *in the holistic sense* and make this their most important responsibility, priority, function, and objective going forward into the future.

In order to do so, political parties, governments, and international institutions will have to change their present administrative structures and systems, create and use cultural models of development, and implement all-inclusive cultural development plans, policies, and practices. To do this successfully, these policies and practices will have to be *transformative, transcendental*, and *redistributive.*

While piecemeal, incremental, partial, and partisan policies and practices are the preferred kinds of developmental policies, procedures, and practices for most governments, politicians, and countries today because they are premised on moving forward slowly and systematically on a number of policy fronts simultaneously and in the same direction, unfortunately there is little room for fundamental change in these matters at present or going forward into the future. This is because they are based on maintaining the status quo and existing way of doing things, and therefore chipping away at problems one at a time rather than dealing with the need for change in holistic terms.

This is no longer a viable or effective political or governmental policy option because it will not solve the most pressing and urgent problems that exist throughout the world at present or create new prospects, possibilities, policies, and practices for the future. This is why a cultural model of development must be created and utilized, since it involves changing direction dramatically. This is the only way to deal effectively with the environmental crisis and all the other complex, severe, and life-threatening problems that exist around the world today.

These recommended policies, procedures and practices should be *transformational* in the sense that they bring about fundamental changes in human behavior, lifestyles, and ways of life by reducing the demands people are making on the natural environment, the world's scarce resources, the globe's fragile ecosystems, other species, and the carrying capacity of the earth. They must also overcome the severe inequalities that exist in the treatment of marginalized and oppressed individuals and groups, as well as deal effectively with the conflicts between different genders, races, religions, countries, cultures, and civilizations in the world. They should be *transcendental* in the sense that they expand and enhance people's awareness of and appreciation for the non-material dimensions and aspects of life, as well as increase their commitment to realizing higher goals and objectives for humanity and living happier, healthier, and more fulfilling and compassionate lives. And finally, they must be *redistributive* in the sense that they allocate income, wealth, resources, and opportunities far more fairly and fully through the adoption and implementation of progressive tax systems and other measures capable of redistributing income, wealth, and financial possibilities from rich, powerful, and wealthy elites to other classes, groups, and sectors in society. If policies and practices such as these are created, adopted, and implemented, they will go a long way towards realizing what Gérard Pelletier, the former Canadian cabinet minister and ambassador to the UN, meant when he said, "Cultural policy is nothing more or less than a plan for civilization."

And this brings us to the roles and responsibilities of the general public, the third and final group in this triumvirate. While the general public will not play as immediate a role as people and organizations working in the cultural field or in governmental, political, and international affairs, its roles and responsibilities are ultimately the most important of all. This is because things will not change—and change substantially and for the better—until the public at large decides they must change and advocates for those changes.

In order to do this, members of the general public will have to reduce the demands they are making on the natural environment, the world's scarce resources, and other species by living a more qualitative and non-material rather than quantitative and material way of life. They will also have to commit to a great deal more environmental preservation and protection, fight for more equality and justice as well as more equitable distributions of income and wealth, live life more compassionately and in communion, community, and solidarity, and elevate their lives to a much higher plane of existence and cultural consciousness. Much of this will depend on people realizing that they not only have basic rights to enjoy but also fundamental responsibilities to implement. While it will take time to achieve this in practical terms, eventually this should lead to the creation and signing of a Universal Declaration of Human Rights and Responsibilities as advocated earlier.

Is it possible for the general public to make these changes and others like them? Surely it is. As people in many parts of the world have demonstrated and demonstrated convincingly in recent years through their involvement in environmental protests, the Black Lives Matter and Indigenous peoples' movements, and countless other activities and calls for reform, it is possible to "get things done" in a collective and systematic way that is not possible on an individual or random basis. Many of these movements have revealed that people are no longer willing to accept huge disparities in income and wealth, lack of interest in their circumstances and needs by corporate and wealthy elites, and procrastination on the part of governments in terms of climate change, global warming, the environmental crisis, oppression, marginalization, and polarization.

Is there room for optimism and excitement rather than pessimism and anxiety in these and other matters? Indeed there is. As a result of the efforts of millions of ordinary people, the effects of the COVID-19 pandemic, and the development of new communications vehicles and digital devices, a profound shift is going on in the world today from elite to popular culture. With this has come a great deal more attention to and interest in people from diverse ethnic and racial groups and classes as well as different parts of the world. This is evident in the transformation that is occurring at present in the character and content of newspapers, radio and television programs, podcasts, social media platforms, and elsewhere. Many of these developments would not have been possible a decade ago, but are bound to have powerful implications and consequences for the future.

One person who has been at the cutting edge of many developments like this is Meg Pier, who founded the People Are Culture (PAC) organization and online magazine to provide in-depth stories of people from around the world and all walks of life, who each offer powerful insights about their culture and its history. In sharing their heritage and traditions, they also reveal their own transformational life lessons and spiritual practices, world-changing ideas, dramatic adventures, and hard-won wisdom. PAC provides a unique perspective, presenting stories of how culture is created and shared by allowing people to tell their own stories in their own voices.

Pier goes on to state that the organization's "philosophy is that culture explains what it means to be human. Culture is all the myriad ways we create, communicate, identify, individuate, and connect. Culture provides ways to both express our individuality, and to see ourselves in others. Culture is the transmission line that makes possible cooperation, peace and prosperity." Many of these stories, and more of the underlying philosophy, is set out in PAC's recently published book, *What is Culture? Why Does it Matter?*[7]

Obviously, we have barely scratched the surface of the rich potential of culture—the potential to bring the world as culture into existence in practical and not just theoretical terms and enable it to flourish, opening the doors to a whole new era in human history. In order to achieve this, it will be necessary to take full advantage of all the major manifestations of culture that have evolved over the course of history, as well as to capitalize on the rich legacy bequeathed to us by generations of cultural scholars, historians, and practitioners over the centuries.

As Jin Li pointed out in her informative book *Cultural Foundations of Learning: East and West* when talking about the fundamental importance of culture for human beings and their development, "Culture, as the largest human created system ... penetrates so profoundly into all spheres of human life that it alters human cognition, emotion, and behavior.... Culture is like the air we breathe; we are completely dependent on it."[8] Eleanora Barbieri Masini, the Italian cultural scholar, echoed these sentiments and reinforced these convictions when she declared, "Culture in the future is the crux of the future."[9]

From the earliest manifestation of culture as "cultivation of the soul" in Roman times to the most recent all-encompassing manifestation of culture as "the cosmic whole" in line with contemporary cosmology, there is no doubt that culture is the key to a better world when everything is considered in totality. Culture makes it possible to move in breadth and depth across virtually all domains, disciplines, and activities, from the human to the non-human, the simple to the profound, the individual to the collective, the local to the global, the artistic to the scientific and technological, and the mundane to the magnificent. It also possesses the potential to move us out of the world as economics and into the world as culture, making a crucial contribution to coming to grips with the problems of the present and entering into a more united, equitable, harmonious, and sustainable world in the future.

Such a world must make it possible to deal effectively with all the injustices and inequalities that exist, as well as to ensure that all people, countries, cultures, and species are able to enjoy a reasonable quality of life without straining the globe's scarce resources and finite carrying capacity to the breaking point. This unique and timely opportunity is far too valuable to pass up. We ignore it at our peril.

Notes

Epigraph

Bernard Ostry, *The Cultural Connection* (Toronto: McClelland and Stewart, 1978), p. 1.

Chapter 1

1. Edward T. Hall, *Beyond Culture* (Garden City, NY: Anchor Press/Doubleday, 1976), p. 195 (insert mine).
2. For a detailed account of the origins, evolution, and functioning of the age of economics or the world as economics, see D. Paul Schafer, *Revolution or Renaissance: Making the Transition from an Economic Age to a Cultural Age* (Ottawa: University of Ottawa Press, 2008), part 1, chapters 1–3, pp. 9–118.
3. See Patrick Gardiner, ed., *Theories of History* (Glencoe, IL: The Free Press, 1959), pp. 126–132 for Marx's statement on the economic interpretation of history—or the materialist conception of history as it is referred to in this book—as well as other interpretations of history by noted scholars.
4. For a detailed assessment of the age of economics or world as economics, see Schafer, *Revolution or Renaissance*, chapter 4, pp. 119–135.
5. *Ibid.*, pp. 124–135.
6. Ruth Benedict. *Patterns of Culture* (London: Routledge and Kegan Paul, 1963), p. 36 (italics mine).
7. Sir Edward Burnett Tylor, *The Origins of Culture* (New York and London: Harper Torchbooks, 1958), p. 1 (italics and insert mine).
8. UNESCO, *A Practical Guide to the World Decade for Cultural Development 1988–1997* (Paris: UNESCO, 1987), p. 16 (italics mine).
9. Fernand Dumont, as quoted in Bernard Ostry, *Cultural Connection*, p. 160.
10. Wole Soyinka, "Culture, Memory, and Development," *International Conference on Culture and Development in Africa, April 2–3, 1992* (Washington: The World Bank, April 1992), p. 21.
11. When all the main manifestations of culture that have been advanced over the centuries are examined in totality and in depth—from the earlier and narrower artistic, humanistic, and historical ones to the more recent and all-encompassing psychological, anthropological, sociological, biological, ecological, and cosmological ones—there is very little in the world that is not concerned with or connected to culture and cultures in one form or another. See Alfred Kroeber and Clyde Kluckhohn, *Culture: A Critical Review of Concepts and Definitions* (New York: Vintage Books, 1963), as well as D. Paul Schafer, *Culture: Beacon of the Future* (Westport, CT: Praeger, 1998), pp. 13–82 for confirmation of this.
12. Nada Švob-Đokić, "Culture as a System: Identity, Development, and Communications," *Razvoj Development International*, 6, no. 2–3 (July–December 1991): 299.
13. Karl J. Weintraub, *Visons of Culture: Voltaire, Guizot, Burckhardt, Lamprecht,*

Huizinga, Ortega y Gasset (Chicago: University of Chicago Press, 1966), p. 216 (insert mine).

14. Edward T. Hall, *The Silent Language* (Garden City, NY: Anchor Press/Doubleday, 1973), p. 20.
15. With the exception of the first manifestation of culture as the cultivation of the soul, all the other manifestations are generally referred to in educational institutions throughout the world as the artistic, humanistic, historical, psychological, anthropological, sociological, biological, ecological, and cosmological ways of seeing and understanding culture in general and cultures in particular.

Chapter 2

1. "*Cultura animi philosophia est*" (in Latin, or "Culture is the philosophy or cultivation of the soul" translated into English) is a statement made by Marcus Cicero, the Roman statesman and orator, when for the first time in history he used the word "*cultura*" from which the word "*culture*" is derived. This occurred several decades before the birth of Christ.
2. Robert Reingold Ergang, *Herder and the Foundations of German Nationalism* (New York: Octagon Books, 1966), p. 90 (inserts mine).
3. Oswald Spengler, *The Decline of the West* (New York: The Modern Library, 1962), p. 97.

Chapter 3

1. Rockefeller Panel Report on the Future of Theatre, Dance, Music in America, *The Performing Arts: Problems and Prospects* (New York: McGraw-Hill, 1965), p. 1.
2. Kamaladevi Chattopadhyay, "The Arts as an Embodiment of the Great Folk Tradition," in UNESCO, *The Arts and Man: A Worldview of the Role and Functions of the Arts in Society* (Englewood Cliffs, NJ: Prentice-Hall, 1960), pp. 45–60.
3. Thelma Barer-Stein, *You Eat What You Are: A Study of Ethnic Food Traditions* (Toronto: McClelland and Stewart, Toronto, 1979), p. vi (insert mine).

Chapter 4

1. This comment by Henry James, the well-known American novelist, is believed to have been made to his nephew Billy James in a conversation, as confirmed in a bibliography of Henry James' life by Leon Edel.
2. Kenneth McLeish, ed., *Key Ideas in Human Thought* (New York: Facts on File, Inc., 1993), p. 356 (italics McLeish's).
3. C.P. Snow, *The Two Cultures and the Scientific Revolution* (Cambridge: Cambridge University Press, 2012 [1959]).
4. C. P. Snow, *The Two Cultures: and a Second Look: An Expanded Version of The Two Culture and the Scientific Revolution* (Cambridge: Cambridge University Press, 1963).
5. The World Commission on Culture and Development, *Our Creative Diversity: Report of the World Commission on Culture and Development* (Paris: UNESCO [printed by EGOPRIM], 1995), p. 33–51.
6. *Ibid.*, p. 35 (italics mine).

Chapter 5

1. Alfred Kroeber and Clyde Kluckhohn, "Culture: A Critical Review of Concepts and Definitions," *Papers of the Peabody Museum of Archaeology and Ethnolo-*

gy, Harvard University 47, no. 1: 44.

2. Alison Mackay, "Program Notes: Tales of Two Cities: The Leipzig-Damascus Coffee House," *Tafelmusik* 6 (May 2015/2016).
3. Javier Pérez de Cuéllar, "Address to the Inaugural Session of the Third Meeting of the World Commission on Culture and Development," San Jose, Costa Rica, February 22, 1994, p. 1.
4. Weintraub, *Visions of Culture*, p. 1.
5. *Ibid.*, p. 4.
6. *Ibid.*, p. 6–7 (insert and italics mine).
7. *Ibid.*, p. 2 (inserts mine).
8. It should be noted that Marx tended to be somewhat more flexible with respect to interpreting the unilateral or one-way relationship between the economic base and the non-economic superstructure than many of the Marxian scholars who followed in his footsteps. He admitted that there may be some cases where there is an interactive rather than unilateral relationship between the economic base and non-economic superstructure, but this was not sufficient to warrant overturning or refuting his general belief concerning the validity of the economic interpretation of history.
9. Weintraub, *Visions of Culture*, p. 3 (inserts and italics mine).
10. E. H. Gombrich, *Ideals and Idols* (Oxford: Phaidon, 1979), p. 56 (insert mine).

Chapter 6

1. James Feibleman, *The Theory of Human Culture* (New York: Humanities Press, 1968), p. 5.
2. Thomas Carlyle, *Critical and Miscellaneous Essays*, vol. 1 (London: Jean Paul Friedrich Richter Buagay: Clay and Taylor Printers, 1869), p. 16 (inserts mine).
3. Matthew Arnold, *Culture and Anarchy* (Cambridge: Cambridge University Press, 1960), pp. 47–48 (italics Arnold's).
4. *Ibid.*, pp. 46, 69, 70 (italics Arnold's, inserts mine).
5. Jan Christiaan Smuts, *Holism and Evolution* (New York: The Viking Press, 1926), p. 263 (insert mine).
6. *Ibid.*, p. 289 (insert mine).
7. Ruth Benedict, *The Chrysanthemum and the Sword: Patterns of Japanese Culture* (Cleveland and New York: Meridian Books/World Publishing Company, 1969).
8. Smuts, *Holism and Evolution*, pp. 296 and 298 (insert mine).
9. John Cowper Powys, *The Meaning of Culture* (New York: W.W. Norton and Company Inc., 1929), p. 77.
10. *Concise Oxford Dictionary* (Oxford: Oxford University Press, 1965).
11. Mircea Malitza, "Culture and the New Order: A Pattern of Integration," *Cultures* 3, no. 4 (1976): 98.
12. Feibleman, *Theory of Human Culture*, pp. 326–27.
13. Milton K. Munitz, *Cosmic Understanding* (Princeton: Princeton University Press, 1986), p. 260.
14. John Cowper Powys, *The Meaning of Culture*, pp. 23, 8 (italics mine).
15. *Ibid.*, p. 11.
16. Ralph Linton, *Cultural Background of Personality* (New York: Appleton-Cen-

tury-Crofts, 1945), p. 3.

17. Francis L.K. Hsu, ed., *Aspects of Culture and Personality: A Symposium* (New York: Abelard-Schuman, 1954), p. 202 (inserts mine).
18. Pitirim Sorokin, *Modern Historical and Social Philosophies* (New York: Dover Publications, 1963), p. 319 (insert mine).
19. Herman Hesse, *The Glass Bead Game* (New York: Bantam Books, 1977), p. 55 (inserts mine).
20. Albert Schweitzer, *Out of My Life and Thought: An Autobiography* (New York: Holt, Rinehart and Winston, 1964), pp. 149–150.
21. Douglas Haring, ed., *Personal Character and Cultural Milieu* (Syracuse, NY: Syracuse University Press, 1964), p. 447 (inserts mine).
22. Charles R. Joy, ed., *Albert Schweitzer: An Anthology* (Boston: The Beacon Press, 1947), p. 131.
23. Pitirim Sorokin, *Social and Cultural Dynamics* (Boston: Sargent Publisher, 1957), p. 628 (inserts mine).
24. Rabindranath Tagore, quoted in Paul J. Braisted, *Cultural Cooperation: Keynote of the Coming Age*, The Hazen Pamphlets, No. 8 (New Haven: The Edward W. Hazen Foundation, 1945), p. 5.
25. Mahatma Gandhi, quoted in *Our Creative Diversity: Report of the World Commission on Culture and Development* (Paris: UNESCO, 1995), p. 73.
26. Quoted in E. Becker, *The Denial of Death* (London: The Free Press, 1972), p. 255 (inserts mine).

Chapter 7

1. Awori Achoka, "Culture, Environment and Development: How?" (comment) (no date).
2. Tylor, *The Origins of Culture*, p. 1 (italics and insert mine).
3. Benedict, *Patterns of Culture*, p. 33.
4. Raymond Williams, *The Long Revolution* (London: Chatto and Windus and New York: Columbia University Press, 1961), p. 46–47.
5. Edward T. Hall, *Beyond Culture* (Garden City, NY: Anchor Press/Doubleday, 1976), p. 195 (italics mine).
6. Benedict, *Patterns of Culture*, p. 36.
7. Giles Gunn, *The Culture of Criticism and the Criticism of Culture* (New York: Oxford University Press, 1987), p. 95.
8. Robert Redfield, *The Little Community: Viewpoints for the Study of a Human Whole* (Chicago: The University of Chicago Press, 1973), p. 161.
9. Clifford Geertz, *The Interpretation of Cultures* (New York: Basic Books, 1973), p. 14.
10. Weintraub, *Visons of Culture*, p. 216 (insert mine).
11. *Ibid.*, p. 219 (italics Weintraub's).
12. *Ibid.*, pp. 219–220 (insert mine).
13. Wade Davis, "A wake-up call to the value of ancient wisdom," *Toronto Star*, October 26, 2009, IN3.
14. Augustin Girard, *Cultural Development: Experience and Policies* (Paris: UNESCO, 1972), p. 142.

Chapter 8

1. Braisted, *Cultural Cooperation*, p. 6.
2. Alfred L. Kroeber and Talcott Parsons, "The Concepts of Culture and Social System," *American Sociological Review*, 23 (1958): 582–583.
3. Harold Innis, *The Bias of Communications* (Toronto: University of Toronto Press, 1951), p. 33 (italics mine).
4. Marshall McLuhan, *Understanding Media* (Toronto: McGraw-Hill Company, 1964), p. 7.
5. *Ibid.*, p. 9 (insert mine)
6. Donald McGregor, "The Prospects for Canadian Identity, Individual and National, in the Global Village," Interdisciplinary Seminar, Institute of Canadian Studies, Carleton University, April 4, 1974.
7. Mary E. Clark, *Ariadne's Thread: The Search for New Modes of Thinking* (New York: St. Martin's Press, 1989), p. 156 (italics Clark's).
8. Antonio Alonso Concheiro, "The Futures of Culture in Latin America," in E. Masini (co-ordinator), *The Futures of Culture*, Vol II: *The Prospects for African and Latin America* (Paris: UNESCO, Future-oriented Studies Programme, 1992), p. 65 (insert mine).
9. Brian Holihan, *Thinking in a New Light: How to Boost Your Creativity and Live More Fully by Exploring World Cultures* (Sunnyvale, CA: Full Humanity Press, 2016), pp. 272–298.

Chapter 9

1. Kroeber and Kluckhohn, *Culture: A Critical Review of Concepts and Definitions*, p. 57.
2. This was confirmed when the delegates at the Second World Conference on Cultural Policies convened by UNESCO in Mexico City in 1982 declared that "Culture ought to be considered today to *whole* collection of distinct traits, spiritual and material, intellectual and effective, which characterize a society or social group. It comprises, besides arts and letters, modes of life, human rights, value system, traditions, and beliefs." UNESCO, Mexico City Declaration on Cultural Policies (Paris: UNESCO, 1982) (italics mine).
3. William J. Broad, "The tantalizing secrets of coral sex," *Toronto Star*, June 26, 2016, IN6.
4. Seth Borenstein and Mayuko Ono, "Feeling sluggish: These sea creatures found a solution," *Toronto Star*, March 13, 2021, p. IN3.
5. Frans de Waal, *Are We Smart Enough to Know How Smart Animals Are?* (New York: W. W. Norton and Company, 2016), p. 275 (italics mine).
6. Peter Wohlleben, *The Hidden Life of Trees: What They Feel, How They Communicate* (Vancouver and Berkeley, CA: Greystone Books, 2016), p. 3.
7. *Ibid.*, p. viii (insert and italics mine).
8. De Waal, *Are We Smart Enough to Know How Smart Animals Are?*, p. 274 (italics de Waal's).
9. Kroeber and Kluckhohn, *Culture: A Critical Review of Concepts and Definitions*, p. 290.

Chapter 10

1. Gregory Bateson, cited in a "A Review of *An Ecology of Mind: A Daughter's*

Portrait, a film by Nora Bateson," by Jan van Boedkel, p. 1.
2. Ruth Benedict, *Patterns of Culture*, p. 34.
3. Van Boeckel, p. 4.
4. W. Scott Morton, *China: Its History and Culture*, 3rd ed. (New York: McGraw-Hill, 1995), p. 105.
5. The four fundamental pillars and sixteen basic principles of the *Earth Charter* are:

   I. *Respect and Care for the Community of Life*

   1. Respect Earth and life in all its diversity.

   2. Care for the community of life with understanding, compassion and love.

   3. Build democratic societies that are just, participatory, sustainable and peaceful.

   4. Secure Earth's bounty and beauty for present and future generations.

   II. *Ecological Integrity*

   5. Protect and restore the integrity of Earth's ecological systems, with special concern for biological diversity and the natural processes that sustain life.

   6. Prevent harm as the best method of environmental protection and, when knowledge is limited, apply a precautionary approach.

   7. Adopt patterns of production, consumption and reproduction that safeguard Earth's regenerative capacities, human rights and community well-being.

   8. Advance the study of ecological sustainability and promote the open exchange and wide application of the knowledge acquired.

   III. *Social and Economic Justice*

   9. Eradicate poverty as an ethical, social and environmental imperative.

   10. Ensure that economic activities and institutions at all levels promote human development in an equitable and sustainable manner.

   11. Affirm gender equality and equity as prerequisites to sustainable development and ensure universal access to education, health care and economic opportunity.

   12. Uphold the right of all, without discrimination, to a natural and social environment supportive of human dignity, bodily health and spiritual well-being, with special attention to the rights of indigenous peoples and minorities.

   IV. *Democracy, Nonviolence, and Peace*

   13. Strengthen democratic institutions at all levels, and provide transparency and accountability in governance, inclusive participation in decision-making, and access to justice.

   14. Integrate into formal education and lifelong learning the knowledge, values and skills needed for a sustainable way of life.

   15. Treat all living beings with respect and consideration.

   16. Promote a culture of tolerance, non-violence and peace.
6. Anthony R. Zelle, Grant Wilson, Rachelle Adam, and Herman Greene (eds.), *Earth Law: Emerging Ecocentric Law—A Guide for Practitioners* (New York: Wolters Kluwer Aspen Coursebook Series, 2021).
7. *Ibid.*, p. 1.
8. B. Jennings, *Ecological Governance toward a New Social Contract with the*

Earth (Morgantown, WV: West Virginia University Press, 2016), p. 44.

9. Pope Francis, *Laudato Si': On Care for Our Common Home* III (2015), as quoted in Jennings, *Ecological Governance*, p. 89.

Chapter 11

1. Pierre Pascallon, "The Cultural Dimension of Development," *Intereconomics* (January-February 1986): 7.
2. Kaj Birket-Smith, *The Paths of Culture: A General Ethnology*, translated from the Danish by Karin Fennow (Madison and Milwaukee: The University of Wisconsin Press, 1965), p. 9 (insert mine).
3. Alexander Eliot and Floyd Yearout (eds.), *Myths* (New York: McGraw-Hill Book Company, 1976), p. 10.
4. Joseph Campbell, with Bill Moyers and Betty Sue Flowers (ed.), *The Power of Myth* (New York: Doubleday, 1988).
5. Ronald Wright, *Stolen Continents: The "New World" through Indian Eyes since 1492* (New York: Viking, 1992), p. 5.
6. Ptolemy quoted in M.S. Suárez Lafuente, "On the Road to Hokitika: The Epics of a New Constellation," *Coolabah* 22 (2017): 96 (inserts mine).
7. Lemaître quoted in "Georges Lemaître, Father of the Big Bang," Cosmic Horizons Curriculum Collection, American Museum of Natural History (https://www.amnh.org/learn-teach/curriculum-collections/cosmic-horizons-book/georges-lemaitre-big-bang).
8. Albert Schweitzer, *Civilization and Ethics* (London: A. and C. Black Ltd., 1923), pp. vii, viii, and ix (inserts mine).
9. Anthony C. Wallace, *Culture and Personality* (New York: Random House, 1967), p. 99 (inserts mine).
10. Robert Redfield, *The Primitive World and Its Transformation* ((Ithaca: Great Seal Books, 1963), pp. 85–86 (italics mine).
11. Jerzy A. Wojeiechowski, "Cultural Pluralism and the Modern State," *Cultures* 4, no. 4 (1977): 54 (inserts mine).
12. This has led in recent years to a distinction between physical (or scientific), religious, and cosmological cosmologies and their various perceptions in many parts of the world.
13. Milton Munitz, *Cosmic Understanding: Philosophy and Science of the Universe* (Princeton: Princeton University Press, 1986), pp. 4–5.
14. Robert V. Wagoner and Donald W. Goldsmith, *Cosmic Horizons: Understanding the Universe* (San Francisco: W. H. Freeman and Company, 1982), p. 1.
15. Edward R. Harrison, *Cosmology: The Science of the Universe* (Cambridge: Cambridge University Press, 1981), pp. 10–12 (italics mine).
16. Review of Rémi Brague's book *The Wisdom of the World: The Human Experience of the Universe in Western Thought* by Herman Greene, presented in February 2005 at a conference on Alfred North Whitehead and Teilhard de Chardin, p. 2.
17. David Schenck, "Cosmology and Wisdom: The Great Teaching Work of Thomas Berry," in *Thomas Berry's Work: Development, Difference, Importance, Applications*, in *The Ecozoic: Reflections on Life in an Ecological-Cultural Age*, 4 (2017): 371, 373.

18. Angela T. Lydon, "Cosmology and Curriculum: A Vision for an Ecozoic Age," Ph.D. thesis, Louisiana State University, 1992, p. 114.
19. Milton Munitz, *Cosmic Understanding*, p. 6.
20. Fritjof Capra, *The Tao of Physics* (New York: Bantam, 1991), p. 130.
21. It should be noted that a great deal of attention has been focused in recent years on what is known as *cosmogenesis*, which is a specific branch of cosmology that deals with the origins of the cosmos as a whole. With this has come an escalating interest in the noosphere (that stage of evolutionary development dominated by the mind and consciousness), as well as what is called *time-developmental consciousness*. The latter starts with the origins of the cosmos and is concerned with its dynamic, evolutionary, regenerative, and expansive rather than static and unchanging character.

Chapter 12

1. S. Takdir Alisjahbana, *Socio-Cultural Creativity in the Converging and Restructuring Process of the New Emerging World* (Jakarta: P.T. Dian Rakyat, 1983), pp. 12–13.
2. John McHale, *The Future of the Future* (New York: George Braziller, 1969), p. 3.
3. Weintraub, *Visions of Culture*, pp. 117–118.
4. Ranji Kothari, *The Schveningen Report: Towards a New International Development Strategy*, Schveningen Symposium, July 25–28, 1979 (Nyon: International Foundation of Development Alternatives, 1979), p. 7.
5. Valerie Lynch Lee (ed.), *Faces of Culture: Viewer's Guide* (Huntington Beach, CA: KOCE-TV Foundation, 1983), p. 69.
6. Margaret Mead, *Letters from the Field 1925–1975* (New York: Harper and Row, 1977), p. 16.
7. More information on the philosophy and activities of People Are Culture (PAC) is available on the PAC website: http://www.peopleareculture.com/. As stated in the material circulated: "While the phenomenon of culture is universal, the meaning is personal. Our interviews and profiles celebrate our unique differences and our shared human contact. We believe we are each special ... and we are all the same. We all matter, we each have an incredible story, and everyone has something to teach us." The stories of cultural standard bearers are presented in 12 categories: Archaeology and Architecture; Dance; Festivals; Folk Art; Food; Gardens and Landscapes; Language and Legends; Maritime; Music; Spirituality; Textiles; and Visual Arts.
8. Jin Li, *Cultural Foundations of Learning: East and West* (New York: Cambridge University Press, 2012), p. 81.
9. Masini, *The Futures of Culture*, vol. 1, p. 6.

A Cultural Timeline, 1700–2000
Some Important Contributions to the History and Development of Cultural Thought

This timeline lists what are generally deemed to be some of the most important contributions to the history and development of cultural thought between 1700 and 2000 by organizations, scholars, and other people working in the cultural field. This list is intended to provide a sense of how this field has evolved during this period of time and is indicative but not definitive in nature.

1700–1800

1725 Giambattista Vico, *The New Science*
1756 Voltaire, *Essai sur les Moeurs et l'Esprit des Nations*
1782 Johann Christoph Adelung, *Versuch einer Geschichte der Cultur des Menschlichen Geschlechts*
1784 Johann Gottfried von Herder, *Outlines of a Philosophy of the History of Man*
1785 Christoph Meiners, *Grundriss der Geschichte der Menschheit*
1795 Marquis de Condorcet, *Esquisse d'un Tableau Historique des Progrès de l'Esprit Humain*

1800–1900

1828 François Guizot, *De la Civilisation en Europe*
1843 Gustav Klemm, *Allegemeine Cultur-Geschichte der Menscheit*
1857 Henry Thomas Buckle, *History of Civilization in England*
1861 Johann Jakob Bachofen, *Das Mutterrecht*
1861 Henry Maine, *Ancient Law*
1863 Theodor Waitz, *Introduction to Anthropology*
1867 Jacob Burckhardt, *Civilization of the Renaissance in Italy*
1869 Matthew Arnold, *Culture and Anarchy*
1870 John Lubbock, *The Origins of Civilization and the Primitive Condition of Man*
1871 Edward Burnett Tylor, *Primitive Culture*
1873 Herbert Spencer, *The Study of Sociology*
1876 Herbert Spencer, *Principles of Sociology*
1877 Lewis Henry Morgan, *Ancient Society*
1882 Friedrich Ratzel, *Anthropogeographie*
1883 Wilhelm Dilthey, *Einleitung in die Geisteswissenschaften*
1890 James George Frazer, *The Golden Bough*
1896 Friedrich Ratzel, *The History of Mankind*
1898 Leo Viktor Frobenius, *Die Weltanschauung der Naturvölker*

1900–1950

1904 Max Weber, *The Protestant Ethic and the Spirit of Capitalism*
1906 Augustus Henry Lane-Fox Pitt Rivers, *The Evolution of Culture and Other Essays*
1910 Alfred Cort Haddon, *A History of Anthropology*
1911 Franz Boas, *The Mind of Primitive Man*
1911 Fritz Graebner, *Die Methode der Ethnologie*
1912 Franz Boas, *Race, Language and Culture*
1914 William Halse Rivers Rivers, *The History of Melanesian Society*
1917 Robert Lowie, *Culture and Ethnology*
1917 Clark David Wissler, *The American Indian*
1918 Oswald Spengler, *The Decline of the West*
1919 Johan Huizinga, *The Waning of the Middle Ages*
1920 Robert Lowie, *Primitive Society*
1921 Edward Sapir, *Language*
1922 Alfred Reginald Radcliffe-Brown, *The Andaman Islanders*
1922 Alexander Goldenweiser, *Early Civilization: An Introduction to Anthropology*
1922 Bronislaw Malinowski, *Argonauts of the Western Pacific*
1922 William Halse Rivers Rivers, *History and Ethnology*
1923 Alfred Louis Kroeber, *Anthropology*
1925 Vere Gordon Childe, *The Dawn of European Civilization*
1925 Marcel Mauss, *The Gift*
1927 Franz Boas, *Primitive Art*
1928 Roland Burrage Dixon, *The Building of Cultures*
1928 Margaret Mead, *Coming of Age in Samoa*
1929 Ruth Bunzel, *The Pueblo Potter*
1929 Lucien Paul Victor Febvre, *Civilisation: Le Mot et L'Idée*
1929 John Cowper Powys, *The Meaning of Culture*
1929 Clark David Wissler, *An Introduction to Social Anthropology*
1930 Sigmund Freud, *Civilization and Its Discontents*
1930 Frank Raymond Leavis, *Mass Civilisation and Minority Culture*
1933 Alexander Goldenweiser, *History, Psychology and Culture*
1934 Ruth Fulton Benedict, *Patterns of Culture*
1934 Arnold Joseph Toynbee, *A Study of History*
1935 Alfred Irving Hallowell, *Culture and Experience*
1936 Raymond Firth, *We, the Tikopia*
1936 Margaret Mead, *Cooperation and Competition among Primitive Peoples*
1937 Robert Lowie, *The History of Ethnological Theory*
1937 Talcott Parsons, *The Structure of Social Action*
1937 Pitirim Alexandrovich Sorokin, *Social and Cultural Dynamics*
1938 Franz Boas, *General Anthropology*
1938 Lewis Mumford, *The Culture of Cities*
1940 Edward Evan Evans-Pritchard, *The Nuer*
1941 Herbert Read, *The Hell with Culture*
1944 Bronislaw Malinowski, *A Scientific Theory of Culture*
1945 Alfred Louis Kroeber, *Configurations of Culture Growth*

1945 Ralph Linton, *The Cultural Background of Personality*
1946 Ruth Fulton Benedict, *The Chrysanthemum and the Sword*
1946 James Kern Feibleman, *The Theory of Human Culture*
1948 Alfred Reginald Radcliffe-Brown, *A Natural Science of Society*
1948 Thomas Stearns Eliot, *Notes Towards the Definition of Culture*
1948 Melville Jean Herskovits, *Man and His Works*
1948 Frank Raymond Leavis, *The Great Tradition*
1949 George Peter Murdock, *Social Structure*
1949 Leslie Alvin White, *The Science of Culture*

1950–2000

1950 Géza Róheim, *Psychoanalysis and Anthropology*
1951 Edward Evan Evans-Pritchard, *Social Anthropology*
1952 Alfred Louis Kroeber and Clyde Kluckhohn, *Culture: A Critical Review of Concepts and Definitions*
1952 Alfred Louis Kroeber, *The Nature of Culture*
1953 Margaret Mead, *Cultural Patterns and Technical Change*
1954 John Joseph Honigmann, *Culture and Personality*
1955 Ralph Linton, *The Tree of Culture*
1955 Julian Haynes Steward, *Theory of Cultural Change*
1957 Richard Hoggart, *The Uses of Literacy*
1958 Alfred Reginald Radcliffe-Brown, *Method in Social Anthropology*
1958 Claude Lévi-Strauss, *Anthropologie Structurale*
1958 Claude Lévi-Strauss, *Tristes Tropiques*
1958 Raymond Williams, *Culture and Society: 1750–1950*
1959 Margaret Mead, *An Anthropologist at Work: Writings of Ruth Benedict*
1959 Edward Twitchell Hall, *The Silent Language*
1959 Leslie Alvin White, *The Evolution of Culture*
1960 Marshall David Sahlins and Elman Rogers Service, *Evolution and Culture*
1961 Anthony Francis Clarke Wallace, *Culture and Personality*
1961 Raymond Williams, *The Long Revolution*
1963 Victor Barnouw, *Culture and Personality*
1963 Jules Henry, *Culture Against Man*
1963 John Joseph Honigmann, *Understanding Culture*
1963 George Peter Murdock, *Outline of World Cultures*
1963 Claude Lévi-Strauss, *Totemism*
1964 Marvin Harris, *The Nature of Cultural Things*
1964 Marshall McLuhan, *Understanding Media*
1964 Montague Francis Ashley-Montagu, *The Concept of Race*
1966 Sutan Takdir Alisjahbana, *Values as Integrating Forces in Personality, Society and Culture*
1966 Edward Twitchell Hall, *The Hidden Dimension*
1968 Marvin Harris, *The Rise of Anthropological Theory*
1972 Gregory Bateson, *Steps to an Ecology of Mind*
1973 Zygmunt Bauman, *Culture as Praxis*
1973 Clifford James Geertz, *The Interpretation of Cultures*

1974 Herbert Gans, *Popular Culture and High Culture*
1976 Ali Al'amin Mazrui, *A World Federation of Cultures: An African Perspective*
1976 Herbert Irving Shiller, *Communications and Cultural Domination*
1976 Raymond Williams, *Keywords: A Vocabulary of Culture and Society*
1978 Edward Wadie Said, *Orientalism*
1980 Geert Hendrik Hofstede, *Culture's Consequences: Comparing Values, Behaviours and Organizations Across Nations*
1981 Raymond Williams, *Culture*
1982 Frijof Capra, *The Turning Point: Science, Society and Rising Culture*
1983 Sutan T. Alisjahbana, *Socio-Cultural Creativity in the Converging and Restructuring Process of The New Emerging World*
1986 James Clifford and George Marcus (eds.), *Writing Culture: the Poetics and Politics of Ethnography*
1986 Michael Fischer and George Emanuel Marcus, *Anthropology as Cultural Critique*
1987 George Stocking Jr., *Victorian Anthropology*
1988 Elise Boulding, *Building a Global Civic Culture*
1988 James Clifford, *The Predicament of Culture*
1988 Clifford James Geertz, *Works and Lives: The Anthropologist as Author*
1989 John Fiske, *Understanding Popular Culture*
1991 Mike Featherstone, *Consumer Culture and Postmodernism*
1991 Geert Hendrik Hofstede, *Cultures and Organizations: Software of the Mind*
1991 John Tomlinson, *Cultural Imperialism*
1992 Mike Featherstone, *Cultural Theory and Social Change*
1993 Christopher Sandy Jencks, *Culture*
1993 Edward Wadie Said, *Culture and Imperialism*
1994 Homi Bhabha, *The Location of Culture*
1994 Jonathan Friedman, *Cultural Identity and Global Process*
1995 Fernand Braudel, *A History of Civilizations*
1995 Néstor Garcia Canclini, *Hybrid Cultures*
1996 Samuel Phillips Huntington, *The Clash of Civilizations and the Remaking of World Order*
1997 Manuel Castells, *The Power of Identity*
1999 Adam Kuper, *Culture: The Anthropologists' Account*
1999 John Tomlinson, *Globalization and Culture*
2000 Elise Boulding, *Cultures of Peace*

Selected Readings

While no books have been written specifically about the world as culture, countless books have been written about various aspects of this matter that are in keeping with the character and contents of this book. I hope the readings that have been selected here will prove helpful for those who would like to pursue this subject further and view the world from a cultural perspective. It should be mentioned that these readings have been provided here because they are relevant to specific chapters in this book and are by no means definitive in these areas.

Abdel-Malek, Anisuzzaman and Abdel-Malek, Anouar, *Culture and Thought in the Transformation of the World* (London: The Macmillan Press, 1983).

Agnew, John A., Mercer, John, and Sopher, David E. (eds.), *The City in Cultural Context* (Boston: Allen and Unwin, 1984).

Ahearne, Jeremy (ed,), *French Cultural Policy Debates* (London: Routledge, 2015).

Allan, Kenneth, and Daynes, Sarah, *Explorations in Sociological Theory: Seeing the Social World*, 4th ed. (London: Sage Publications, 2016).

Alisjahbana, S. Takdir, *Socio-Cultural Creativity in the Converging and Restructuring Process of the New Emerging World* (Jakarta: P.T. Dian Rakyat, 1983).

Alisjahbana, S. Takdir, *Values as Integrating Forces in Personality, Society and Culture* (Kuala Lumpur: University of Malaya Press, 1966).

Allport, Gordon, *Pattern and Growth in Personality* (New York: Holt, Rinehart and Winston, 1963).

Anderson, Victor, *Alternative Economic Indicators* (London: Routledge, 2015).

Arnold, Matthew, *Culture and Anarchy* (Cambridge: Cambridge University Press, 1960).

Attfield, Robin, *Environmental Thought: A Short History* (Cambridge and Boston: Polity Press, 2021).

Baldwin, John R., Faulkner, Sandra L., Hecht, Michael L., and Lindsley, Sheryl L., (eds.), *Redefining Culture: Perspectives Across the Disciplines* (London: Routledge, 2005).

Bauman, Zygmunt, *Culture as Praxis* (London: Routledge and Kegan Paul, 1973).

Bauman, Zygmunt, *Globalization: The Human Consequences* (New York: Columbia University Press, 1998).

Behar, Ruth, and Gordon, Deborah, A. (eds.), *Women Writing Culture: Twentieth Century Women American Anthropologists* (Berkeley and Los Angeles: University of California Press, 1995).

Bekoff, Marc (ed.), *Encyclopedia of Animal Behavior* (Westport, Conn.: Greenwood Press, 2004).

Bekoff, Marc, *The Emotional Lives of Animals: A Leading Scientist Explores Animal Joy, Sorrow and Empathy—and Why This Matters* (Novato. CA.: New World Library, 2008).

Benedict, Ruth, *Patterns of Culture* (London: Routledge and Kegan Paul, 1963).

Berger, Peter, I. and Huntington, Samuel (eds.), *Many Globalizations: Cultural Diversity in the Contemporary World* (New York: Oxford University Press, 2002).

Bernardi, Bernado (ed.), *The Concept and Dynamics of Culture* (The Hague: Mouton Publishers, 1977).

Berry, Thomas, *Dream of the Earth* (New York: Random House, 1988).

Berry, Thomas, *The Great Work: Our Way into the Future* (New York: Three Rivers Press, 1999).

Berry, Thomas, and Tucker, Mary Evelyn (eds.), *The Sacred Universe: Earth, Spirituality and Religion in the Twenty-First Century* (New York: Columbia University Press, 2009).

Bickley, Verner, and Philip, Puthenparampil John (eds.), *Cultural Relations in the Global Community* (New Delhi: Abhinav Publications, 1981).

Bird, Jon, et al. (eds.), *Mapping the Futures: Local Cultures, Global Change* (London: Routledge, 1993).

Blacker, Carmen, and Loewe, Michael (eds.), *Ancient Cosmologies* (London: George Allen and Unwin Ltd., 1975).

Bloom, William (ed.), *Holistic Revolution: The Essential New Age Reader* (New York: Allen Lane and Penguin Press, 2000).

Bohm, David, *Wholeness and the Implicate Order* (London: Routledge, 2002).

Bonner, John R., *The Evolution of Culture in Animals* (Princeton: Princeton University Press,1983).

Boulding, Elise, *Cultures of Peace: The Hidden Side of History* (Syracuse, NY: Syracuse University Press, 2000).

Boxx, T. William, and Quinlivan, Gary M. (eds.), *The Cultural Context of Economics and Politics* (Landan, MD: University Press of America, 1994).

Bradford, G., Gary, M., and Wallach, G. (eds.), *The Politics of Culture: Policy Perspectives for Individuals, Institutions and Communities*, (New York: The New Press and The Center for Arts and Culture, 2000).

Brague, Rémi, *The Wisdom of the World: The Human Experience of the Universe in Western Thought*, trans. Teresa Lavender Fagan (Chicago: Chicago University Press, 2003).

Braudel, Fernand, *A History of Civilizations*, trans. Richard Mayne (New York: Penguin Books, 1995).

Buhner, Stephen Harrod, *Plant Intelligence and the Imaginal Realm* (Rochester, VT: Bear and Company, 2014).

Burckhardt, Jacob, *The Civilization of the Renaissance in Italy* (Washington, DC: Washington Square Press, 1966).

Burke, Peter, *Varieties of Cultural History* (Cambridge: Polity Press, 1997).

Call, William, *Cultural Revolution: From the Decay of a Dying World Comes the Birth of a New Age* (Salt Lake City: Freethinker Press, 2000).

Canclini, Néstor Garcia, *Hybrid Cultures: Strategies for Entering and Leaving Modernity* (Minneapolis: University of Minnesota Press, 1995).

Capra, Fritjof, *The Tao of Physics* (New York: Bantam, 1991).

Capra, Fritjof, *The Turning Point: Science, Society and the Rising Culture* (New York: Simon and Schuster, 1982).

Carroll, Sean, *The Big Picture: On the Origins of Life, Meaning, and the Universe* (New York: Dutton, 2016).
Chay, Jongsuk, (ed.), *Culture and International Relations* (New York: Praeger Publishers, 1990).
Chisholm, Anne, *Philosophers of the Earth: Conversations with Ecologists* (New York: Dutton, 1972).
Clifford, James, and Marcus, George (eds.), *Writing Culture: The Poetics and Politics of Ethnography* (Berkeley: University of California Press, 1986).
Commoner, Barry, *The Closing Circle: Nature, Man and Technology* (New York: Knopf, 1971).
Coser, Lewis A., *Masters of Sociological Thought: Ideas in Historical and Social Context*, 2nd ed. (Long Grove, IL: Waveland Press, 2003).
Coyle, Daniel, *The Culture Code: The Secrets of Highly Successful Groups* (New York: Bantam, 2018).
Cronk, Lee, *That Complex Whole: Culture and the Evolution of Human Behaviour* (Boulder, CO: Westview Press, 1999).
Crump, Donald, J. (ed.) *Splendors of the Past: Lost Cities of the Ancient World* (Washington, DC: National Geographic Society, 1981).
Cunningham, Lawrence, Reich, John. J., and Fichner-Rathus, Lois, *Culture and Values: A Survey of the Humanities*, vol. 1, 8th ed. (Andover, UK: Cengage Learning, 2014).
Dennis, Kingsley L., *New Consciousness for a New World* (Rochester, VT: Inner Traditions, 2001).
Davis, Wade, *Light At The Edge Of The World: Journey Through The Realm of Vanishing Cultures* (Toronto: Douglas and McIntyre, 2000).
Devall, Bill, *Deep Ecology: Living as If Nature Mattered* (Layton, UT: Smith Publisher, 2007).
Diamond, Jared, *Guns, Germs and Steel: The Fate of Human Societies* (New York: W.W. Norton, 1999).
Dirks, Nicholas B., Eley, Geoff, and Ortner, Sherry B. (eds.), *Culture/Power/History: A Reader in Contemporary Social Theory* (Princeton, NJ: Princeton University Press, 1994).
Dixon, R.B., *The Building of Cultures* (New York: Charles Scribner's Sons, 1928).
Dorian, Frederick *Commitment to Culture* (Pittsburgh: Pittsburgh University Press, 1964).
Ehrlich, Anne and Paul, *Healing the Planet: Strategies for Resolving the Environmental Crisis* (Reading, MA: Addison-Wesley, 1991).
Eliot, Alexander, *Myths* (New York: McGraw-Hill Book Company, 1976).
Eliot, T. S., *Notes Towards the Definition of Culture* (London: Faber and Faber, 1963).
Featherstone, Mike (ed.), *Global Culture: Nationalism, Globalization and Modernity* (London: Sage Publications, 1990).
Featherstone, Mike, and Lash, Scott (eds.), *Spaces of Culture: City-Nation-World* (London: Sage Publications Ltd., 1999).
Feibleman, James, *The Theory of Human Culture* (New York: Humanities Press, 1968).

Fiero, Gloria, *Landmarks in Humanities*, 4th ed. (New York: McGraw-Hill, 2016).
Frazer, James George, *The Golden Bough: A Study in Magic and Religion* (New York: The Macmillan Company, 1951).
Friedman, J., *Cultural Identity and Global Process* (London: Sage Publishers, 1994).
Friedman, Thomas L., *The Lexus and the Olive Tree: Understanding Globalization* (New York: Anchor Books, 2000).
Gacs, Uta, et al. (eds.), *Women Anthropologists: A Biographical Dictionary* (Westport, CT: Greenwood Press, 1988).
Gaisford, John (ed.), *Atlas of Man* (London: Marshall Cavendish Editions, 1978).
Gamst, Frederick C., and Norbeck, Edward (eds.), *Ideas of Culture: Sources and Uses* (New York: Holt, Rinehart and Winston, 1978).
Geertz, Clifford, and Darnton, Robert, *The Interpretation of Cultures*, 3rd ed. (New York: Basic Books, 2017).
Girard, Augustin, *Cultural Development: Experience and Policies* (Paris: UNESCO, 1972).
Gombrich, E. H., *Ideals and Idols: Essays on Values in History and in Art* (Oxford: Phaidon, 1979).
Grossberg, L., Nelson, Cary, and Treichler, P. (eds.), *Cultural Studies* (London: Routledge, 1992).
Haberland, Eike (ed.), *Frobenius 1873 to 1973: An Anthology* (Wiesbaden: Franz Steiner Verlag GmbH, 1973).
Haeckel, Ernst, *The History of Creation*, vol. 1, ed. Janice M. Hughes (Thunder Bay, ON: Briar Bird Press, 2018).
Hall, Edward T., *The Hidden Dimension* (Garden City, NY: Doubleday and Company, 1966).
Hall, Edward, T., *Beyond Culture* (Garden City, NY: Anchor Press/Doubleday, 1976).
Hallowell, Irving, A., *Culture and Experience* (Philadelphia: University of Pennsylvania Press, 1995).
Haq, Mahbub ul, *Reflections on Human Development* (New York and Oxford: Oxford University Press, 1995).
Haring, Douglas (ed.), *Personal Character and Cultural Milieu* (New York: Syracuse University Press, 1949).
Harris, Marvin, *The Rise of Anthropological Theory: A History of Theories of Culture* (New York: Thomas Y. Crowell Company, 1968).
Harris, Marvin, *Theories of Culture in Postmodern Times* (Walnut Creek, London and New Delhi: Altamira Press, 1999).
Harrison, Lawrence E, and Huntingtin, Samuel P. (eds.), *Culture Matters: How Values Shape Human Progress* (New York: Basic Books, 2001).
Haught, John F. *The New Cosmic Story: Inside Our Awakening Universe* (New Haven: Yale University Press, 2017).
Herskovits, Melville, *Cultural Anthropology* (New York: Alfred Knopf, 1963).
Herskovits, Melville, *Cultural Relativism: Perspectives in Cultural Pluralism,* ed. Frances Herskovits (New York: Random House, 1979).
Hirschberg, Stuart, and Hirschberg, Terry, *One World, Many Cultures*, 4th ed. (Boston: Allyn and Bacon, 2001).
Hofstede, Geert, *Culture's Consequences: Comparing Values, Behaviours, Institu-*

tions and Organizations Across Nations (London: Sage Publications, 2001).
Hoggart, Richard, *The Uses of Literacy* (London: Routledge, 1998).
Holihan, Brian, *Thinking in a New Light: How to Boost Your Creativity and Live More Fully by Exploring World Cultures* (Sunnyvale, CA.: Full Humanity Press, 2016).
Honigmann, J. J., *Understanding Culture* (New York: Harper and Row, 1963).
Honigmann, J. J., *Personality in Culture* (New York: Harper and Row, 1967).
Honigmann, J. J., *The Development of Anthropological Ideas* (Homewood, IL: The Dorsey Press, 1976).
Hughes, Donald J., *An Environmental History of the World: Humankind's Changing Role in the Community of Life* (London: Routledge, 2009).
Huntington, Samuel P., *The Clash of Civilizations and the Remaking of World Order* (New York: Touchstone Books, 1998).
Hutcheon, Pat Duffy, *Building Character and Culture* (Westport, CT: Praeger, 1999).
Hsu, Francis, L. K. (ed.), *Aspects of Culture and Personality* (New York: Abelard-Schuman, 1954).
Huizinga, Johan, *The Waning of the Middle Ages* ((New York: Penguin Books, 1979).
Inglehart, Ronald, F., *Cultural Evolution: People's Motives are Changing, and Reshaping the World* (Cambridge: Cambridge University Press, 2019).
Innis, Harold, A., *The Bias of Communications*, 2nd ed. (Toronto: University of Toronto Press, 2008).
Iriye, Akira, *Cultural Internationalism and World Order* (Baltimore, MD.: John Hopkins University Press, 1997).
Jameson, Fredric, and Miyoshi, Masao, *Cultures of Globalization* (Durham, NC: Duke University Press, 1998).
Janson, A.E, and Janson, H.W., *The History of Art*, 6th ed. (New York: Harry N. Abrams, Inc., 2001).
Jencks, Chris, *Culture* (London, Routledge, 1993).
Jenkins, Hugh, *The Culture Gap: An Experience in Government and the Arts* (London: Marion Boyers, 1979).
Jennings, Bruce, *Ecological Governance: Toward a New Social Contract with the Earth* (Morgantown, WV: West Virginia University Press, 2016).
Johnson, Leslie, *The Cultural Critics: From Matthew Arnold to Raymond Williams* (London: Routledge and Kegan Paul, 1979).
Kahn, Joel S., *Culture, Multiculture, Postculture* (London: Sage Publications, 1995).
Kaplan, Max, *The Arts: A Social Perspective* (Cranbury, NJ: Associated University Presses, 1990).
Kaufmann, Walter, *Religions in Four Dimensions: Existential, Aesthetic, Historical, Comparative* (New York: Reader's Digest Press, 1976).
Kenny, Michael G., and Smillie, Kirsten, *Stories of Culture and Place: An Introduction to Anthropology*, 2nd ed. (Toronto: University of Toronto Press, 2017).
King, A. D. (ed.), *Culture, Globalization and the World System* (London: Macmillan, 1991).
Klein, Richard G., and Edgar, Blake, *The Dawn of Human Culture* (New York: John Wiley and Sons, 2002).
Kottak, Conrad Phillip, *Mirror for Humanity: A Concise Introduction to Cultural*

Anthropology, 9th ed. (New York: McGraw-Hill, 2013).

Kragh, Helge, *Conceptions of Cosmos: From Myths to the Accelerating Universe: A History of Cosmology* (Oxford: Oxford University Press, 2013).

Kragh, Helge, *Entropic Creation: Religious Contexts of Thermodymamics and Cosmology* (London: Routledge, 2016).

Kragh, Helge, and Longair, Malcolm (eds.), *The Oxford Handbook of the History of Modern Cosmology* (Oxford: Oxford University Press, 2019).

Kroeber, Alfred L., *The Nature of Culture* (Chicago: University of Chicago Press, 1952).

Kroeber, Alfred L., and Kluckhohn, Clyde, *Culture: A Critical Review of Concepts and Definitions* (New York: Vintage Books, 1963).

Kroeber, Alfred, L., *Configurations of Culture Growth* (Berkeley: University of California Press, 1969).

Kuper, Adam, *Culture: The Anthropologists' Account* (Cambridge: Harvard University Press, 1999).

Lavrenova, Olga, *Spaces and Meanings: Semantics of the Cultural Landscape* (New York: Springer, 2019).

Langness, L. L, *The Study of Culture* (San Francisco: Chandler & Sharp Publishers, Inc., 1974).

Lederach, John Paul, *Preparing for Peace: Conflict Transformation Across Cultures* (Syracuse, NY: Syracuse University Press, 1996).

Legrand, Thomas, *Politics of Being: Wisdom and Science for a New Development Paradigm* (N.p.: Ocean of Wisdom Press, 2021).

Lemkow, Anna, F., *The Wholeness Principle: Dynamics of Unity Within Science, Religion and Society* (Wheaton, IL: Quest Books, 1990).

Lent, Jeremy, *The Pattering Instinct: A Cultural History of Humanity's Search for Meaning* (Amherst, NY: Prometheus Books, 2017).

Lévi-Strauss, Claude. *Tristes Tropiques* (New York: Atheneum, 1974).

Lévi-Strauss, Claude, *Structural Anthropology* (New York: Basic Books, 1963).

Lewis, Jeff, *Cultural Studies: The Basics* (London: Sage Publications, 2002).

Lewis, Richard D., *When Cultures Collide: Leading Across Cultures* (Boston: Nicholas Brealey Publishers, 2018).

Li, Jin, *Cultural Foundations of Learning: East and West* (Cambridge: Cambridge University Press, 2012).

Linton, Ralph, *The Cultural Background of Personality* (New York: Appleton-Century-Crofts, Inc. 1945).

Linton, Ralph, *The Tree of Culture* (New York: Alfred A. Knopf, 1955).

Lovelock, James, *Gaia: A New Look at Life on Earth* (Oxford: Oxford University Press, 1995).

Lovelock, James, *Gaia* (Oxford: Oxford University Press, 1979).

Lowie, Robert H., *Primitive Society* (New York: Boni and Liveright, 1925).

Lowie, Robert H., *The History of Ethnological Theory* (London: George G. Harrap, 1937).

MacLachlan, Colin M., and Rodriguez O., Jamie E., *The Forging of the Cosmic Race: A Reinterpretation of Colonial Mexico* (Berkeley: University of California Press, 1980).

Malinowski, Bronislaw, *A Scientific Theory of Culture* (Chapel Hill, University of North Carolina Press, 1965).

Maritain, Jacques, *The Twilight of Civilization* (New York: Sheed and Ward, 1943).

Masini, Eleanora Barbieri, and Atal, Yogesh (eds.), *The Futures of Asian Cultures* (Bangkok: UNESCO Principal Regional Office for Asia and the Pacific, 1993).

Masini, Eleanora, Barbieri (ed.), *The Futures of Cultures*, vols. 1 and 2 (Paris: UNESCO Publishing, 1994 and 1995).

Mayr, Ernst, *The Growth of Biological Thought* (Cambridge: Belknap/Harvard University Press, 1982).

Mazrui, Ali, A., *A World Federation of Cultures: An African Perspective* (New York: Free Press, 1976).

McKibbon, Bill, *The End of Nature* (New York: Random House, 2006).

McLeish, Kenneth (ed.), *Key Ideas in Human Thought* (New York: Facts On File, 1993).

McLuhan, Marshall, *The Gutenberg Galaxy*, "Centennial edition" (Toronto: University of Toronto Press, 2011).

McLuhan, Marshall, *Understanding Media* (New York: McGraw-Hill Book Company, 1964).

McMurray, Ruth Emily, *The Cultural Approach: Another Way to International Relations* (Chapel Hill, NC: University of North Carolina Press, 1947).

Mead, Margaret, *An Anthropologist at Work* (New York: Avon Books, 1959).

Mead, Margaret, and Métraux, Rhoda, *The Study of Culture at a Distance* (Chicago: University of Chicago Press, 1962).

Mengozzi, Chiara (ed.), *Outside the Anthropological Machine: Crossing the Human-Animal Divide and Other Exit Strategies* (London: Routledge, 2020).

Meyer, Erin, *The Culture Map: Breaking Through the Invisible Boundaries of Global Business* (New York: Public Affairs, 2014).

Mitchell, J. M., *International Cultural Relations* (London: Allen and Unwin/British Council, 1986).

Montagu, M. F. Ashley (ed.), *Culture and the Evolution of Man* (New York: Oxford University Press, 1962).

Moore, Jerry D. *Visions of Culture: An Introduction to Anthropological Theories and Theorists*, 5th ed. (New York: Rowman and Littlefield, 2019).

Mumford, Lewis, *The Culture of Cities* (New York: Harcourt, 1938).

Naess, Arne, *Ecology, Community and Lifestyle* (Cambridge: Cambridge University Press, 1989).

North, John, *An Illustrated History of Astronomy and Cosmology*, revised ed. (Chicago: University of Chicago Press, 2008).

Northrop, F.S.C., *The Meeting of East and West* (New York: The Macmilllan Company, 1946).

Peters-Golden, Holly, *Culture Sketches: Case Studies in Anthropology*, 6th ed. (New York: McGraw-Hill Education, 2011.)

Petrie, W. M. Flanders, *The Revolutions of Civilizations* (New York: Haskell House Publishers, 1971).

Pier, Meg, *What Is Culture?: Why Does it Matter?* (Boston: People Are Culture, 2021).

Powys, John Cowper, *The Meaning of Culture* (New York: W. W. Norton and Company, Inc., 1929).
Quammen, David, *The Tangled Tree: A Radical New History of Life* (New York: Simon and Schuster, 2018).
Rapaille, Clotaire, *The Culture Code* (Toronto: Random House Canada, 2007).
Ray, Larry, and Sayer, Andrew (eds.), *Culture and Economy After the Cultural Turn* (London: Sage Publications, 1999).
Redford, Robert, *The Little Community: Viewpoints for the Study of a Human Whole* (Chicago: University of Chicago Press, 1973).
Redpath, Peter A. (ed.), *From Twilight to Dawn: The Cultural Vision of Jacques Maritain* (Notre Dame, IN: University of Notre Dame Press, 1990).
Ricklefs, Robert E. *Ecology* (New York: Chiron Press, 1979).
Ritzer, George, and Stepnisky, Jeffrey, *Classical Sociological Theory*, 8th ed. (London: Sage Publications, 2020).
Rogoff, Barbara, *The Cultural Nature of Human Development* (New York: Oxford University Press, 2003).
Rosaldo, Renato, *Culture and Truth: The Remaking of Social Analysis* (Boston: Beacon Press, 1990).
Ryden, Barbara, *Introduction to Cosmology*, 2nd ed. (Cambridge: Cambridge University Press, 2016).
Sachs, Wolfgang (ed.), *Global Ecology: A New Arena of Political Conflict* (London: Zed Books, 1993).
Saggs, H. W. E., *Civilization Before Greece and Rome* (New Haven: Yale University Press, 1989).
Said, Edward W., *Cultural Imperialism* (New York: Vintage Books, 1994).
Sajep, Alina, and Persaud, Randolph (eds.), *Race, Gender, and Culture in International Relations* (London: Routledge, 2018).
Salins, Marshall, *Culture and Practical Reason* (Chicago: University of Chicago Press, 1976).
Sapir, Edward, *Selected Writings of Edward Sapir on Language, Culture, and Personality* (Berkeley: University of California Press, 1963).
Sartika, Mira, *The Map of Civilization: A Geo-cultural Synthesis* (Jakarta: Mira Sartika and the Chakra Cultural Foundation, 2015).
Sartika, Mira, *Cultural Genetics* (Jakarta: Mira Sartika and the Chakra Cultural Foundation, 2018).
Schama, Simon, *The Embarrassment of Riches: An Interpretation of Dutch Culture in the Golden Age* (New York: Alfred A. Knopf, 1987).
Schumacher, E. F., *Small is Beautiful: Economics as if People Mattered* (New York: Harper and Row, 1973).
Scott, Bonnie Kime, Cayleff, Susan E, and Donadey, Anne, and Lara, Irene (eds.), *Women in Culture: An Intersectional Anthology of Gender and Women's Studies*, 2nd ed. (London: Wiley/Blackwell, 2016).
Sennett, Richard (ed.), *Classic Essays on the Culture of Cities* (Englewood Cliffs, NJ: Prentice-Hall, 1969).
Sessions, George (ed.), *Deep Ecology for the 21st Century: Readings on the Philosophy and Practice of the New Environmentalism* (Boston: Shambhala, 1994).

Shore, Herbert, *Cultural Policy: UNESCO's First Cultural Development Decade* (Washington: U.S. National Commission for UNESCO, 1981).

Sorokin, Pitirim, *Social and Cultural Dynamics: A Study of Change in Major Systems of Art, Truth, Ethics, Law and Social Relationships* (Boston: Extending Horizons Books/Porter Sargent Publishers, 1970).

Sorokin, Pitirim, *Modern Historical and Social Philosophies* (New York: Dover Publications, 1963).

Spengler, Oswald, *The Decline of the West* (New York: Alfred A. Knopf/The Modern Library, 1962).

Steward, Julian, *Theory of Culture Change: The Methodology of Multilineal Evolution* (Urbana, IL: University of Illinois Press, 1955).

Streeten, Paul, Burki, S. J., Haq, Mahbub ul, Hicks, Norman, and Stewart, Frances, *First Things First: Meeting Basic Human Needs in Developing Countries* (London: Oxford University Press, 1981).

Švob-Đokić, Nada (ed.), *Redefining Cultural Identities: The Multicultural Contexts of the Central European and Mediterranean Regions* (Zagreb: Institute for International Relations/Royaumont Process, 2001).

Swimme, Brian, and Berry, Thomas, *The Universe Story: From the Primordial Flaring Forth to the Ecozoic Age—A Celebration of the Unfolding of the Cosmos* (New York: HarperCollins, 1994).

Toffler, Alvin, and Toffler, Heidi, *Creating a New Civilization* (Atlanta: Turner Publishing Inc., 1994).

Tomlinson, John, *Cultural Imperialism* (London: Pinter, 1991).

Tomlinson, John, *Globalization and Culture* (Cambridge: Polity Press, 1999).

Toynbee, Arnold, *A Study of History* (London: Oxford University Press, 1934).

Turner, Ralph, *The Great Cultural Traditions: The Foundations of Civilizations: The Ancient Cities*, vol. 1 (New York: McGraw-Hill, 1941).

Turner, Ralph, *The Great Cultural Traditions: The Foundations of Civilizations: The Classical Cities*, vol. 2 (New York: McGraw-Hill, 1941).

Tylor, Edward Burnett, *The Origins of Culture* (New York: Harper Torchbooks, 1958).

UNESCO, *The Arts and Man: A World View of the Role and Functions of the Arts in Society* (Englewood Cliffs, NJ: Prentice-Hall, 1969).

UNESCO, *Cultural Rights as Human Rights* (Paris: UNESCO, 1970).

UNESCO, *Cultural Development: Some Regional Experiences* (Paris: UNESCO, 1981).

Van der Elst, Dirk, *Culture as Given, Culture as Choice*, 2nd ed. (New York: Waveland Press, 2003).

Van Loon, Hendrik Willem, *The Arts* (New York: Simon and Schuster, 1937).

Virel, André, Lenars, Charles, and Lenars, Josette, *Decorated Man: The Human Body as Art* (New York: Harry N. Abrams, Inc., Publishers, 1979).

Wagner, Roy, *The Invention of Cultures* (Chicago: University of Chicago Press, Second Edition, 2006).

Wallace, Anthony, *Culture and Personality* (New York, Random House, 1970).

Wallerstein, Immanuel, *The Modern World System* (New York: Academic Press, 1974).

Weintraub, Karl J., *Visions of Culture: Voltaire, Guizot, Burckhardt, Lamprecht, Huizinga and Ortega y Gasset* (Chicago: University of Chicago Press, 1966).
White, Leslie A., *The Evolution of Culture* (New York: McGraw-Hill, 1959).
White, Leslie A. *The Concept of Culture* (Minneapolis: Burgess Publishing Company, 1973).
White, Leslie A., *The Concept of Cultural Systems: A Key to Understanding Tribes and Nations* (New York: Columbia University Press, 1975).
Whitehead, Alfred North, *Adventures of Ideas* (New York: The Free Press, 1967 [1933]).
Whitehead, Alfred North, *Process and Reality*, 2nd ed. (London: The Free Press, 1979).
Williams, Raymond, *Culture and Society 1780–1950* (London: Penguin Books, 1966).
Williams, Raymond, *Culture* (Glasgow: Fontana Paperbacks, 1981).
Williams, Raymond, *Keywords: A Vocabulary of Culture and Society* (New York: Oxford University Press, 1976).
Wohlleben, Peter, *The Hidden Life of Trees: What They Feel, How They Communicate* (Vancouver: Greystone Books, 2015).
Wohlleben, Peter, *The Inner Lives of Animals: Love, Grief, and Compassion* (Vancouver: Greystone Books, 2017).
Wood, D. (ed.), *Craft is Political* (London: Bloomsbury Publishing, 2021).
World Commission on Environment and Development, *Our Common Future* (Oxford: Oxford University Press, 1987).
World Commission on Culture and Development, *Our Creative Diversity* (Paris: UNESCO, 1995).
Worsley, Peter, *The Three Worlds: Culture and World Development* (Chicago: University of Chicago Press, 1984).
Zelle, Anthony R., Wilson, Grant, Adam, Rachel, and Greene, Herman (eds.), *Earth Law: Emerging Ecocentric Law: A Guide for Practitioners* (New York: Wolters Kluwer, 2020).

Index

Achoka, Awori, 145
Adam, Rachelle, 230
Adelung, Johann Christoph, 97
Adorno, Theodor, 179
Age of Surveillance Capitalism, The (Zuboff), 183
Alisjahbana, S. Takdir, 253
Al-Muqaddimah (Khaldun), 169
Alonso-Concheiro, Antonio, 185–186
American Soul, The (Needleman), 43
Anderson, Hans Christian, 54
Animal rights, 228–229
Animals, as national symbols, 37–38; *see also* Living organisms *and specific animals*
Anthropological manifestation of culture, 145–168
Anthropology, 145–168, 213; sociology and, 173–175
Ants, as traffic engineers, 197–198
Architecture, 57–58
Are We Smart Enough to Know How Smart Animals Are? (de Wahl), 206
Ariadne's Thread (Clark), 185
Aristarchus, 239
Arnold, Matthew, 120–122, 135–136
Arts Council of Great Britain, 33
Arts, benefits to communities, 64–66; capacity for holism, 67–68; career training and, 62; creativity and, 62; diversity and, 63; excellence and, 62–63; as gateway to culture, 72, 157–158, 258; health and, 70–71; model for resource conservation, 224; nature of, 46–47; perception and, 63–64; political advocacy and, 66–67; significance of, 48–49; social bonds and, 64–65
Arts, The: Gateway to a Fulfilling Life and Cultural Age (Schafer), 53
Auguries of Innocence (Blake), 55–56
Bach, Johann Sebastian, 55, 106, 261
Backster, Clive, 207
Barer-Stein, Thelma, 61
Basho, Matsuo, 56
Bateson, Gregory, 213, 214, 219
Beatles, 54
Bees, culture of, 197–198
Beethoven, Ludwig, 258
Benedict, Ruth, 124, 147, 152, 188, 213
Berry, Thomas, 39–40, 248, 249–250
Big Bang theory, 83–84, 240, 241, 245
Bio-archives, 100
Biological manifestation of culture, 193–211
Birket-Smith, Kaj, 236
Blake, William, 55–56
Boas, Franz, 18
Burdain, Anthony, 60, 152
Bourdieu, Pierre, 179
Brague, Rémi, 248
Braisted, Paul J., 169
Browning, Elizabeth Barrett, 56
Brush painting, 221
Buddhas of Bamiyan, 109
Burckhardt, Jacob, 114, 259
Burns, Ken, 158
Butler, Samuel, 136
Calvin, John, 120
Campbell, Joseph, 120, 144, 237, 238
Candide (Voltaire), 24
Canon (Pachelbel), 261
Capra, Fritjof, 251
Carème, Marie-Antoine, 59–60
Carlyle, Thomas, 119
Carnival of the Animals (Saint-Saëns), 200, 223–224
Carson, Rachel, 216
Cave paintings, 45
Centre for Contemporary Cultural Studies, 180
Chagall, Marc, 219, 227
Chakra Cultural Foundation, 151
Chapouthier, Georges, 205–206
Cheong Koon, 227
Child, Julia, 60
Chimpanzees, 199
China, ecological civilization in, 215–216; landscape painting in, 222
Choir, The (BBC), 64
Chopin, Frédéric, 54
Chrysanthemum and the Sword, The (Benedict), 124
Cicero, Marcus, 21, 22, 23, 38, 40, 44
Civilization of the Renaissance in Italy, The (Burckhardt), 114
Clark, Mary E., 185
Cocteau, Jean, 48
"Coffee Cantata" (Bach), 106
Coffee houses, 105–106
Communications technology, 151ff., 183–185
Comte, August, 170
"Concepts of Culture and of Social System" (Parsons and Kroeber), 173–175
Convention Concerning Protection of the World's Cultural and Natural Heritage, 103–104
Convention on the Protection and Promotion of the Diversity of Cultural Expressions, 111
Copernicus, Nicolaus, 239
Corals, 201
Cosmic Adventure, The (Haught), 250

Cosmic background radiation, 245
Cosmic Understanding (Munitz), 132–133
Cosmological manifestation of culture, 235–251
Cosmology and Curriculum (Lydon), 250–251
Cosmology, 240–251; and astronomy, 246–247; definition, 245
Cosmos (flower), 245
"Country Gardens" (Grainger), 32
Creation myths, 237
Crows, 199–200
Culinary arts, 59–60
Cultural appropriation, 181
Cultural conflict, 160–161
Cultural consciousness, 262
Cultural conservation, 103
Cultural contact points, 12
Cultural continuum, 259
Cultural education, 187–189
Cultural Foundations of Learning (Li), 270
Cultural heritage, intangible, 105–107; negative aspects, 109–110; personal, 99–100; role of women in preserving, 102–103; threats to, 108–109
Cultural History of Mankind (Klemm), 97
Cultural history, collective, 100–102
Cultural indicators, 165–167
Cultural lives, 125–126
Cultural myths, 237
Cultural personality, 119–144; creativity of, 133–135; humane nature of, 137–138; idealism of, 136–137; philosophy of life, 132; qualities of, 128ff.; reverential thinking and, 139
Cultural scholars, role in creating world as culture, 260–261
Cultural studies, 180–181
Cultural tragedy, 172
Culture of Criticism and the Criticism of Culture, The (Gunn), 153
Culture, as the arts, 45–72; of bees, 197–198; big picture and, 13, 148, 255; biological manifestation of, 193–211; and communication, 151ff.; as complex whole or total way of life, 145–168; cosmological manifestation of, 235–251; as cultivation of the soul, 21–44; and cultures, 148–151; development in breadth and depth, 161–162; ecological manifestation of, 213–233; environment and, 164–165; and ethics, 93–94; harmony and, 14–15, 162–163; as heritage of history, 87–118; as human characteristic, 195–196; as the humanities, 73–95; macro-elements of, 11; manifestations of, 16–19, 254–255, 258; micro-elements of, 11; of other species, 196ff.; personality development and, 119–144; sociology and, 169–191; as source, 247; Spengler's three types, 41–42; traits, 213; as tree, 236; as the whole, 9–10, 243, 247, 255–257; as unifying force, 13, 255
Culture wars, 178
Cultures, appreciation of other, 186; wolf, 203–204; lamb, 204–205
d'Ormesson, Jean, 262
Dagg, Anne, 200
Dahl, Roald, 68
Dance, 57
Data, personal, commercial use, 182–183
Davis, Wade, 167–168
de Wahl, Frans, 206, 210
Decline of the West, The (Spengler), 41, 42–43
Development, sustainable, 216ff.
Dibdin, Charles, 208
#DiCultHer, 108
Diodato, Johannes, 105
Dodd, Diane, 60
Dogs, 202
Dolphins, 199
Don Quixote at Camacho's Wedding (Telemann), 58–59
Drama, 58
Dudley, Susan, 207
Dumont, Fernand, 10
Durkheim, Émile, 171–172
Earth Charter, 228, 229–230, 231
Earth Law, 228, 230–231
Earth Law: Emerging Ecocentric Law (Zelle, Wilson, Adam, and Greene), 230–231
Ecological civilization, 214–216
Ecological culture, 214
Ecological footprint, 217–218
Ecological Governance (Jennings), 231
Ecological manifestation of culture, 213–233
Eco-museums, 101
Economic personality, 126–127
Economics, importance of, 5–6, 260; natural environment and, 1, 4–5, 6, 7, 113; as part of culture, 15, 149; as the whole, 2, 4, 8, 9
Einstein, Albert, 240, 250
Elephants, 199, 202–203
Enchanted Forest (Schafer), 226
"England's Tree of Liberty" (Dibdin), 208
Environmental art/artists, 226
Escoffier, Auguste, 59–60
Essay on the History of Culture of the Human Species (Adelung), 97
Ethics, decline in, 87; need for new global ethics, 87–90, 92–93
Face, Chinese notions of, 140
Faces of Culture (Lee), 262
Feibleman, James, 119, 326–327
Film, 59
Finlandia (Sibelius), 258
Flannery, Tim, 209
Flowers, in art, 225
Floyd, George, 182
Folk music, preservation of, 107
Forbush, E.H., 199
Four Horsemen of the Apocalypse, The (film), 106
Friedmann, Alexander, 82–83
Fundamentals of Ecology (Odum and Odum), 216
Galileo, 240
Galtung, Johan, 123

Gandhi, Mahatma, 110, 122, 141, 143, 157, 258
Gardens, relation to culture, 25ff.; famous, 31; types, 32–33
Gare, Arran, 215
Gasset, José Ortega y, 193
Geertz, Clifford, 159
Genocide, 177
Glass Bead Game, The (Hesse), 136–137
Global warming, 218
Globalization, 3, 117
Goethe, Johann Wolfgang von, 128, 141, 144
Golden Rule, 78–79, 89
Gombrich, Ernst, 118
Gonzalez-Carrasco, Carlos A., 67
Goodall, Jane, 200
Gorbachev, Mikhail, 229
Gould, Glenn, 53
Graham, Martha, 57
Grainger, Percy, 32
Great law of culture, 119–120
Greene, Herman, 230
Guide Culinaire, Le (Escoffier), 60
Gunn, Giles, 153, 159
Gutenberg Galaxy, The (McLuhan), 184
Gutenberg, Johannes, 184
Hall, Edward T., 1, 16, 152
Hall, Stuart, 180
Handel, George Frideric, 36
Harmony of the spheres, 245
Haught, John F., 250
"Heart of Oak," 208
Herder, Johann Gottfried, 24–25, 26, 29, 30
Hesse, Herman, 136–137
Hidden Life of Trees, The (Wohlleben), 208–209
Hierarchy of needs, 123–124
History, cultural interpretation of, 114–117; heritage of, versions, 98; interpretations of, 112–114
Hobbes, Thomas, 231
Hoggart, Richard, 180
Holihan, Brian, 190
Holism, 130
Homespun, 258
Hu Hsien-Chin, 140
Huizinga, Johan, 14, 163
Humanism, 75–77, 79
Humanist Society of Western New York, 77
Humanist, The (magazine), 76
Humanities, definition of, 75; lower priority of, 82; makeup of, 74; rise to prominence, 73
IMAGINEzine, 43
Indigenous peoples, 232
Inequality, economic, 7–8
Innis, Harold, 151, 183–184
International Child Art Foundation, 49
International Institute of Gastronomy, Culture, Arts, and Tourism (IGCAT), 60
Interpretation of Cultures (Geertz), 159
Ishaq, Ashfaq, 49
James, Henry, 73
Jennings, Bruce, 231
Johnson, Maisha A., 181
Joyless Economy, The (Scitovsky), 225
Jung, Carl, 43
Kant, Immanuel, 143
Katz, Ruth J., 71
Keats, John, 55
Kenyatta, Uhura, 208
Kepler, Johannes, 239, 245
Keynes, John Maynard, 3, 205
Khaldun, Ibn, 169
Kilmer, Alfred Joyce, 222–223
King, Martin Luther, Jr., 143
Kipling, Rudyard, 204
Ki-Zerbo, J., 18
Klemm, Gustav, 97
Kluckhohn, Clyde, 97, 210
Kothari, Rajni, 259
Kroeber, Alfred, 97, 173–175, 210
Kuznets, Simon, 3
La Bourse (Telemann), 58–59
Latour, Bruno, 231
Laudato Si': On Care of Our Common Home (Pope Francis), 40, 231
Lee Kuan Yew, 227
Lee, Harper, 199
Lee, Valerie Lynch, 262
Lemaître, Georges, 83, 84, 240, 241
Jin Li, 270
Linton, Ralph, 134
List of Intangible Cultural Heritage of Humanity, 105
Literature, 59
Locke, John, 231
Long Revolution, The (Williams), 114
Longfellow, Henry Wadsworth, 54
Lydon, Angela T., 250–251
Macdonald, Sir John A., 182
Magsamen, Susan, 71
Malikowski, Bronislaw, 123
Malitza, Mircea, 130
Malone, Gareth, 64
Malthus, Thomas, 119
Marcuse, Herbert, 179–180
Marinucci, Carmine, 108
Marshall, Alfred, 3
Marx, Karl, 2–3, 112–113, 116, 171
Masini, Eleanora Barbieri, 270
Maslow, Abraham, 123–124
May, Rollo, 48
Mayor, Federico, 110
McHale, John, 254
McLuhan, Marshall, 151, 183–184; historical periods according to, 184
Meacham, Jon, 43
Mead, Margaret, 124, 265
Meerkats, 203
Mendelssohn, Felix, 261
Midsummer Night's Dream, A (Shakespeare), 29
Mockingbird, 199
Monet, Claude, 221
Morrison, Roy, 215
Motivation and Personality (Maslow), 124
Mozart, Wolfgang, 199, 224; Mozart's starling, 199, 224

Muir, John, 41, 225–226
Munitz, Milton K., 132–133, 246, 251
Muses, 46
Music for Wlderness Lake (Schafer), 226
Musical Joke, A (Mozart), 199
Music, 54; Afghan, 224; capacity for transcendence, 68–69
Mythology, 235ff.; Greek, 238
Nash, Ogden, 200
National Museum of Brazil, 111
Nature, human relationship with, 219ff.; arts and, 220–226; music and, 220, 224; poetry and, 222–223; reverence of, 226, 232; as spiritual entity, 232; visual arts and, 220–221, 224–225
Needleman, Jacob, 43
NeuroArts Blueprint, 71
Newton, Isaac, 240
Niglio, Olimpia, 188–189
Nineteen Eight-Four (Orwell), 182
Ninth Symphony (Beethoven), 258
Notre Dame Cathedral, 42
O'Shaughnessy, Arthur, 68
O-City project, 189
"Ode" (O'Shaughnessy), 58
Odum, Eugene, 216
Odum, Howard, 216
Ombre mai fù (Handel), 36
On Heroes, Hero Worship, and the Heroic in History (Carlyle), 119
One World, One Health initiative, 228
Opera, 58–59
Organisms, living, attachment to others, 201–202; care of offspring, 201, 207; communication among, 198–199, 203, 209; emotions of, 200, 207; habitats, 197–198; intelligence of, 199–200, 205–206; largest, 196; mating customs, 200–201; needs of, 194–195, 206–207; regenerative capacity, 205; sensory abilities, 198, 207; sexual practices, 201
Origins of Culture, The (Tylor), 10, 146
Orwell, George, 182
Outlines of a Philosophy of the History of Man (Herder), 25
Pachelbel, Johann, 261
Padmanbhan, Thanu, 251
Pan Yue, 215
Parsons, Talcott, 173–175
Pascallion, Pierre, 235
Paths of Culture, The (Birket-Smith), 236
Patterns of Culture (Benedict), 152, 213
Pearson, T. Gilbert, 199
People Are Culture (PAC), 269
Pérez de Cuéllar, Javier, 113
Performing Arts, The: Problems and Prospects (Rockefeller Panel), 45
Personology, 122
Perspectives of World History (Spengler), 41
Philosophical Foundations of Ecological Civilization (Gare), 215
Piazolla, Astor, 106
Pier, Meg, 269
Plants, as national symbols, 36–38; similarities to people, 28–29; *see also* Living organisms *and specific plants*
Plato, 54, 237–238
Poetry, 55–56
Pope Francis, 40, 231
Power of Myth, The (Campbell), 237
Powys, John Cooper, 129–130, 133
Primates, 194
Princess of the Stars (Schafer), 226
Ptolemy, 239
Pythagoras, 245
Raccoons, 200
Rasbach, Oscar, 223
Read, Sir Herbert, 49
Reconnecting With Your Culture (RWYC), 189
Redfield, Robert, 155–156
Rees, William, 217
Religion, benefits of, 86; decline in, 84–86
Republic, The (Plato), 54
Respighi, Ottorino, 224
Responsibilities, human, 91–92
Revolution or Renaissance (Schafer), 5
Ricardo, David, 2
Rite of Spring, The (Stravinsky), 66
Riva, Mark, 43
Robinson, Sir Kenneth, 51
Rousseau, Jean Jacques, 231
Ryerson, Egerton, 182
Saint-Saëns, Camille, 200, 223–224
Sardar, Ziauddin, 18
Sartika, Mira, 151
Schafer, R. Murray, 226
Schenck, David, 249–250
Schumann, Robert, 55
Schweitzer, Albert, 138–139, 141–142, 241–242
Science of Culture (Klemm), 97
Science, 79–80
Scitovsky, Tibor, 225
Second World Conference on Cultural Policies, 193
Secret Lives of Plants, The (Backster), 207
Senghor, Léopold Sédar, 168
Shakespeare, William, 29, 56, 59
Shevchenko, Galyna, 189
Sibelius, Jean, 258
Silent Spring (Carson), 216
Silk Road, 108
Simard, Suzanne, 209
Simmel, Georg, 172
Singapore, 226–227
Singh, Rana P.B., 251
Skinner, B.F., 225
Sleeping Beauty (Tchaikovsky), 57
Smith, Adam, 2, 126
Smuts, Jan Christiaan, 122–123, 129
Snow thesis, 80–81
Snow, C.P., 80–81
Social contract, 231
Social problems, 176–179
Social protests, 182
Sociological manifestation of culture, 169–191
Sociology, 169–191; anthropology and,

173–175; founders of, 169–171
Sorokin, Pitirim, 136, 142
Soul of America, The (Meacham), 43
South Oxhey, England, 64–65
Soyinka, Wole, 10, 247
Specialist personality, 126–127
Species, similarities and differences between, 194, 207
Spencer, Herbert, 170
Spengler, Oswald, 41–42, 43
Story, arts based in, 58–59
Stravinsky, Igor, 66
Strong, Maurice, 229
Super tools, 206
Švob-Đokić, Nada, 12
Swami Vivekananda, 251
Swan Lake (Tchaikovsky), 57
Swimme, Brian, 39–40, 249
Symbols of cultures, 153–158; buildings, 155; carpets, 155; food, 153–154; material arts, 154–155; music, 156–157
Tagore, Rabindranath, 193
Taj Mahal, 57
Tango (dance), 106–107
Tchaikovsky, Pyotr Ilyich, 57
Teilhard de Chardin, Pierre, 250
Telemann, Georg Philipp, 58
Thick description, 159
Thinking in a New Light (Holihan), 190
Thoreau, Henry David, 63
Thucydides, 23
Thunberg, Greta, 5
To Kill a Mockingbird (Lee), 199
Toselli, Enrico, 224
Tree Cultures (Cloke and Jones), 207–208
Trees (Kilmer), 222–223
Trees, 207–208; as cultural symbols, 208; cultures of, 209; fig, 208; in poetry, 222–223; roots, 209
Trump, Donald, 178
Turner, Joseph Mallord William, 54–55
Two Cultures and the Scientific Revolution, The (Snow), 80
Two Cultures, The: And A Second Look (Snow), 81
Tylor, Edward Burnett, 9–10, 16, 146, 149, 159
UNESCO, 193
United Nations Declaration of Human Rights, 90, 91
United Nations, environmental programs and conferences, 217
Universal Declaration of Human Rights and Responsibilities (proposed), 92
Universe Story, The (Swimme and Berry), 40, 249
Universe, origin of, 84, 240–241; *see also* Big Bang theory, Cosmology
Valentino, Rudolph, 106
Values, 130–132
van Gogh, Vincent, 221
Visions of Culture (Weintraub), 115
Visual arts, 54–55
Voltaire, 23–24, 26, 29, 30, 97
Wackernagel, Mathis, 217
Walden II (Skinner), 225
Wallace, Anthony, 242–243
Ward, Barbara, 247
Wayfinders, The (Davis), 167
Wealth of Nations, The (Smith), 2, 126
Weber, Max, 172
Weintraub, Karl J., 115–117
"What's Wrong with Cultural Appropriation?" (Johnson), 181
Whitehead, Alfred North, 248
Whole person, 122
Wilber, Ken, 63
Williams, Raymond, 114, 148, 180
Willy Wonka and the Chocolate Factory (Dahl), 68
Wilson, Grant, 230
Wisdom of the World, The (Brague), 248
Wohlleben, Peter, 208–209
Wojciechowski, Jerzy A., 243–244
Wolves, 203–205; culture of, 203–205
Wood wide web, 209
World Commission on Culture and Development, 87, 92
World Heritage Sites, 104–105
World of culture, achieving, 253–271; contributions by workers in cultural field, 263–265; contributions by workers in politics and government, 265–268; role of general public, 268–269
Worldview, 235ff., 242–243, 244
Wright, Ronald, 237
Xi Jinping, 215
Ye Quianji, 215
You Eat What You Are (Barer-Stein), 61
Zak, Paul, 201
Zelle, Anthony R., 230
Zuboff, Shoshana, 183

www.ingramcontent.com/pod-product-compliance
Lightning Source LLC
Chambersburg PA
CBHW060311030426
42336CB00011B/996

* 9 7 8 1 7 7 2 4 4 2 4 7 2 *